Women's Voice
in Latin American Literature

Women's Voice
in Latin American Literature

by
Naomi Lindstrom

A THREE CONTINENTS BOOK
LYNNE RIENNER PUBLISHERS
BOULDER & LONDON

A Three Continents Book

Published in the United States of America by
Lynne Rienner Publishers, Inc.
1800 30th Street, Boulder, Colorado 80301

Library of Congress Cataloging-in-Publication Data:

Lindstrom, Naomi.
    Women's Voice in Latin American Literature/Naomi Lindstrom.
       p.   cm.
    Bibliography: p.
    Includes index.

    ISBN 0-89410-295-8   ISBN 0-89410-296-6 (pbk.)
    1. Latin American fiction—Women authors—History and criticism.
    2. Latin American fiction—20th century—History and criticism.
    3. Lispector, Clarice. *Laços de família*. 4. Castellanos, Rosario.
    Oficio de tinieblas. 5. Lynch, Marta, 1929— *Señora Ordóñez*.
    6. Bullrich, Silvina, 1915— *Mañana digo basta*. 7. Sex role in
    literature. 8. Women in literature. 9. Feminism in literature.
    I. Title.
PQ7082.N7L54 1989   89-32391
863—dc20   CIP

Cover art by Todd Wiggins
©Three Continents Press 1989

Caricatures by Max Winkler
©Three Continents Press 1989

Acknowledgment

Support for this research came from a Faculty Research Assignment from the University Research Institute of the University of Texas at Austin.

To L.L. Johnson

Table of Contents

Preface

During the decade of the 1980's, there has been an increasing focus on the critical presuppositions and methods of critics who choose to study literary texts written by women. Considerable debate has centered on such issues as whether women's texts display distinctive characteristics indicating female authorship. Other critics seek to identify a category of writing that is "feminine" in deviating from, and calling into question, criteria of well-writtenness or significance that embody the "masculine" values of mainstream culture. Additional discussion has centered on the possibility, or advisability, of developing new critical approaches exclusively for the purpose of studying women's writing or femininty as a property of certain texts.

This study stands somewhat apart from these debates and their central issues. The works that here receive detailed commentary (novels by Rosario Castellanos of Mexico and Marta Lynch and Silvina Bullrich of Argentina; short stories by Clarice Lispector of Brazil) have been selected for their utilization of the illustrative and persuasive powers of literature to examine critically one aspect of women's cultural and social situation. All four focus attention upon the special problems of expression and communication women may encounter in many societies (the fictional settings include modern and traditional Latin cultures and an Indian community in Southern Mexico). These works show women as disadvantaged, because of their role and status, as participants in communication. The treatment of an issue that particularly affects women is what makes these works either feminist or implicitly feminist texts (among other ways they may be categorized). It is reasonable to suppose that the authors of the four works, all women, drew upon the experience of living as women when they composed their work. Nonetheless, it is not women's distinctive experience, or the inscription of this experience, that receives consideration. Rather, attention goes to the critical vision of women's situation projected in each text, together with the textual construction that projects it.

For purposes of this study, the feminist element in writing is one manifestation of literature's special ability to generate complex, provocatively indirect statements about society. In developing my critical approach, my primary loyalty has been to the texts under analysis. The goal has been to identify fairly the propositions and assertions made by these works and to explicate the literary means through which these notions are made convincing and memorable to the reader. No claim is being made that the form the analysis takes will necessarily prove generally applicable to other works written by women or concerned with women and their characteristics. While some works display significant commonalities—as do these four in their concern over women's expression—each text, if it is of sufficient interest, deserves attention to its distinctive persuasive and critical mechanisms.

The ideal here has been to avoid, insofar as possible, recourse to terminology other than that normally used in analyzing literary texts. However, in some cases an infusion of expressions from other types of discussion has occurred in identifying and drawing out tendencies inherent in the works in question. Marta Lynch in *La señora Ordóñez*, for example, frequently pursues a novelistic inquiry that at moments parallels discourse analysis. Silvina Bullrich, as an author of popular fiction, often includes in her literary writing passages similar to social criticism or popularized sociology. Again, the strongest efforts have been made to understand and explain the texts under consideration.

I would like to mention developments that have taken place since this book went to press, a number of which represent the continuation or the fulfillment of tendencies and projects discussed here.

English-language readers' access to the writings of Rosario Castellanos has increased with the 1988 publication, by the University of Texas Press, of *A Rosario Castellanos Reader: An Anthology of Her Poetry, Short Fiction, Essays, and Drama*, edited and with a critical introduction by Maureen Ahern with translations by Ahern and others. This volume includes the translation of *The Eternal Feminine*, mentioned in the author bibliography for Castellanos, (Diane E. Marting and Betty Tyree Osiek combined their work in translating this play), as well as many previously unpublished or uncollected translations of poetry and essays. Other projects to translate Castellanos' work into English are presently at various stages of completion and future years should bring the publication of some of the results.

Lispector's work has also reached new English-language readers. The University of Texas Press recently reissued in paperback Lispector's celebrated existential novel, *The Apple in the Dark* in Gregory Rabassa's English version (originally published by Knopf in 1967). Also made newly available was *Family Ties*, in the 1972 translation by Giovanni Pontiero from which Lispector translations in this study are taken. Pontiero continues to take a special interest in bringing into English not only this author's recognized classics, but also her more fragmentary and experimental writings. Notable in this respect is the *Foreign Legion: Stories and Chronicles* (published in London by Carcanet Press, 1986). Translated and with an afterword by Pontiero, this work presents for the first time in English a selection of Lispector's elliptical, evocative *crónicas* or brief journalistic notes.

The availability of English versions of work by a number of Latin American women rose with the publication of new anthologies. Alberto Manguel, ed., *Other Fires: Short Fiction by Latin American Women* (Avenal, NJ: Clarkson N. Potter, 1986) proved a popular offering, while translations appeared accompanied by scholarly background in Angel Flores and Kate Flores, eds., *Hispanic Feminist Poems from the Middle Ages to the Present* (New York: Feminist Press of CUNY, 1986; in series *The Defiant Muse*), and Marian Arkin and Barbara Schollar, ed., *Longman Anthology of World Literature by Women, 1875-1975* (White Plains, NJ: Longman Press, 1988; includes sections on Brazil, Spanish America, and the Caribbean.) All four authors featured in this study receive critical consideration and/or have their writing represented in the *Longman Anthoogy*. Of related interest is a thematic anthology of both male- and female- authored works: Ann Venture Young, *The Image of Black Women in 20th Century South American Poetry* (Washington, D.C.: Three Continents Press, 1987.

Women's writing from Latin America has had an increasingly visible representative to the international literary world in the person of Isabel Allende, the Chilean-born writer mentioned in the introduction to this study. Allende's complex, but highly readable novels have swiftly enjoyed success in translation without precedent for a Latin American woman author. *La casa de los espiritus* (1982; *The House of Spirits*, Magda Bogen, trans., 1985), *De amor y de sombra* (1984; *Of Love and Shadow*, Margaret Sayers Peden, trans., 1987), and *Eva Luna* (1987; Peden trans., 1988) have reached both an academic and a more general English-language public in Knopf editions, and there has been considerable fascination with the author, fluent in English and active on the U.S. cultural scene. The ideal outcome of this phenomenon would be for Allende's fame to draw readers toward the writings of other Latin American women, including works from earlier decades.

Less broadly popular than Allende, in her newly-attained prominence is the recent surge of interest in Sor Juana Inés de la Cruz. This seventeenth-century nun has lately attracted translators eager to make her work available in a number of languages, resulting in the publication of different versions of long-untranslated works. Scholars have, in increasing numbers, investigated and interpreted her statements on women's role, her acquisition of an education despite discouraging circumstances, and her baroque verse and writings for the stage. Beyond any doubt, current discussion derives an important stimulus from a work whose influence continues to expand: Octavio Paz's *Sor Juana Inés de la Cruz o las trampas de la fe* (original version 1982; revised 1983), which Harvard University Press published in 1988 as *Sor Juana* (Peden, trans.).

The bibliographic work noted here has also continued. Marting's long-running project, discussed here in the chapter "Feminist Criticism of Latin American Literature: Bibliographic Notes," resulted in her section "Spanish America," in Margery Resnick and Isabelle de Courtviron, eds., *Women Writers in Translation: An Annotated Bibliography 1945-1982* (New York: Garland Press, 1984), and the 1987 *Women Writers of Spanish America: An Annotated Bio-Bibliographical Guide*, published by Greenwood Press of Westport, Connecticut. She continues to work in biographical and bibliographical guidance and is currently coordinating the team preparing *Fifty Spanish American Women Writers* for Greenwood Press. The same publishing house had brought out, in 1986, *Women Writers of Spain: An Annotated Bio-Bibliographical Guide*, edited by the late Carolyn L.

Galerstein and Kathleen McNerney. Also worthy of mention in this category is Sidonia Rosenbaum, *Modern Women Poets of Spanish America* (New York: Garland Press, 1985).

To the discussion, in "Feminist Criticism," of anthologies of articles, an item should be added. Scholars with widely differing approaches to women and femininity in literature are represented in Carmelo Virgillo and Naomi Lindstrom, eds., *Woman as Myth and Metaphor in Latin American Literature* (Columbia, MO: University of Missouri Press, © 1985, appeared 1986). As well as pursuing the global topic of the anthology, with its essentially women's-studies emphasis, the essays exemplify the varieties of critical approaches to the element of myth in literature.

Particularly extensive interviews with women authors are collected in Evelyn Picon Garfield's, *Women's Voices from Latin America: Interviews with Six Contemporary Authors*. The emphasis is on presenting to English-language readers authors who are still less known and who are still producing new work.

In journals and their contents, two tendencies of change are observable. The journal *Letras Femeninas*, discussed in the section on "Feminist Criticism," has taken on a more professional form under the editorship of Adelaida López Martínez. *Letras Femeninas*, which in its early years gave importance simply to making known the names and work of Spanish and Latin American women authors, now functions more like an academic journal in expecting contributors to investigate designated literary aspects of particular texts or other specific research problems. The journal has moved increasingly toward speciifc thematic issues such as 11. 1-2 (1985), *Sor Juana Inés de la Cruz. Mexico 1651-1695*. It is a fair speculation that a women's studies undertaking of this type can become more focused on specialized literary investigations in part because the work of bringing women authors and issues of femininity and masculinity into literary discussion has already been, to a considerable extent, accomplished. Journals of no special feminist or women's studies orientation are increasingly likely to include more frequent mention and discussion of women writers and of the literary presentation of concepts male and female.

Another tendency of recent significance, although in a field somewhat adjacent to that of the present study, is that the examination of texts by women from the various U.S. Hispanic groups has become increasingly visible in the past few years. The first book to draw widespread attention to this area of research is María Ester Sánchez's *Contemporary Chicana Poetry: A Critical Approach to an Emerging Literature* (Berkeley: University of California Press, 1986).

Finally, note should be made of the deaths, in 1988, of two of the authors mentioned in this study: Sara Gallardo and Beatriz Guido, both of Argentina.

Naomi Lindstrom

Introduction

Recent years have witnessed a resurgence of interest, both popular and scholarly in the question of women's role. When Simone de Beauvoir's *Le Deuxième Sexe* appeared (1949; English translation, *The Second Sex*, 1952), its treatment of this issue placed it outside the mainstream of social criticism. By expressing profound dissatisfaction with the way in which our society apportions what is properly male and what female, the work initiated a widespread, productive discussion. Sex-role analysis and debate assumed an important place in social writings of the fifties and sixties. Such well-publicized works as Betty Friedan's *The Feminine Mystique* (1963), Kate Millett's *Sexual Politics* (1970) and Germaine Greer's *The Female Eunuch* (1971) helped increase public awareness of the constraints society places upon its female members. Less visible but more rigorous studies sought to construct feminist models for research in various fields. An instance of this attempt is Juliet Mitchell's 1972 *Woman's Estate*, an economic analysis. One need only look at the recent offerings of scholarly publishers to see what inroads sex-role analysis has made in sociology, social services administration and psychology.

It is highly reasonable that literary studies, too, should participate in the general intellectual inquiry into sex roles. Creative writers are known for their great willingness to make manifest the least satisfactory aspects of the prevailing social arrangement. The restriction of women's role, as a troubling matter, has often served as the theme of literary works. For instance, in Samuel Richardson's *Clarissa Harlowe* (1747-48), the eponymous heroine seeks to furnish an improving role model to members of her sex. Her failure makes evident how rigidly her society circumscribes acceptable female behavior. Denis Diderot's 1760 *La Religieuse* points out how few options women enjoy. The nun of the title takes vows, though lacking a vocation, because she cannot aspire to the only other status permissible to her, that of married woman. Such works provide a foreground for sex-role analysis with emphasis on the inequities of existing patterns. They invite a critical reading with the same concern. Such writings are numerous in the twentieth century, as more feminist or feminist-influenced authors express their views through the rhetoric of literature (e.g., Rosario Castellanos in Mexico, Monique Wittig in France, Jean Rhys in England).

A second body of works has also attracted the notice of feminist commen-

1

tators. These writings do not stress women's need for choice; indeed, many suggest a more rigid system of restrictions as the ideal. They interest sex-role analysts because they constitute "documents" of commonly held views about women. While some of these texts are non-literary, for example, manuals of proper comportment, others have full literary stature. Beauvoir utilizes a great variety of creative writings for their testimonial value. To gauge the historical variations in attitudes toward women, she examines exemplary tales, the *Thousand and One Nights*, the *Decameron*, amorous verse, and other creative writings. In some cases, such as that of courtly love literature, women's image becomes a manifest topic. In these instances, Beauvoir's procedure is to hold the portrait of women projected in the text to her own standard of women as fully existent creatures. She also discusses works that only imply what women are or might be. In particular, she pursues the notion of literature as a mythmaking activity. Her critical premise is that artist-made myths exhibit reflexes of societal myths and, in that sense, furnish indirect documentation of widespread attitudes. Her chapter on "The Myth of Woman in Five Authors" applies this analysis to the writings of Henri de Montherlant, D. H. Lawrence, Paul Claudel, André Breton and Stendhal.[1] Millett's *Sexual Politics* makes use of this procedure as well.

A third type of evidence that has interested commentators is the biographical and historical side of literary life. Beauvoir cites the correspondence of Jules Laforgue, Stendhal and others. Millett looks at the personal beliefs of authors. Her justification is a need to identify the personality factors underlying sexual inequity. Nonetheless, it is startling to find her comparing Swinburne to "a prurient schoolboy jerking off."[2]

Related are inquiries into women's participation in literary life. A celebrated discussion is Virginia Woolf's 1929 "A Room of One's Own," given a further elaboration by the Mexican writer Ulalume González de León in the latter's 1970 collection of short stories, *A cada rato lunes* (*Every So Often Monday*). These works point out that women's role limits access to privacy and life experience, key factors in the genesis of much literary work.[3]

A corollary of this idea is that literary women are role deviants. Many studies of women authors stress the importance of this aberrance. Both Juan José Sebreli and H. Ernest Lewald have gauged the impact of the "confessional" women poets who scandalized many Latin Americans early in this century. Sebreli considers defiant women authors too removed from ordinary life to create a new role model.[4] Lewald, on the other hand, finds their lives and work an *avant la lettre* manifestation of women's liberation.[5] The issue of role deviance has also been raised in regard to George Sand, Gertrude Stein, and the seventeenth-century Mexican nun Sor Juana Inés de la Cruz, among others.[6] Needless to say, this question figures prominently in the personal and public writings of these women, as well as being a question of biography.

Women as consumers of literature have also been the object of study. One such inquiry is Ann Douglas' 1977 *The Feminization of American Culture*. Douglas examines the emergence, in the nineteenth-century United States, of writings notable for their overt sentimentality and moralizing. Members of both sexes created this product, but its character was determined by the demands of an essentially female audience.

Very popular writings aimed at a mass female audience have also figured as the subject matter of feminist study. Castellanos, in *Mujer que sabe latín...* (*A Woman Who Knows Latin*, 1973), discusses the endlessly serialized love stories of Corín Tellado. "Lección de cocina (Cooking Lesson)," a short story in the same author's 1971 *Album de familia* consists of a sex-role analysis of cookbook prose. Popular jingles, homilies, television, radio and press images of women form part of the documentation for Castellanos' feminist statements in *Mujer que sabe latín . . .* and *El uso de la palabra (Speaking Up),* 1974). Greer's *The Female Eunuch* denounces the so-called "Gothic novel" marketed to English-reading women. Beauvoir, in *The Second Sex*, deplores the impact of fashion magazines; Friedan's *The Feminine Mystique* includes an angry critique of housewifely periodicals. Sebreli's *Eva Perón ¿militante o aventurera? (Eva Peron: Revolutionary or Adventuress?)* evaluates the feminist content of Eva's radio interpretations of celebrated women. The larger question of the glamorization of women in mass culture also interests Sebreli. Though it is not a sex-role analysis, Roland Barthes' 1967 study of women's-magazine texts, *Système de la mode (The System of Fashion)* has much to interest feminists. Barthes shows how these publications trivialize the fashion-conscious bourgeoise who is their ideal reader. This same body of writings has also been studied, with similar results, by Edgar Morin.[7]

II

In sum, a vast range of materials lend themselves to the study of sex roles in literature. The present inquiry looks at a small but highly significant portion: four texts by Latin American women writers. It would be reductive to label them "feminist" works, since many other concerns are also evident in the writings. Yet each is an instance of a deliberate and explicit literary response to the current-day sex-role debate. Every one of the writers in question has demonstrated her strong interest in the controversy. These women have involved themselves not only literarily but also as public figures willing to comment upon the issue.

The first representative of feminine expression dealt with here is Clarice Lispector (1925-77), born in the Ukraine but Brazilian in her formation. Her inclusion involves crossing a linguistic barrier that often keeps Brazilian writers from winning a readership in Spanish America. However, the transcendence of this barrier has come to seem a desirable move. Major creative writers as well as critics have over the past two decades sought to move their readers away from the concept of two separate Latin American literatures.[8] The joint critical consideration of Luso-Brazilian and Spanish-American authors is becoming increasingly common. At any rate, since all citations appear here with their English translations, the reader of the present study will not face a linguistic barrier.

The discussion of a Brazilian woman author is especially significant.

Brazil presents an impressive case of the full incorporation of women into literary life. Lispector and Nélida Piñon enjoy the stature of truly major novelists. Not only does Brazil produce women writers of note, but it publicizes them and accords them equal participation in the public activities of literary celebrities. The Brazilian Academy of Literature broke ground in 1977 by inducting Rachel de Queiroz. This circumstance stands in contrast to the situation in Spanish American literature, where the most highly visible figures of the *nueva narrativa* are all male writers.

Lispector cannot be considered a programmatic feminist, either in her public remarks or in her writings. Yet the strength of her concern for women's relation to literature is manifest in both. Her covert approach to these matters is evident in her 1976 intreview with *Crisis* [Buenos Aires]. The creator is unreceptive to the interviewer's assertion that her fiction is "essentially feminine."[9] However, she becomes articulate in describing the relation between maternity and literary production. Lispector considers several aspects of the topic: the difficulty of combining a career and motherhood, maternity as a stimulus to and influence upon creative work, the literary representation of children and mothers and the writing of children's literature as an extension of her own mothering activities. Developing these topics, she reveals a good deal of insight into issues central to women's studies.

The *Crisis* interviewer is not alone in finding Lispector's work feminine in character. Castellanos uses the Brazilian's writings to support the tenet that women's consciousness may manifest itself in literature. Teresinha Alves Pereira emphasizes the influence of notably "feminine" writers on Lispector; see the critic's 1975 *Estudo sòbre Clarice Lispector*.

Laços de família (1960; English translation *Family Ties*, 1972) here represents Lispector's achievement in this vein. This volume of short stories has an abundance of female-related subject matter. To elaborate the feminine theme, Lispector creates a number of emblematic women's and girls' voices. These created voices are heard as narrators of or characters in the stories, providing a point of entry into the working of Lispector's much mentioned "femaleness."

Rosario Castellanos (1925-74) was a prominent voice for feminism in Mexico. Eager to explore the transformation of women's experience into artistic forms, she wrote a 1950 thesis on feminine culture at the Universidad Nacional Autónoma de México. However, as she notes, the elaboration of this study coincided with her realization that a strictly academic approach was not well suited to her proposed endeavor.[10] Subsequently, Castellanos continued to look into the relation between women's role and art, but through journalism, essay-writing, lecturing and public appearances, meetings with other creative women, classroom teaching and, of course, her own literary production, which merits a chapter's discussion in this study.

As a highly visible public person, Castellanos worked toward several feminist-related goals. Her most abstract labor was the elaboration of a feminist model of criticism that would still respect the specifically literary properties of the text. The theoretical question of how literature is able to structure female experience is ever-present in her writings. More pragmatically, Castellanos promoted the work of women writers, such as María Luisa Mendoza of Mexico and the Catalonian Mercè Rodoreda, who might otherwise have escaped public notice.[11] Both in her teaching and in her writing, she urged readers to accept even the most blatantly feminine writings (e.g. Colette's novels, the letters and diaries of well-born ladies) as potentially significant.[12] Through her very personal journalism in the Mexican newspaper *Excélsior*, she made her own experience exemplary of the problems and satisfactions an independent, outspoken woman faces. Her frankness about her divorce and its social consequences was an especially bold move to increase public awareness of these matters.[13] Serving as Mexican ambassador to Israel must surely represent, at least in part, her campaign to demonstrate women's all around competence. Along with her diplomatic duties, she continued her literary activities up to her death in 1974. Her comedy *El eterno femenino* (*The Eternal Feminine*), published in 1975, reveals her most overt feminist didactics within a literary work. At the same time, it continues her practice of conserving the complex elaboration and humorous component in even the most "useful" literature.

Of Castellanos' literary output, the 1962 novel *Oficio de tinieblas* (*In Darkness*) receives consideration here. This work depicts the unstable relations between white and Indian during President Lázaro Cárdenas' vigorous attempts to institute social reforms. Though the indigenist theme is in the foreground, the novel also constitutes a cross-cultural inquiry into the factors that hinder women's effective self-expression and self-determination. Because it includes such a wide range of female characters and, more specifically, an implicit analysis of role-related communication difficulties, it is feminist writing.

Marta Lynch (Argentina, 1930-85) was a writer distinguished not only by her social commentary but by her notable narrative skill. Her feminism was less patent than the direct statements characteristic of Bullrich's fiction. Nonetheless, the representation of women is one of the features of Lynch's work that has drawn most attention. Lewald cited her and Bullrich as the leading fiction-writing "witnesses" of Argentine women. Another commentator, Amy Kaminsky, turns to Lynch and Bullrich in search of novelistic documentation or quasi-documentation of the maternal role in Latin America.[14] *La señora Ordóñez* (*Mrs. Ordóñez*, 1967), the Lynch novel this study examines, is an exceptionally complex and troubling portrait in literature of a woman confused about her role. Although firmly anchored in the specifics of recent Argentine history, the work is germane to all countries where roles are undergoing a painful redefinition.

Lynch has also provided nonfictional statements that further demonstrate her awareness of the problem. In a 1974 declaration, "Testimonio: con mi obra (Testimony: With My Work)," published in *Hispamérica*, she speaks of her efforts to portray women from diverse social backgrounds.[15] Her journalistic comments frequently touch on issues affecting women, such as abortion and divorce.[16] Representative of her feminist remarks is a 1975 interview in which Lynch said:

Si yo fuera hombre, hubiera tenido la mitad de los problemas y el triple del éxito que he tenido. [Cita a Ernesto Sábato:] 'Vos sos una desdichada, que paga el pato de ser mujer.' En Europa (tanto qu se jactan los europeos de su desarrollo cultural), no tienen absolutamente ningún interés en la literatura escrita por mujeres, habiendo mujeres como Carson McCullers, Mary McCarthy, Virginia Woolf, o Elsa Morante, ¿no?

If I were a man, I would have had half the problems and three times the success I've had. [She quotes the Argentine writer Ernesto Sábato, who told her:] 'You get the short end of the stick just for being a woman.' In Europe (and here the Europeans make such a big thing of their cultural development), they have absolutely no interest in literature written by women, when they have women like Carson McCullers, Mary McCarthy, Virginia Woolf, or Elsa Morante.[17]

Lynch recalls an episode in which a literary colleague, apparently unnerved by the oddity of a woman writer, had to reassure himself that she really could cook.[18] She finds this question symptomatic of a widespread conviction that active and competent public women must somehow not quite belong to the female sex.

Silvina Bullrich (Argentina, 1915) is an extremely popular author, notable for her insistence in bringing the sex-role debate to public attention. H. Ernest Lewald, the most prominent and enthusiastic commentator of her writings, had been principally attracted to them by their feminist aspect.[19] In his discussion of *Bodas de cristal (Crystal Anniversary*, 1952), *Historias inmorales (Immoral Stories,* 1965), *Mañana digo basta (Tomorrow I'll Tell Them I've Had it,* 1968), and *Será justicia (Just Deserts,* 1976), Lewald finds an almost sociological or anthropological exploration of women's status in present-day Argentina. He parallels the points Bullrich makes through the rhetoric of fiction with the assertions of, among others, Helen Deutsch (*The Psychology of Women,* 1944) and Margaret Mead (*Male and Female,* 1949).[20] Another critic notes the polemic strain running through the author's novels: "Bullrich—herself from the upper class—deplores its attitude that women of her class had only one future—marriage, and she condemns the uselessness of such women. In *Bodas de cristal* and *Teléfono ocupado (Busy Signal)*, apparently emancipated women rebel ineffectually against the old mores."[21]

Apart from her fictional didacticism, which is a topic of the chapter here on Bullrich, she has utilized essays, personal journalism, and public appearances to promote her feminist views. A good example of her nonfiction is *George Sand: una mujer como yo (George Sand: A Woman Like Me,* 1972). Bullrich moves from the specifics of Sand's life to a general evaluation of "las mujeres que surgen antes que las demás, que se adelantan a su tiempo (women who are ahead of the rest, who are ahead of their time)."[22] Although Bullrich does not grant unquestioning approval to Sand's behavior, she hails it as a salutary rupture with delimited sex roles. Sand's pronouncements on women's status figure prominently in her study. The biographer makes it clear that she shares Sand's underlying premises, if not the vehemence of their expression.

A "Nota autobiográfica" appended to the anthology *Entre mis veinte y treinta años* makes a similar instructive point about Bullrich herself. As a deviant from traditional roles, she found others reluctant to attribute human needs and feelings: "a mí, a quien todos consideraban una leona o un ventarrón (to me, whom everyone considered some lioness or unleashed force of nature)."[23] Autobiographical fact becomes an illustration of several sex-related issues: the insecurity of a woman living alone, repressive anti-divorce legislation and so forth.

Mañana digo basta is the Bullrich novel discussed here. Its enormous sales and its emphasis on feminist concerns make it a monument to the resurgence of interest in women's studies. Although, as will become evident, this work ranks below the expertly constructed novels of Castellanos and Lynch, it is of interest as an endeavor to make a rather blatant sex-role polemic accessible to a wide fiction-reading public. Also important is the question of how the conventions of the "best-seller" format may be accommodated to the presentation of the sex-role question, a complicated issue indeed.

At this point, it might be well to justify an obvious circumstance: two of the four representative women writers come from one country, Argentina. The factor most able to account for this apparent imbalance is the vigorous public sex-role debate that has occupied a salient place in Argentine intellectual life.[24] Contributors to this exchange have included Victoria Ocampo, Julio Mafud, Esther Vilar, Juan José Sebreli, Arturo Jauretche and other polemicists, social critics and opinionated celebrities.[25] The inescapability of the dispute, whether in scholarly inquiry or mass media, encourages its infiltration into the realm of creation. A good index of this situation is the special 1970-71 issue of the magazine *Sur* devoted to women's issues. Women in the arts, with one notable exception, responded to the magazine's questionnaires by expressing the most programmatically feminist opinions.

The four women studied here by no means exhaust the list of fine contemporary women writing in Latin America. In the prose genres alone, many important works are female-authored. Especially outstanding are *Los recuerdos del porvenir* (1963; *Recollections of Things to Come*, 1969), by Elena Garro (Mexico, 1920); *As três Marias* (1931; *The Three Marias*, 1963), by Rachel de Queiroz (Brazil, 1910); the many fantastic stories authored by Silvina Ocampo (Argentina, 1903); *La última niebla* (1934; *The House of Mist*, 1947) and *La amortajada* (1938; *The Shrouded Woman*, 1948) by María Luisa Bombal (Chile, 1910-1980); *Ifigenia* (1924) and *Las memorias de la Mamá Blanca* (1929; Mama Blanca's Souvenirs, 1959) by Teresa de la Parra (Venezuela, 1891-1936); *Cartucho* (*Cartridge*, 1931) and *Las manos de Mamá* (*Mama's Hands,* 1937) by Nellie Campobello (Mexico, 1909); and *Floradas na serra* (*Mountain Blossom*, 1938) by Dinah Silveira de Queiroz (Brazil, 1911-1982). Beatriz Guido (Argentina, 1925) reached many through novels and screenwriting, though some deem her too "pop."[26] Women have also won recognition and sizable readerships for their work in other genres. Gabriela Mistral of Chile (b. Lucila Godoy Alcayaga, 1889-1957, Nobel prize 1945) is a vital presence for her poetry and her extensive writings about women. Alfonsina Storni (Argentina, 1892-1936) is being rediscovered as a poet and feminist; her Uruguayan contemporaries Delmira Agustini (1887-1914) and Juana de Ibarbourou (1895-1979) merit reconsideration. Cecília Meireles (1901-1964) and Henriqueta Lisboa (1904-1985) are Brazil's great women poets. In drama, Griselda Gambaro of Argentina (1928),

Leilah Assunção of Brazil (1940) and Luisa Josefina Hernández of Mexico (1928) are three major names. Women have been active in literary criticism; rather than single out a few individual contributors, it would be fitting to recognize their collective contribution.

There are many women novelists still evolving, among them María Luisa Mendoza and Elena Poniatowska (Mexico), Nélida Piñon and Lygia Fagundes Telles (Brazil), Sara Gallardo and Luisa Valenzuela (Argentina), and Isabel Allende (Chile).

The four authors focused upon here stand out for their public prominence as contributors to the ongoing reconsideration of women. For this reason, it becomes especially important to see how they translate their evident concern with women into fictional expression. This is the factor that must justify their inclusion and the exclusion—with regret—of so many other women worthy of study.

III

The above considerations delimit the corpus of literary works to be studied. The next step is to establish a critical procedure capable of revealing ways in which literature gives a form to female experience. To do so, one should first look at what previous commentators have done in this vein.

The joint discussion of sex role and artistic expression far antedates the current revival of feminism. Plato, to cite an early example, worries lest young boys be caused to recite poetry written for a female "voice" or that of an unmanly man.[27] The idealization of women as a characteristic poetic labor draws much attention to this day. The artist's exaltation of the female concerns academics (Dante scholars) as well as essayists (Robert Graves, *The White Goddess*, 1948) and creative writers (Henry James, "The Madonna of the Future," 1874). Discussion of Anthony Trollope's "political" cycle of novels frequently contrasts male and female strategies for the wielding of power. Critics' perceptions of masculinity and femininity in art could, indeed, serve as the subject-matter for a lengthy examination.

1949 stands as the base year for this study; it is the year in which Simone de Beauvoir and Margaret Mead brought forth their now-famous role analyses. Each utilizes literary material, Beauvoir more extensively and more systematically than Mead. In *Male and Female*, Mead treats literary works as she would any cultural artifacts. For example, she remarks that anyone uncertain as to how seriously to take amorous passion will find few clues to this riddle anywhere in our society. Even a reading of *Romeo and Juliet*, which presents an extreme case of this attachment, sheds remarkably little light on the real-world question.[28] She also looks to literature to provide documentation of prevalent practices or attitudes.

In many cases, Beauvoir also follows this simple procedure of utilizing literature as a record of common behavior and notions. In some of the most interesting of her remarks, though, she calls upon literature to "bear witness" in a much more complex fashion. This analysis appears in her previously mentioned commentary on "The Myth of Woman in Five Authors."

Beauvoir's work on myth is interesting, but its applicability to an essentially literary study is limited by two factors. One is Beauvoir's premise that the mythification of women, whether through literary or other means, is a grievous culture-wide mistake. Her ideal is a presentation of women without the mediating element of myth. Authors she salutes for achieving this straightforward depiction include Denis Diderot and Ernest Hemingway. Needless to say, the literary critic cannot reasonably view myth as a negative phenomenon. Current literary theory has laid much emphasis on the creation of myth as a productive and illuminating literary task.[29]

Since Beauvoir's goal is to expose a social wrong, she calls on creative writers as witnesses to the offense. Friendly witnesses willing to make manifest the inequity include several social philosophers of the Enlightenment, Choderlos de Laclos, Percy Bysshe Shelley and his circle, Virginia Woolf and the Bloomsbury group and Colette. Others, such as D.H. Lawrence, are hostile witnesses whose words tend to obscure the problem or misrepresent its causes, obliging Beauvoir to demonstrate inadequacies in their testimony. In either case, her attention goes directly to the version of reality the writer communicates. She does not ask how literary work may be so constructed as to permit this good or bad communication to occur. The absence of specifically literary commentary by no means invalidates her remarks, but is merely a result of her focus. Indeed, Beauvoir deserves credit for recognizing that literature does not transmit meaning with the pragmatic directness of, say, a treatise.

An attempt to move from Beauvoir's social-criticism model to one allowing cultural and literary criticism is Millett's *Sexual Politics*. Millett's method is to alternate literary discussion with the examination of nonliterary documents on women: legal declarations, manuals of proper comportment, social doctrine, sermons and scientific or pseudo-scientific findings.

The proposed synthesis of literary and cultural analysis is worthwhile, but Millett's realization of her plan has certain worrisome features. Whereas Beauvoir cites many sympathetic and truthful depictions of women by men, Millett's evaluations of male authors tend heavily toward the negative side. Of the four writers to receive lengthy discussion, three are condemned: D.H. Lawrence, Henry Miller and Norman Mailer. The attack on Mailer is so severe and so personal that he felt compelled to write a book-length rebuttal and self-defense, *The Prisoner of Sex* (1971). One creator, Jean Genet, finds favor with Millett. The reason for this positive response is that Genet, as homosexual, stands outside the male role and is capable of directing at it a corrosive irony. Like Millett herself, Genet makes untenable male attitudes his target of denunciation.

Yet, it would be procedurally justifiable to base a study largely on deficient works. What is more troubling is the nature of Millett's complaint against many male writers. Typically, she sees too many negative features and too few worthwhile traits in the women characters these men portray. For example, these are her observations on Vivian in Alfred Lord Tennyson's *The Idylls of the King*:

> Vivian, who renders Merlin helpless and so hastens the ruin of Arthur's

kingdom and Tennyson's ideal state, is another matter. She is carnality unrelieved by a single sympathetic trait; a vaginal trap, a *vagina dentata*, a snakelike presence whose every cell is another bit of guile. In Tennyson's adherence to the separate-spheres dogma, the male is given over to intellect, rule, warfare and other altruistic projects calculated to serve mankind and promote civilization, but the female, as Vivian obligingly confesses, knows only the animal level of sexuality.[30]

As this passage reveals, Millett is also against the polarization of male and female roles. In her estimation, the exaggeration of either masculinity or femininity generally tends to be advantageous to male interests.

The limitations of Millett's model became evident in a polemic which appeared in *Journal of Spanish Studies: Twentieth Century*. In 1973, Patricia O'Connor published an article, "Francisco García Pavón's Sexual Politics," applying the Millett treatment to the sophisticated detective novels of a Spanish writer.[31] In 1974, the same journal printed "The Great Clash: Feminist Criticism Meets up with Spanish Reality," by Birgitta Vance. For Vance, O'Connor's article is almost an illustrated map of the pitfalls into which feminist criticism may fall. As she points out, O'Connor fails to differentiate between García Pavón's works and the man who wrote them. The author's remarks in nonliterary contexts appear mingled indiscriminately with statements made by his fictional narrators and characters, as if all proceeded from one mouth. O'Connor speculates about the influence of two figures from García Pavón's childhood and the ambience of Tomelloso, his home town. Thus she implicitly falls into what have long been defined as the biographical and the intentional fallacies.

After pointing out these procedural shortcomings, Vance raises a question crucial to the future direction of feminist criticism. She complains that O'Connor is, in effect, "requesting that García Pavón falsify his experience in the service of a better society and the Women's Liberation Movement," adding, "I doubt that many critics or teachers of literature, other than those subjugated by Socialist Realism, would go along with such a pragmatic view of the author's role."[32] In Vance's judgment, the negative features of Pavón's fictional women reflect, with harsh accuracy, the deformation of the female character in an unjustly-delineated sex role. O'Connor, though, holds the novelist responsible for deficiencies in his country's social arrangement. A key instance of alleged sexism is a scene in which a woman, waking to find her lover dead, can think only of how to keep their relation a secret. Surely this woman's numbness can also be seen as a natural reflex of the societal demand that women present themselves as chaste, no matter what the personal cost. Common sense would indicate that the oppressed learn duplicity and cold-heartedness in order to survive.

The point Vance makes also shows why an approach such as Millett's or O'Connor's leads so often to denunciation. The model demands that female characters be presented as noble victims of male oppression or else as inhabitants of a utopian world in which female potential may express itself freely. This requirement makes it highly dangerous for writers to depict women as they occur in real-world, flawed societies. It is notable that Genet, the writer most favorably treated in *Sexual Politics*, does not treat women directly, but rather portrays, in an allegorical mode, the behavior of men.

IV

Because Castellanos made such an original and important contribution to the development of feminist literary and cultural discussion, a review of her efforts in this area is in order. She succeeded in mapping out the work that would need to be done in order to integrate sex-role analysis into the critical endeavor.

After exposure to so much denunciatory commentary, one finds in the work of Rosario Castellanos fresh hope for feminist criticism. Castellanos, like any number of committed critics, situates a literary work within its societal context and tries to see how truthfully and how responsibly the work represents that context. However, she is especially interested in finding in fiction the accurate reflection of the harmful effects of socially-imposed sex-role distinctions. Whether the author in question was conscious of anything resembling the feminist point of view or whether the work of literature expresses feminist concepts are not important points. Castellanos seems to presuppose that the injustices of women's role have always been salient enough that a sensitive writer ought to be able to perceive them and to translate them into fictional terms.

An instance of this approach is her original reading of *Les Liaisons dangereuses*, the eighteenth-century novel by Choderlos de Laclos.[33] Although the author cannot have read Simone de Beauvoir, Castellanos finds in his novel a true reflection of women's frustration in a male-dominated society, in person of the infamous Marquise.

Critical consensus considers the Marquise as a paradigmatically evil figure. Castellanos, though, would modify this view somewhat. She views the Marquise's course of action as the only one open to her as an intelligent, ambitious woman in a society that allows only males an outlet for intelligence and ambition. In Castellanos's reading, the Marquise is less emblematic of evil than of the frustration and blockage that distort the female personality.

To make this point, Castellanos prefaces her discussion of the fictional Marquise with a description of women's place in eighteenth-century France. By situating the Marquise in a societal context, Castellanos aims to throw all of her behavior within the novel into a different perspective, and to establish her both as a victim and a victimizer. The Marquise's context is a society which allows promising young men to compete in the church and military hierarchies, but relegates all women, regardless of their potential, to such limited roles as nun or gracious hostess. Castellanos argues that the pathological form which the Marquise's ambition takes is the fault of the society which offered her no healthier form of fulfillment; to view the character as purely and arbitrarily evil is a displacement of guilt. One must also consider the strong societally-imposed constraints which deformed her character and conduct.

The essay on *Les Liaisons dangereuses* offers not only an unusual reading of that work but, more importantly, some hopeful implications for the further development of a feminist criticism. First, it does not condemn the author or his work for presenting a number of female characters with deficient personalities. Nor does Castellanos fault the work for not setting forth in programmatic fashion the underlying causes of the behavior of the female characters along with a statement of proposed remedies. As critic, she demands no more of the work than that it reflect in a truthful way the position of women. This would seem a more reasonable demand than the requirement that all works of literature, regardless of their date of composition, express a set of beliefs which are essentially those of twentieth-century feminism. Thus one is spared the prospect of feminist criticism becoming only the labor of condemning heretical or morally deficient works to some Male Chauvinist Index.

Secondly, Castellanos' approach has a good deal of applicability to other literary works. Certainly it is no new thing for a critic to situate a literary work within its historical or social context, or to evaluate the actions of characters taking into account their social milieu. However, it is a recent development to include social rules about sex roles as part of that milieu. We have all seen many commentaries on literary works stressing such factors as class distinctions, economic injustices, immigration, attitudes toward deviance and the formation of elites and elitist attitudes.

Perhaps the eventual impact of feminist criticism will be the inclusion of sex-role analysis into sociologically-based literary criticism. Such a development would give feminist concepts much wider applicability since, in literature as in real-life society, sexism does not operate independently of other forces, and often cannot reasonably be studied in isolation.

The women's movement could affect not only literary criticism but the relationship between readers and works, in Castellanos' view. Castellanos tried to make her students aware of the expectations and presuppositions that they brought to the reading of a literary work. She deplored the skewed outlook that overrates works that depict predominantly male sectors of existence and relegates to a lesser status works that dwell on feminine aspects of life. Her prime instance of this bias was the evaluation of Hemingway's fiction, celebrated for a manly vigor which manifested itself in an obsession with bullfights, weaponry, demonstrations of physical courage and so forth. To Castellanos' mind, this praise of Hemingway was nothing but an extension of the pervasive notion that what a male does is more interesting than what a female does. To her, a literary work that presented to its readers a unipolar, all-male, truncated scheme of the universe ought to be considered as seriously flawed, not as more worthwhile and significant on that account.[34]

The incorporation of such subjects as housework and church bazaars does not trivialize a work of literature, as Castellanos points out. Rather it is a weighty matter, and one deserving of literary comment, that women who could think and create should be limited solely to such pursuits. As a newlywed in a Castellanos story observes: "Yo anduve extraviada en aulas, en calles, en oficinas, en cafés: desperdiciada en destrezas que ahora he de olvidar para adquirir otras. Por ejemplo, elegir el menú. (By some mistake, I wandered around in classrooms, in the street, in offices, in cafes; wasting my time learning skills I must now forget in order to acquire others. For instance, to plan the menu.)"[35]

As a positive example of the serious literary treatment of purely female experience, Castellanos singled out the character of Alberto's mother in Mario Vargas Llosa's *La ciudad y los perros* (1963; *The Time of the Hero*, 1968). Accustomed to defining herself solely as self-abnegating mother and long-suffering wife, this woman finds herself without an appreciative audience for her self-abnegation when her husband and son both have absented themselves. She must entertain herself with pursuits such as religious fanaticism and martyrdom. Castellanos acted out the part of this frustrated creature for her classes, imploring the cosmos, "¿A quién le importan mis manos? Soy una pobre mujer abandonada. (Who cares about my hands? I'm a poor abandoned woman.)"[36]

Like the Marquise and many of Castellanos' characters, Alberto's mother is a grotesque, hyperbolic representation of women. Castellanos, though, refrained from blaming authors for presenting Latin American womanhood in caricatured form. Rather she saw in such grotesque characters confirmation of her theory that when female energies cannot be discharged through creative and satisfying work, those blocked forces will assume pathological forms. In the creation of this character and her admission into an altogether serious novel, Castellanos saw the act of a novelist willing to present some unpleasant societal realities, to show society what it does to women.

As noted, one should not limit the study of Castellanos' literary feminism to her criticism and her teaching, in obeisance to an arbitrary distinction between creative and critical work. As Fredric R. Jameson pointed out in his 1971 essay "Metacommentary," not only is criticism about literature, but literature itself is about literature, a fact especially inherent in twentieth-century works.[37] According to Jameson, each work of literature implies why that work is necessary. In the case of a writer with such strong notions of what was needed in literature, we may expect the creative work to be in large part an attempt to supply what is missing. Since Castellanos felt that literature had been skewed away from feminine experience and female sectors of life, she demonstrated serious literature could present those missing elements.

Indeed, we find in the stories of the 1971 *Album de familia* a veritable barrage of the thoughts of women, the language of women among themselves and the repertory of female life: household items, complaints about servants needlework. Perhaps the most extreme instance of this incorporation of female trivia into a story of serious intent is "Lección de cocina (Cooking Lesson)." The reader is initially startled to find a cookbook playing a major part in the story, but its inclusion is not primarily whimsical. By the end of the story, the reader is conscious that the seemingly insignificant cookbook is nothing less than an instrument of the transmission and perpetuation of certain generally-held attitudes toward women.

The cookbook is being consulted by a new bride, who must learn to renounce the small degree of freedom she enjoyed as a single woman. She discovers that the language of the cookbook makes evident some presuppositions about the women who will consult it. With its vague phrasing, the cookbook "me supone una intuición que, según mi sexo, debo poseer pero no poseo, que me permitiría advirtir el momento preciso en que la carne está a punto (suppose I have some intuition that, as a member of the female sex, I'm supposed to have, only I don't have it, that will let me know exactly when the roast is done)."[38] While the manual's language requires a high degree of intuition from its readership, it seems to expect little intelligence from the readers, for it says that the roasting spit "previamente ha de untarse con un poco de grasa para que la carne no se pegue (should first be greased lightly to keep the meat from sticking to it)."[39] Humiliated and misinformed by this sinister document, the bride ruins her cooking and is left to brood on her married future. Besides the immediate point of the story, a presentation of the status of married women, Castellanos makes a literary point. It is highly eccentric to include the dull, condescending prose of the manual in what is obviously a competently written literary effort. But it is dangerously eccentric for a society to relegate clever young women to the status which the cookbook so clearly gives them: that of instinctive housekeepers lacking in brains. The inclusion of this banal text is justified because it is through literary means that the reader is made aware of the manual's coercive, subjugating implications.

Many of Castellanos' poems also reflect her concern with giving voice to feminine experience through literature. In her "Lamentación de Dido," written in the early fifties, the voice of Dido is not that of a woman ashamed of her failure to live up to her royal status. Rather the voice in the poem is that of a woman keenly aware of the constricted female life she has led and the freedom enjoyed by her departing lover: "La mujer es la que permanece (The woman is the one who stays behind)."[40] The free-roaming Aeneas is described as "hombre de paso, hombre con el corazón puesto en el futuro (man passing through, man with his heart set on the future)." [41] Dido speaks as a woman with a feminist awareness of the gulf between her lover's open life experience and her own closed upbringing: "De mi madre, que no desdeñó mis manos y que me las ungió desde el amanecer con la destreza/heredé oficios varios; cargadora de lana, escogedora del fruto que ilustra la estación y su clima/despabiladora de lámparas (From my mother, who knew the worth of my hands and anointed them from daybreak on with skills/I learned to fill my roles: the gatherer of wool, the one who picks the best fruit for the season and the climate/the one who trims the lamps)."[42] By making the lamentation that of a woman who conceives of herself as a woman rather than a queen, and of her lover as a man rather than a special, questing hero, Castellanos has made the epic tale relevant to encounters between men and women.

V

Using the above-described approach, Castellanos comments on many aspects of literary work. Some of her discussions are purely thematic in character. On other occasions, she is especially interested in linguistic features, in the synthesis of documentary testimony and imaginative literature, in the meta-literary component of a fictional work or in specific structural characteristics. Of these last, the creation of fictional and poetic female voices has a special importance for its efficacy in representing what women experience in life. As is evident from the above survey, Castellanos herself creates many feminine "I's" capable of testifying to women's situation. She also hails the achievements of other writers who pursue the same structural tactic. Particularly interesting in this respect is her essay on Mercè Rodoreda, whose female protagonist-narrator expresses reactions emblematic of the thoughts and feelings of real-life women.[43] The autobiographical voice merits special attention when it can be made paradigmatic of a uniform womanhood; Castellanos finds such universal voices in the reminiscences of Mary McCarthy, Simone Weil, Betty Friedan, and others writing "directly" from life.

It is from this aspect of Castellanos' discussion that the present study takes its focus. The creator's ability to speak in a "fashioned" voice representative of some class of people has long fascinated literary critics.[44] One student of this phenomenon, Ludomir Doluzel, characterizes the "text with a speaker" as having a "subjective semantics" rich in information about that speaker. This feature allows the reader to glimpse the speaker's temporal and spatial orientation, his attitudes and preoccupations. In this way, the "text with a speaker" becomes an effective means of revealing how experience is registered, organized and made the basis of significant generalizations.[45] It may also show the falsification of experience. Wayne Booth, in *The Rhetoric of Fiction* (1961), identifies the "unreliable narrator" whose testimony is patently inaccurate. This recourse draws attention to the question of why the speaker cannot or will not narrate events faithfully.

The structural feature of literary work has a special relevance to a socio-cultural issue. Women's inability to "make their voices heard" or to have a "say" in the governance of society has been a major target of recent feminist writings. Feminist linguists, for example, have looked at the features of the present social arrangement that discourage and inhibit female expression. Typical of this inquiry is Robin Lakoff's 1975 *Language and Woman's Place*. The cover depicts a woman with her mouth taped shut—an image emblematic of the author's conclusions. The difficulties of making government responsive to women's statements of need continues to draw considerable commentary.[46]

To combine this issue of sociocultural value dimensions with explicit structural analyses of works, this study begins by looking at narrative voice, the formal aspect of literature studied by Doluzel, Booth, Tzvetan Todorov, and others. However, the identification of technique is only the point of entry into each writer's presentation of the problem of *voice* in a rather different sense. Here one should clarify a point of critical terminology. In this study, *voice* designates the individual's ability to participate in activities of discourse. These activities include both self-addressed communications (e.g., soliloquies, utterances that are only understood by the speaker, unuttered interior formulations) as well as verbal transactions involving interaction between two or more individuals. The writers studied here use a variety of narrative strategies in order to bring to the forefront women's difficulties in achieving voice in this sense.

Thus, while narrative voice studies tend to concern themselves principally with the central narrator in a text, we need to look at the total pattern of speech

acts represented in that text. Patterns of dialogue, silences, aborted communication, all become indicative of the social structuring of discourse—a structuring
that most often, proves to be unfavorable to women's expression. These
feminist writers display a concern that is parallel to that of discourse analysts.
For example, Mary Louise Pratt's 1977 *Toward a Speech Act Theory of
Literary Discourse* describes tacit "contracts," conventional expectations
about who shall speak in a given situation. "Contractual" expectations govern
much of the individual's own production of speech and affect one's responses to
the speech of others. This is because each member of a society carries with him
that society's notions of what constitutes normal discourse.[47] In the work of
feminist writers, the reader sees how these tacit contracts work against women.
When women characters have something that must be expressed, they frequently
find no space in which to make their voices heard. Moreover, they may have no
effective voice to use, because their formation has not included experience in
"stating one's case." The intended audience, even when favorably disposed to
women speakers, may have difficulty grasping their assertions. The listeners
have neither the expectation of nor the past experience in listening to women
voice their deepest concerns. The result is, often as not, a trivialization,
banalization or simple ignoring of women speakers' message. In addition,
many of the women characters depicted cannot formalize their experience in
words, even to themselves. To see this range of discourse problems, and to
make the reader see it, feminist writers utilize all the devices literature
possesses for the representation of uttered and unuttered verbal formulations
by characters and by the central narrator.

Oficio de tinieblas gives us an example of this overall approach. In this
novel, the central narrator has no feature either of masculinity or femininity.
This narrator takes a special interest in the discourse problems of the novel's
female characters. Through editorializing remarks to the reader, the story-
teller draws attention to these women's severe communication problems.
Concurrently, it falls to this narrator to tell the reader what the women would
have said had they possessed the means to speak out, i.e., a voice. Thus the
contrast between what the women say in their own voices and what the narrator
must say for them is telling. While the former is poor in information and
frequently full of misrepresentations, the latter supplies the nuances and extra
data needed for comprehension of the women's situations. This device constantly
emphasizes the women's disturbance—a disturbance closely related to the
status of women in society. Here one must look at the narrator's voice, the
women's voices and sometimes the men's voices that engage the women's in
dialogue. The total pattern that emerges constitutes a denunciatory portrait of
the ways in which women's expression is silenced, deformed or ignored. The
framework Castellanos sets up in this novel is similar to that used in Lynch's *La
señora Ordóñez*, with one notable exception: Lynch places much less reliance on
a central omniscient narrator capable of offering full and trustworthy information.

Even when the central narrator is the troubled woman herself, as in the
pseudo-diary *Mañana digo basta*, the interaction of her voice with other,
mostly female voices is impressive and revealing. In this novel, the narrator
engages in a power struggle with her three daughters. In their conversations, the

aggressive young women attempt to push her into a disadvantageous grand-motherly role. In addition, one reads her accounts of dialogues with women friends of her own generation. Her age-peers represent a more authentic set of values, to which they hope to convert the vacillating diarist. Again, the exchange of words becomes important as one follows who is "winning" these interrelated struggles. One comes to see why the heroine, heavily socialized into a ladylike role, cannot make her voice heard among more assertive types. Also of great importance is the heroine's ability to formalize her experience into statements—the self-addressed statements that form the bulk of the pseudo-diary text. While considerably above her social self-assertion ability, her capacity to speak frankly to herself is also somewhat inhibited by considerations of "proper" femininity. Indeed, the very title of the work, in which the heroine promises herself that she will state her case more forcefully in the proximate future, is an impressive case of self-delusion by verbal means. The reader is continually perceiving discrepancies between what the heroine's voice is saying and what she patently "ought" to have said in order to gain control over her situation.

Lispector's *Laços de família* presents quite a different variety of feminist fiction. While Castellanos, Lynch and Bullrich all address the sex-role issue overtly, Lispector places existential thematics in the foreground of her work. Women, as constricted and trivialized beings, become paradigmatic of human beings who cannot or will not confront the drama of existence. The patterns of discourse one finds here reveal the women's evasion of problematic aspects of the human condition: nothingness, absurdity, the need to make conscious life choices. Lispector's women characters frequently refrain from formulating their experiences and perceptions, even to themselves. On other occasions, their inner voices (indirect and direct interior monologues) and utterances revert to stereotypic models when the terrors of existence begin to enter their minds. The reader finds the recognizable voices of the dutiful housewife, the langorous belle or the fantasy princess rather than those of responsible, self-aware human beings. As a character struggles toward a greater degree of awareness, her voice may undergo abrupt alterations: as she reverts to routine, her voice may disappear from the narrative. These complex patterns produce an implicit denunciation of socialized discourse, with its ability to stifle the fully existent human being.[48]

In all four works, this study seeks an exposition of two allied questions. First, how does women's voice become inefficacious? Presenting paradigmatic instances of stymied expression, these authors reveal the workings of the blockage. Secondly, one finds answers to the question: how are women to achieve their own voice? Even in such a bleak work as *La señora Ordóñez*, women occasionally speak clearly and directly, overcoming their confusion and inhibition.

A common tenet underlying all four authors' works is the conviction that women have something especially worth expressing. The frustration of the female voice is not only disadvantageous to the women affected, but prevents the society as a whole from hearing the insights that can be obtained from a female perspective. Each of these four works serves, among other purposes, that of encouraging and celebrating the female voice.

Notes

1 Simone de Beauvoir, *The Second Sex*, trans. H.M. Parshley (New York: Knopf, 1952), pp. 199-252.
2 Kate Millett, *Sexual Politics* (Garden City: Doubleday, 1970), p. 150.
3 Virginia Woolf, *A Room of One's Own* (London: Hogarth Press, 1929).
4 Juan José Sebreli, *Eva Perón, ¿aventurera o militante?*, 4a. ed. rev. (Buenos Aires: La Pléyade, 1971), p. 47. See also Marta Colomina, *La Celestina mecánica* (Caracas: Monte Avila, 1976), feminist denunciation of mass culture.
5 H. Ernest Lewald argues that the presence of celebrated literary women has had an "opening" effect on the definition of woman's role in Argentine society; see his general remarks to this effect in "Aspects of the Modern Argentine Woman," *Chasqui*, 5, 3 (1976), 19-20. Reviewing Silvina Bullrich, *Será justicia*, in *Chasqui*, 6, 2 (1977), 94, Lewald speaks of "Alfonsina Storni, whose poetry heralded the emergence of the emancipated woman as early as 1918."
6 See Rosario Castellanos' testimony to her own sense of isolation and deviance as a woman writer in her *El uso de la palabra* (México: Excélsior, 1974) and *Mujer que sabe latín...* (México: SepSetentas, 1973). The latter volume makes note of the marginal position of several literarily productive women.
7 See, for example, Edgar Morin's analysis of mass-media texts in Morin et al., *La Française aujourd'hui* (Paris: Julliard, 1960), pp. 83-88. Morin explores the writing of movie magazines in *Les Stars* (Paris: Seuil, 1972).
8 Creative writers of considerable prominence decry the separation of Brazilian literature from that of Spanish-speaking Latin America in "Encuesta: argentinos y brasileños en la literatura," *La Nación* [Buenos Aires], 3a sección, 30 de mayo, 1976, 1.
9 María Ester Gilio, remark to Clarice Lispector in "Mis libros son mis cachorros," interview-article in *Crisis* [Buenos Aires], 39 (1976), 42.
10 Castellanos, "Si 'poesía no eres tú' entonces ¿qué es?" in her *Mujer que sabe latín...*, pp. 204-205.
11 Castellanos, "María Luisa Mendoza: el lenguaje como instrumento" and "Mercedes Rodoreda: el sentimiento de la vida," in her *Mujer que sabe latín...*, pp. 165-70, pp. 133-38 respectively.
12 See Castellanos' discussion of the writings of the Marquesa Calderón de la Barca, a fashion-conscious ambassador's wife, "La mujer mexicana del siglo XX," in her *Mujer que sabe latín...*, pp. 159-65. Castellanos insisted on the testimonial value of writers like Mme. de Sévignée, Colette and Anita Loos, whose work could too easily be dismissed as "frilly." She made this point in a course I took from her at the Universidad Ibero-Americana, summer of 1970.

[13] The *Excélsior* articles have been made accessible in the above-cited *El uso de la palabra*.

[14] Amy Kaminsky, "The Real Circle of Iron: Mothers and Children, Children and Mothers, in Four Argentine Novels," *Latin American Literary Review*, 4, 9 (1976), 77-86.

[15] Marta Lynch, "Testimonio: con mi obra," *Hispamérica*, 3, 7 (1974), 61-64.

[16] Lynch discusses these matters in, for example, "El paso de Lefebvre no ha significado nada," *Extra* [Buenos Aires], 13, 146 (1977), 63.

[17] Lynch, interview with Martha Paley de Francescato, *Hispamérica*, 4, 10 (1975), 34.

[18] Lynch, *Hispamérica* interview, 35.

[19] As well as the above-cited article and review, see Lewald's comments in his anthology, *Escritores platenses: ficciones del siglo XX* (New York: Houghton-Mifflin, 1971), pp. 20-21, and his *Eduardo Mallea* (New York: Twayne, 1977), pp. 41-42.

[20] Lewald makes this implicit social essayism central to his discussion of Bullrich and Marta Lynch in "Aspects of the Modern Argentine Woman," and in his anthology, *Diez cuentistas argentinas* (Buenos Aires: Ediciones Riomar, 1968), p. 8, p. 88.

[21] Katherine K. Phillips, "Silvina Bullrich," in David William Foster, ed., *A Dictionary of Contemporary Latin American Authors* (Tempe: Center for Latin American Studies, Arizona State University, 1975), p. 18.

[22] Silvina Bullrich, *George Sand: una mujer como yo* (Buenos Aires: Emecé, 1972), p. 461; see also her *La mujer argentina en la literatura* (Buenos Aires: Centro Nacional de Documentación e Información Educativa, 1972).

[23] Bullrich, "Nota autobiográfica," in her *Entre mis veinte y treinta años* (Buenos Aires: Emecé, 1971), p. 619 (entire essay, pp. 609-22).

[24] For examples of the variety of this debate, see Julio Mafud, *El desarraigo argentino: claves argentinas para un estudio social americano* (Buenos Aires: Américalee, 1966), pp. 16-18, 100-103; Esther Vilar, *El varón domado*, trans. Máximo Estrella (México: Editorial Grijalbo, 1973); *Sur*, special issue on women, 326-28 (1970-71); Beatriz Guido, *Una madre* (Buenos Aires: Emecé, 1963); Dalmiro Sáenz' consideration of masculinity and femininity in *Diálogo con un homosexual* (Buenos Aires: Merlín, 1974), and *Carta abierta a mi futura ex mujer* (Buenos Aires: Emecé, 1974); María Angélica Bosco, *Cartas de mujeres* (Buenos Aires: Emecé, 1975), especially her reply to Esther Vilar, pp. 188-236, and *Carta abierta a Judas* (Buenos Aires: Emecé, 1971); Victoria Ocampo, essays on women writers and feminism in the ten volumes of her journalistic essays, *Testimonios* (Madrid: Revista del Occidente. 1935; Buenos Aires: Sur. 1941; Buenos Aires: Sudamericana, 1950; subsequent volumes through 1977, Sur); Darío Cantón, *El mundo de los tangos de Gardel* (Buenos Aires: Instituto Torcuato di Tella, Centro de Investigaciones Sociales, 1969).

[25] Lewald makes this point in his Bullrich review.

[26] Arturo Jauretche, *El medio pelo en la sociedad argentina* (Buenos Aires: A. Peña Lillo, 1966), pp. 193-211. Guido receives serious consideration in Noé Jitrik, *Seis novelistas de la nueva promoción* (Mendoza, Argentina: Cuadernos de Versión, 1959); her work has appeared in *Sur* and received favorable review there, e.g., Adolfo Bioy Casares on Guido's *La caída*, *Sur*, 243 (1956), 82-83.

[27] Plato, *The Republic*, Book III, Argument 395. It will be remembered that Plato's unease over the poet's ability to speak in a voice not his own, transgressing gender and social class distinctions, led him to banish poets from his ideal republic.

[28] Margaret Mead, *Male and Female: A Study of the Sexes in a Changing Society*

(New York: William Morrow, 1949), p. 36.

29 For instance, Leslie Fiedler stresses positive and negative aspects of literary mythmaking in the widely-read *Love and Death in the American Novel* (New York: Criterion Books, 1960).

30 Millett, p. 148.

31 Patricia O'Connor, "Francisco García Pavón's Sexual Politics," *Journal of Spanish Studies: Twentieth Century*, 1, 1 (1973), 65-81.

32 Birgitta Vance, "The Great Clash: Feminist Literary Criticism meets up with Spanish Reality," *Journal of Spanish Studies: Twentieth Century*, 2, 2 (1974), 111.

33 Castellanos, *Las amistades peligrosas*, in her *Juicios sumarios* (Xalapa, México: Universidad Veracruzana, 1966), pp. 221-30.

34 Castellanos, remarks in above-cited seminar.

35 Castellanos, "Lección de cocina," in her *Album de familia* (México: Joaquín Mortiz, 1971), p. 7.

36 Mario Vargas Llosa, *La ciudad y los perros* (Barcelona: Seix Barral, 1967), p.75.

37 Fredric R. Jameson, "Metacommentary," *PMLA*, 86 (1971), 9-18.

38 Castellanos, "Lección de cocina," p. 13.

39 Castellanos, "Lección de cocina," p. 16.

40 Castellanos, "Lamentación de Dido," in her *Poemas 1953-1955* (México: Colección Metáfora, 1957), p. 58.

41 Castellanos, "Lamentación de Dido," p. 58.

42 Castellanos, "Lamentación de Dido," p. 56.

43 Castellanos, "Mercedes Rodoreda: el sentimiento de la vida," pp. 133-38.

44 Plato, of course, found the writer's practice of creating or feigning new voices exceptionally troublesome, potentially deceitful or confusing. Present-day discussion of the phenomenon includes Norman Friedman, "Point of View in Fiction: The Development of a Critical Concept," *PMLA*, 70 (1955), 1160-84; Wayne C. Booth, *The Rhetoric of Fiction* (Chicago: University of Chicago, 1961); Tzvetan Todorov, "Poétique," in Oswald Ducrot et al., *Qu'est-ce que le structuralisme?* (Paris: Seuil, 1968), pp. 97-166.

45 Ludomir Doluzel develops these concepts in *Narrative Modes in Czech Literature* (Toronto: University of Toronto, 1973).

46 Especially good commentary on this question is found in the above-cited volume by Morin et al., *La Française aujourd'hui*. Millett deals with the practical problems of making marginal women politically articulate in *The Prostitution Papers* (New York: Basic Books, 1971). Millett's remarks are interesting because she worked with women whose ability to state their case effectively was originally very poor and showed notable improvement through organized effort.

47 Mary Louise Pratt, *Toward a Speech Act Theory of Literary Discourse* (Bloomington: Indiana University, 1977).

48 Bella Jozef has pointed out Lispector's mocking exposé of the socialized conventions of discourse. Jozef sees this ironic treatment as directed at both the fossilized tradition of literature and the stereotyped behavior of Lispector's characters. See "Clarice Lispector: La transgresión como acto de libertad," *Revista Iberoamericana*, Nos. 98-99 (1977), 225-31.

Clarice
Lispector

Clarice Lispector:
Articulating Women's Experience

I

Looking at the critical commentary on the fiction of Clarice Lispector, one immediately notes how much attention has been given to the existential themes that run through her work. Benedito Nunes and others have studied Lispector's writings as the literary elaboration of a set of philosophical concerns: the human being's need to make choices and take responsibility; the terror of contemplating nothingness and meaninglessness; the evasions with which people avoid consideration of such terrifying phenomena. Criticism that focuses on these issues has established Lispector as an artistic explorer of the human condition, an "existential writer" comparable to Jean-Paul Sartre and Albert Camus.[1]

A second feature of Lispector's work has drawn the attention of literary analysts with a more structural approach. The Brazilian writer shows great inventiveness in her handling of narrative voice or fictional point of view. Maria Luisa Nunes, for instance, studies the many narrative strategies employed in the short stories of *Laços de família* (1960; English translation, *Family Ties*, 1972). She finds this multiplicity of techniques exceptionally efficacious in providing access to the characters' consciousness.[2] Sílvio Castro, too, makes the variegated treatment of the narration the point of departure for his study. In his analysis, the very fact that so many techniques are used in conjunction is a significant break with traditional fiction. The fusion of "discurso indireto radical, monólogo interior como fonte de revelação da ficção (radical indirect discourse, interior monologue as the source of fictional exposition)" as part of the innovation that "permitirá a Clarice Lispector uma nova linguagem (allows Clarice Lispector [to develop] a new language)." In Castro's analysis, the use of swiftly varying narrative techniques structures "uma montagem psicológica, montagem que se realiza antes do recolhimento do material a ser montado (a psychological montage, a montage that is set up before acquiring the matter to be placed in it)."[3] Bella Jozef discusses the meta-literary implications of the "estructura polifónica (polyphonic structure)" of the fiction, which presents a "diálogo de varios discursos (dialogue of several discourses)."[4] These discussants underline the functionality of such patterning in conveying the inner upheaval occasioned by sudden insights into the nature of one's existence. Owen

23

Kellerman's formal typological study again reveals the complex multiplicity characteristic of this aspect of Lispector's writings.[5]

This study takes as its point of departure these already-established features of Lispector's work: her existential questioning and her shifting-about of narrative control. I propose to show how these two aspects of her work function jointly in the generation of a commentary upon the condition of being female. The "femininity" of the Brazilian's work has often attracted notice. For instance, María Ester Gilio calls Lispector's fiction "esencialmente femenina (essentially feminine),"[6] while Dennis Seniff praises her "keen insight into feminine psychology."[7] Rosario Castellanos made the Brazilian one of the subjects of an inquiry into the literary manifestations of feminine consciousness. In her 1973 *Mujer que sabe latín...(A Woman Who Knows Latin...),* the Mexican feminist critic shows the implicit examination of the female role that runs through Lispector's writings.[8] Moreover, one of Clarice Lispector's early literary models and a writer with whom she is often compared is Virginia Woolf, perhaps the literary feminist *par excellence.*[9]

At first, it might seem an eccentric displacement to seek an examination of societally-determined sex roles in writings so focused on the individual's existence. Bella Jozef, to cite one critic, states that Lispector "no busca un explicación social, al nivel ideológico (does not look for a social explanation, at the ideological level)."[10] Yet, Jozef's analysis ably reveals Lispector's abrasive irony intended to "desmitificar la sociedad (demythify society)," whose "padrones y normas sociales ya consagrados (pre-sanctified social norms and patterns)" force people into "formas cristalizadas de comportamiento (rigidly fixed forms of behavior)."[11] Social factors enter this fictional world insofar as they constrict the characters, stifle awareness, and prevent the emergence of fully existent humanity. Since this constraining effect is most severe for those in a too-circumscribed role, it is significant that in *Laços de família,* considered the best working-out of the author's existential subject-matter, several protagonists are found living in very delimited, traditional-housewife roles. Among these are the heroines of two of the stories to be examined here, "Amor (Love)" and "Devaneio e embriaguez duma rapariga (Daydreams of a Drunken Woman)." The adolescent heroine of the third story under discussion, "Preciosidade (Preciousness)" also finds herself troubled and confused by society's notions of femininity and the female role.[12]

For a perspective on women's diminished existential possibilities, one should refer to Simone de Beauvoir's *Le Deuxième Sexe (The Second Sex,* 1949). Beauvoir's complaint about women's role is. precisely, that woman is not treated as one capable of becoming "an autonomous existent."[13] Under the current social arrangement, men are led to believe that women, unlike themselves, do not confront doubt, decision, nothingness and absurdity and hence are not fully human:

> Appearing as the Other, woman appears at the same time as an abundance of being in contrast to that existence, the nothingness of which man senses in himself; the Other, being regarded as the object in the eyes of the subject, is regarded as *en soi;* therefore as a being. In woman is incarnated in

positive form the lack that the existent carries in his heart, and it is in seeking to be made whole through her that man hopes to attain self-realization.[14]

In Beauvoir's judgement, this view of women is not peculiar to men, nor are men the only ones to derive gratification from it. Women, too, come to believe that they cannot be other than they are, that their female nature freezes them into established patterns and obviates the human need to create oneself continually anew. Diffused throughout the culture, this tenet becomes both an oppressive constraint and an excuse for women not to take a voice in determining their own actions.

Beauvoir does not, of course, claim that all males enjoy optimum conditions for realizing an authentic and responsible existence. A life lived by Sartrean standards of "good faith" is massively demanding for any member of modern Western society. Nor is the feeling of having "no say" in the running of one's affairs an experience exclusive to women. Nonetheless, women are more vulnerable to this apparently voiceless, stagnant plight. This is because society maintains them in a restrictive role and discourages them from articulating life choices. At the same time, at least as a social ideal, "man is defined as a being who is not fixed, who makes himself what he is," and who can assert his will.[15] Of particular importance in Beauvoir's analysis, is the fact that women are discouraged from formulating, either inwardly or in overt speech and writing, the alternatives to their present pattern of life. Rather, the social arrangement pushes women toward a trivial, limited manner of thought and verbal expression that tends to preserve their narrowly-defined role.

Before applying these concepts in the analysis of three short stories, I should reemphasize that I am using *voice* in the sense of efficacy in discourse activities. The issue of narrative voice or narrative point of view is important as the technical device that helps lay bare patterns of discourse. In analyzing shifts in point of view. I am looking for structures that reveal women's difficulty in achieving an efficacious inner and outer voice.

II

The female malaise Beauvoir describes finds a fictional representative in Ana, the housewifely protagonist of the short story "Amor." When the reader first meets Ana, she has spent years in a muted and suppressed form of life, as far removed as possible from the anxieties of freedom. Her unwillingness to address herself to any but routine domestic matters results in a virtual silencing of her most vital self. Ana's evasive tactic is, notably, an exaggerated compliance with the socially-prescribed wife-and-mother role. For instance, the narrator explains Ana's habitual strategy for warding off the stirrings of existential terror: "Mas na sua vida não havia lugar para que sentisse ternura pelo seu espanto—ela o abafava com a mesma habilidade que as lides em casa lhe haviam transmitido. Saía então para fazer compras ou levar objetos para consertar, cuidando do lar e dal família á revelia dêles. Quando voltasse era o fim da tarde e as crianças vindas do colégio exigiam-na. Assim chegaria a noite, com sua tranqüila vibração (But in her life there was no opportunity to cherish her fears—she suppressed them with that same ingenuity she had acquired from domestic struggles. Then she would go out shopping or take things to be mended, unobtrusively looking after her home and her family. When she returned it would already be late afternoon and the children back from school would absorb her attention. And so the evening descended with its quiet excitement)."[16] The event upon which "Amor" turns is a dramatic attitudinal upheaval in which Ana comes to see her fixed, rigid housewifeliness as "um modo moralmente louco de viver (a morally crazy way to live; p. 26)."

Maria Luisa Nunes has identified a multiplicity of narrative strategies within this one story: narrated monologue (or indirect interior monologue), internal analysis of the character by a third-person narrator, as well as direct quotation from Ana's mental processes (to use Nunes' terminology).[17] For Nunes, the interest of these various structures is their efficacy in the vivid rendering of consciousness.

In terms of the present study, the very fact that there should be so much intervention on the narrator's part and that the mediation should vary so greatly in degree is highly significant. The text has as its foremost task to communicate the mechanical quality of Ana's life in the years preceding her crisis and to narrate her crisis and its aftermath. It effects this labor through, on the one hand, the narrator's reportage, editorializing and summary and, on the other, the direct and indirect transmission of Ana's perception, formulation and attempted communication of this same subject-matter. By comparing passages in which the narrator's skillful elaboration is apparent with passages in which Ana's thoughts and speech are salient, the reader receives a commentary on the heroine's relatively poor powers of articulation. This becomes a commentary on her womanly role.

An example of a matter treated twice, once with much editorial participation by the narrator and once with very little, is how Ana has avoided all contemplation of the drama of existence. The first account appears before the "plot," such as it is, begins. The narrator provides a preliminary summation of Ana, supplementing the character's limited vision with wit, eloquence, insight, and mastery of metaphorical and abstract language:

No fundo, Ana sempre tivera necessidade de sentir a raiz firme das coisas. E isso um lar perplexamente lhe dera. Por caminhos tortos, viera a cair num destino de mulher, com a surprêsa de nêle caber como se o tivesse inventado. O homem com quem casara era um homem verdadeiro, os filhos que tivera eram filhos verdadeiros .... Havia ... emergido para descobrir que também sem a felicidade se vivia: abolindo-a, encontrara uma legião de pessoas, antes invisíveis, que viviam como quem trabalha .... O que sucedera a Ana antes de ter o lar estava para sempre fora de seu alcance: uma exaltação perturbada que tantas vezes se confundira com felicidade insuportável.

Deep down, Ana had always found it necessary to feel the firm roots of things. And this is what a home had surprisingly provided. Through tortuous paths, she had achieved a woman's destiny, with the surprise of conforming to it almost as if she had invented that destiny herself. The man whom she

had married was a real man, the children she mothered were real children . . . .
She had . . . emerged to discover that life could be lived without happiness;
by abolishing it she had found a legion of persons, previously invisible, who
lived as one works . . . . What had happened to Ana before possessing a
home of her own stood forever beyond her reach: that disturbing exaltation
she had often confused with unbearable happiness (pp. 18-19).

Four pages later, one finds a second elaboration of the same subject-matter. This time, the topic appears as part of Ana's ongoing thoughts during her crisis, which is now fully underway. The language of narration is assimilated to that of Ana herself. There is still a mediator interposed between heroine and reader, relaying Ana's thoughts, but the narrator refrains from tampering with the material. Maria Luisa Nunes describes such passages in *Laços* as a reporting of the character's consciously formalized thoughts. Nunes finds that, essentially, only the verb forms have been changed and the pronouns transferred from first to third person; everything else is the character's "own."[18] Here, then, is Ana's retrospective look at her lost, pre-crisis life:

Ela apaziguara tão bem a vida, cuidara tanto para que esta não explodisse.
Mantinha tudo em serena compreensão, separava uma pessoa das outras,
as roupas eram claramente feitas para serem usadas e podia-se escolher
pelo jornal o filme da noite—tudo feito de modo a que um dia se seguisse
ao outro.

She had skillfully pacified life; she had taken so much care to avoid
upheavals. She had cultivated an atmosphere of serene understanding,
separating each person from the others. Her clothes were clearly designed
to be practical, and she could choose the evening's film from the newspaper—
and everything was done in such a manner that each day should smoothly
succeed the previous one (p. 22).

What immediately differentiates the two summaries is the homely, pedestrian quality of the second: the references to quotidian things, the absence of complex, thought-demanding figures such as appear in the first version (e.g., "a legion of persons, previously invisible . . . "), the comparatively low level of abstraction. It is now possible to see, by comparing the two accounts, signs of Ana's weak ability to register experience fully and structure coherent thoughts about it.

The first indication of her problem is the tremendous amount of upheaval she must experience before she is able to assemble this portrait of her life. In this connection, the four pages that elapse between the two versions are important. When one first reads of Ana's mechanical housewife routine, she is still immersed in it, incapable of standing outside it. The narrator points out that up until she takes a seat on a trolley, she has had no free moment for observation or reflection, being occupied with errands. Indeed, she clings to unreflective habits of mind to the last possible moment; even as she enters her crisis of doubt, "Ana ainda teve tempo de pensar por um segundo que os irmãos viriam jantar (Ana still had time to reflect for a second that her brothers were coming to dinner: p. 20)."

Because Ana has forbidden herself to formulate thoughts on the nature of existence, she finds it difficult to explain to herself what is happening to her. Her first reactions are nonverbal and inchoate: allowing her shopping bag to drop to the floor, letting out a shriek, paling, staring at the blind man who has somehow triggered her turmoil. She then registers perceptions that metaphorically express her discomfort in her role. Especially prominent is her net shopping bag, emblematic of her neatly-contained, tied-in domesticity: "A rêde de tricô era áspera entre os dedos, não íntima como quando a tricotara (The string bag felt rough between her fingers, not soft and familiar as when she had knitted it; (p. 21)." Not only is the confining network now chafing and oppressive, but its contents are no longer held intact: "Vários anos ruíam, as gemas amarelas escorriam (Several years fell away, the yellow yolks trickled; p. 21)."

As Ana's awareness of her situation grows, these metaphorical displacements finally lead to a recognition that the discomfort and rupture are not in her shopping bag or eggs, but within her being: "O que chamava de crise viera afinal (What she called a crisis had come at last; p. 22)." With this sentence the narrator emphasizes that Ana has reached the point where she can now use words to confront and pattern her turbulent experience. Only after Ana has reached this level of aware articulation is she able to produce a summary of her previous unreflective life.

However, Ana's review of her past is still not as fully elaborated as the one in which the narrator editorializes. Looking at the two versions, one notes that the narrator has laid bare the connection between Ana's exaggerated female role and her existential absurdity. In the first version, *home, husband* and *children* figure saliently; it is clear that forming a home was Ana's pretext for rejecting the dangerous part of her human condition. Ana's version completely omits what the narrator stresses, her hyperbolic "cair num destino de mulher ([having)] achieved a woman's destiny; p. 18)," The woman also fails to account for another aspect of her ultradomesticity: the fact that it obliges her to live "sem a felicidad (without happiness; p. 18)," as the narrator puts it, closed to the stimulation of a more widely-lived existence. In short, Ana's self-accounting is good in comparison with her previous inarticulate condition, but poor compared with the narrator's richer elaboration. She has attained an inner voice, but an incomplete one.

III

In the second part of "Amor," these mediated renderings of Ana's consciousness are supplemented with direct quotations, including actual utterances addressed to other characters. The first of these direct manifestations occurs when Ana attempts to communicate her new-found insights to another person. Upon arriving home after her crisis, the woman faces an evening of discourse tasks: greetings, dinner-table conversation. These verbal transactions require a good deal of social skill, but none of them can possibly be accommodated to her new and urgent concerns. Her wife-and-hostess role is so patterned as to leave no room for the critical discussion of such questions as life's ultimate meaning.

Because of this inadequacy in her normal speech opportunities, Ana steps entirely outside the rules and improvises a strange interchange with her small son. This event is intended to create a conduit for her "unspeakable" existential concerns: "Abraçou o filho, quase a ponto de machucá-lo . . . A vida é horrível, disse-lhe baixo, faminta (She embraced her son, almost hurting him . . . 'Life is horrible,' she said to him in a low voice, as if famished; p. 26)." Here Ana has no trouble verbalizing her discovery in a way that is accurate and conscious. However, she has not taken into account the character and probable reaction of her intended confidant. When she adds to this first statement "Tenho mêdo (I am afraid)," the child bursts into frightened weeping. The encounter degenerates still further when the mother instructs the child: "Não deixe mamãe te esquecer (Don't let Mummy forget you; p. 26.)." The transaction becomes so weird that the chosen recipient of Ana's new vision flees, directing at her "o pior olhar que jamais recebera (the worst look that she had ever received; p. 26)."

Ana's remarkably inept handling of this encounter indicates that she has no verbal skills—no "voice"—suitable to the overt questioning and criticism of basic assumptions. Here one sees the fictional laying-bare of a problem that has much interested feminist linguists. As Robin Lakoff observes in her 1975 *Language and Women's Voice*, even women who are fluent in the discussion of routine topics may be virtually voiceless concerning crucial or potentially threatening issues. Lakoff specifies that this silencing is not primarily the result of overt repressive measures, such as forbidding women to speak. Rather, the social-ization of girl children into the female role provides an insufficient apprenticeship in the verbal questioning of certain highly sensitive matters. Moreover, when women do attempt to speak out on these charged subjects, they may be returned to a more harmless form of discourse through a variety of covert, often uncon-scious strategies.[19]

The displacement of discourse from disturbing questions to housewifely ones becomes evident in an exchange between Ana and her husband. Ana expresses what appears to her husband to be a disproportionate amount of anxiety. However, he resolves the matter by attributing all of her distress to excessive concern over the malfunctioning kitchen stove. Thus when Ana proclaims sweepingly, "Não quero que lhe aconteca nada, nunca! (I don't want anything ever to happen to you!)," her husband narrows that statement in scope by replying: "Deixe que pelo menos me aconteça o fogão dar um estouro (You can't prevent the stove from having its little explosions; p. 29)." His wry humor and smile succeed in reducing Ana's terror at the instability of existence to a womanly case of over-apprehension about trifles, which he can dissipate with an embrace and soothing utterance.

This brief verbal transaction illustrates Lispector's satisfyingly complex critique of social roles. It would be ridiculous to blame Ana's husband for exhibiting a condescending attitude toward his wife or for circumscribing her horizons. The husband is only trying to bring an inexplicable, threatening situation back within the bounds of an exchange between damsel-in-distress and manly protector. The "villain" here is neither masculine nor feminine, but abstract. The rigidity of structuring in socialized discourse prevents Ana from making manifest the source of her terror. In turn, her inability to share her vision of absurdity leads to the rapid dimming of that vision. After this conversation, with its trivializing and neutralizing effect, the narrator describes Ana's husband as "afastando-a do perigo de viver (removing her from the danger of living; p. 30)."

Most telling, in this respect, is the fact that the narrator assigns no names to those with whom Ana speaks; they remain the husband, the child, the brothers, the maid. This manner of reference suggests that the conversational partners are playing their socially assigned parts around Ana, nudging her back into her own proper role as wife, mother and hostess. Ana possesses not only a name but, through her special awareness, an individuality highly incompatible with the performance of her prescribed womanly functions.

IV

During the second half of the story, the narrator begins to signal that there is now a more direct transmission of the "utterances" of Ana's inner voice. This is the case, for example, when the heroine becomes aware of her deviant reaction to the stranger she saw on the trolley: "Oh! mas ela amava o cego! pensou com os olhos molhados. No entanto não era com êste sentimento que se iria a uma igreja ('Oh! but she loved the blond man.' she thought with tears in her eyes. Meanwhile. it was not with this sentiment that one would go to church: p. 27)."

Here Ana makes perhaps her most direct confession of deep-seated aberrance. Yet, her self-characterization falls short of being overt, either in what is admitted or in the form that admission takes. Impressively, although the narrator's *she thought* signals a direct quotation from Ana's mental processes, the third-person, past-tense statement does not look like anything Ana could actually think. Jozef sees Ana's presentation as a form of duplication in which the woman's fragmented self allows her to be both the commentator and commented-upon: "El comportamiento artístico se caracteriza por el desdoblamiento del yo que se ve en el acto de producción, actor y espectador de sí mismo, sujeto del espectáculo y objeto del juego, captando una conciencia en fraccionamiento por la disociación del yo (The artistic procedure is characterized by a duplication of the *I* which is seen in the act of production, actor and spectator of itself, the subject of the spectacle and the object of the game, capturing a consciousness that has been fragmented by the tearing-asunder of the *I*)."[20] Whether or not the form of Ana's self-characterization reflects such a divided self, its ambiguity is purposely troubling. Its equivocal character is yet another sign of Ana's extreme difficulty in formalizing insights not proper to her official, housewifely sense of self.

A further ambiguity appears when the reader attempts to attribute the second assertion ("Meanwhile . . .") either to the narrator or to Ana. This statement, with its implications of unruly eroticism, may be too upsetting for the heroine to voice, even to herself. In that case, the narrator is once again supplementing Ana's incomplete elaboration and, in so doing, revealing its limited, censored character. Alternatively, the sentence may be a continuation of the quotation from Ana's mind marked by *she thought*; both statements are in the third person and past tense. Sharing Ana's disorientation to some extent, the reader is unable to ascertain what the woman really knows, admits, and formalizes in her unspoken verbal material.

V

Throughout the greater part of the story, one observes Ana's painful coming to consciousness. From an unreflective immersion in household routine, she progresses to a chaotic flow of disconcerting perceptions that metaphorically correspond to her plight and moves on to a partial articulation of her human problem. As Ana gains awareness, the narrator entrusts a greater burden of the story to her, calling upon her inner and even her spoken voice to tell the reader where she stands.

The last paragraphs, however, present a swift change. Ana's new insight has come to an end, as the narrator explicitly announces. Now nothing of Ana's voice is heard as the third-person narrator does all the work of explaining how her husband calms her supposedly stove-related fears and the couple retires for the night.

The handling of narrative voice in this story gives an artistic representation to a phenomenon frequently explored in the social essays of feminists.[21] Ana is voiceless largely through acquiescence to her wife-and-mother role. Nonetheless, the reader sees her acquire the beginnings of a voice when, for example, she correctly identifies the nature of her problem by saying "Life is horrible (p. 26)." Here is the implication that even the most suppressed individual can yet generate a voice capable of speaking out and questioning. The acquisition of this voice is painful; early attempts at articulation may be disastrous. If the new voice finds no support from the social environment, it may disappear, and the individual may resume the predictable patterns of socialized discourse.

For this reason, the narrator's intervention and stepping-back give an index to Ana's varying progress in being her own spokeswoman. The reader sees how much of Ana's situation cannot be stated by the woman herself and, hence, falls to the narrator. Woman here epitomizes the human being silenced in a narrow role. The shifting pattern of voices shows how such an individual must develop in order to become able to enunciate life decisions and vital awareness—in sum, to become fully existent.

VI

The heroine of "Devaneio e embriaguez duma rapariga (The Daydreams of a Drunken Woman)," another short story included in the same volume, differs superficially from the verbally stifled Ana. The nameless *rapariga* provides plentiful outpourings from both her inner and outer voices. Large portions of the text represent her rambling interior monologues. These passages are patently marked as the character's "own" by their adherence to a Lusitanian standard of speech proper of the heroine's Portuguese origin.[22] There is no reason for the narrator's occasional summaries and intercalated remarks to assume this notably European form. Thus, one can see that the overt editorial presence and participation is relatively slight; often the narrator's only task is to pass on to the reader what the heroine thought or said. Apart from her interior soliloquies, the heroine gives audible voice to a wide, rather random variety of material. She bursts into song, recites ritualized verbal formulae and talks to herself, her husband and imaginary conversation partners.

Moreover, the *rapariga* considers her skill as a conversationalist to be one of her accomplishments in life. Early in the story she is heard rehearsing, in front of a mirror, coquettish repartee. Later, immersed in a social occasion, she secretly glories in her participation: "Naturalmente que ela palestrava. Pois que lhe não faltavam os assuntos nem as capacidades (Naturally she talked, since she lacked neither the ability to converse nor topics to discuss; p. 10)." In her judgment, her fluent production of sociable "palestras (conversation)" proves that "ela não era nenhuma parola d'aldeia (she was no provincial ninny; p. 9)." Indeed, her narcissistic obsession with her imagined verbal prowess becomes a recurring topic in the text. Repeatedly, she defines herself as a woman who has a voice and knows how to use it smoothly and efficaciously. This insistence, however, is one of the text's ironic strategies. The reader cannot possibly concur with the *rapariga*'s self-assessment. From the outset of the story signs of conflict, uncertainty and inadequacy are manifest in the woman's habits of speech and thought.

The *rapariga* first appears at a moment when the demands of her mothering role have suddenly diminished. With her children away, she lacks her routine patterning and cannot manage to structure her own time. In an empty house with an empty day ahead, she fills time with lengthy sleeping, primping and reflection.

During this first part of the story, the narrator's presence is more evident than it will be subsequently. Authorial presence is visible in occasional summaries of the heroine's thoughts and actions and in verbs of declarandi following quotations from her uttered and unuttered speech. As in "Amor," the narrator's burden of telling the story is greatest before the heroine enters the crisis that brings her inner turbulence to a conscious level. Once agitation forces her to begin formalizing her existential terrors, her direct and indirect interior monologues can become the substance of the narration. However, even before she achieves this involuntary eloquence, the *rapariga* formulates a good many telling phrases without being aware of their significance.

Her early formulations lay bare a deep-seated conflict in her view of herself and her life situation. She harbors within her mind two mutually contradictory voices. One, cheerful and given to romanticizing, insists she is a langorous belle luxuriating in a stretch of leisure. Indirect interior monologue reports such thoughts as "Ai, ai, vinha da rua como uma borboleta (Oh my!—she would come fluttering in from the street like a butterfly; p. 6)." A darker voice, though, hints that she is beginning to face nothingness and meaninglessness: "que chatura (how boring; p. 6)." The omniscient narrator's remarks favor this latter view, for they describe the heroine as "colérica (irritated)" and "com leve rancor (slightly annoyed; p. 6)." Nonetheless, it remains uncertain whether or not one should consider matters to be seriously amiss.

The next segment resolves the ambiguity of the woman's behavior. Her wildly inappropriate responses to her homecoming husband reveal that crisis, not delightful leisure, is her true state, and that her self-lyricizing contains an element of self-misrepresentation. In this scene, each of the woman's unusual behaviors represents a further rupture with her normally-defined wife-and-mother role. Her patterning of her life has already been thrown into question by the removal of her child-care duties. Now she refuses to make any of the expected wifely responses to her husband: she fails to greet him, to care about his food, clothing or activities and finally she rejects, with impressive crudity, his sexual overtures.

The *rapariga*'s lack of insight into her inchoate rebellion is reflected in the fact that her thoughts on the issue are not heard. The implication is that her notions are not yet sufficiently formed to appear represented even as unuttered speech. It falls to the narrator to describe the chaos of this household in which the wife refuses to play the part of wife. The heroine remains opaque even when the narrator speaks of her mental processes, for one only learns what she is not thinking: "O marido apareceu-lhe já trajado e ela nem sabia o que o homem fizera para o seu pequeno-almôço, e nem olhou-lhe o fato, se estava ou não por escovar, pouco se lhe importava se hoje era dia dele tratar os negócios na cidade (Her husband appeared before her, having already dressed, and she did not even know what he had prepared for his breakfast. She avoided examining his suit to see whether it needed brushing . . . little did she care if this was his day for attending to his business in the city; p. 7)." All that is heard from her overt voice is two harsh rebuffs to her husband; she seems unwilling to recognize or comment upon her obvious disturbance. The husband does offer an interpretation that brings his wife's baffling unwifeliness back within the bounds of normal actions: "estás doente (you're ill; p. 7)." Despite the lack of any somatic disturbance, the heroine accepts this soothing normalization, further delaying recognition of or confrontation with her life crisis.

This scene of household interaction precedes two segments that highlight the heroine's mental processes. These two explorations of consciousness employ, again, a variety of techniques to provide a mass of verbal material documenting what the heroine was saying to herself. The two stand in marked opposition to one another. In the first, the *rapariga* stands outside her everyday housewife persona and thinks in an extraordinary "voice." In the second, she has abruptly returned to her old self and to her routine habits of organizing her world.

As her aberrant, nonwifely self, the woman imagines her life as one open to all possibilities. The real-world constraints on her choices—the result of her family circumstance—now disappear. What replaces them is a vision of freedom and availability to new experience, this vision being strongly colored by an element of Bovarization: "Ela amava . . . . Estava previamente a amar o homem que um dia ela ia amar. Quem sabe lá, isso às vêzes acontecia, e sem culpas nem danos para nenhum dos dois (She was in love . . . . She was anticipating her love for the man whom she would love one day. Who knows, this sometimes happened, and without guilt and injury for either partner; p. 8)."

After these timeless, unfettered imaginings, one is startled to hear the down-to-earth housewife's voice suddenly reassert itself. The woman reminds herself of "as batatas por descascar, os miúdos que voltariam à tarde das titias ai que até me faltei ao respeito!, dia de lavar roupa e serzir as peúgas . . . (the potatoes waiting to be peeled, the kids expected home that same evening from their visit to the country. God, I've lost my self-respect, I have! My day for washing and darning socks . . . ; p. 8)."

What is interesting here is that, in all her ramblings, the heroine avoids referring to the issues underlying her crisis. Indeed, she seeks to mask her turmoil through a euphemistic subterfuge. Scolding herself, she transmutes her conflicted rejection of her role into a simple case of neglectful housekeeping. The notion that she is "vagabunda (lazy; p. 8)," like her husband's assertion that she is unwell, gives an incomprehensible situation the features of recognizability and quotidian verisimilitude.

Nonetheless, in the juxtaposition of her two identities, one can see implicit the matters that generate her trouble. Simone de Beauvoir's characterization of the housewife is descriptive of the *rapariga*'s problem:

> The tragedy of marriage is not that it fails to assure woman the promised happiness—there is no such thing as assurance in regard to happiness—but that it mutilates her; it dooms her to repetition and routine. The first twenty years of a woman's life are extraordinarily rich, as we have seen; she discovers the world and her destiny. At twenty or thereabouts, mistress of a home, bound permanently to a man, a child in her arms, she stands with her life virtually finished forever. Real activities, real work are the prerogative of her man; she has mere things to occupy her which are sometimes tiring but never fully satisfying.[23]

VII

The next segment of the story moves the heroine out of her housebound languor and into the city's nightlife. Accompanied by her husband and his employer, she makes a display of coquettish charm and drinks massive quantities of wine. The wine, along with the turmoil she already harbors, produces a state of almost transcendent excitation.

This section offers copious documentation of the thoughts the woman formulates to herself. These inner reflections reveal still further her inability to take one coherent stance toward the topic, which nonetheless becomes the repeated focus of her anxiety. On the one hand, she reviles her housewife self as a banal and trivialized one from which she has now escaped: "No sábado à noite a alma diária perdida, e que bom perdê-la, e como lembrança dos outros dias apenas as mãos pequenas tão maltratadas (Saturday night, her every-day soul lost, and how satisfying to lose it, and to remind her of former days, only her small, ill-kempt hands; p. 10)." Contradictorily, she glories in the respectability that her matronly status confers upon her. She reassures herself that she can afford to be drunk in public, because she is "protegida pela posição que

alcançara na vida (protected by the position she had attained in life; p. 11).''
The fact that the woman can tell herself such patently opposed things reflects
the contradictions that Beauvoir diagnoses in the traditionally-defined female.
In Beauvoir's analysis, when women chafe under the restraints imposed upon
them, they "simultaneously demand and detest their feminine condition; they
live through it in a state of resentment."[24]

This resentment finally finds a suitable object in the person of a blonde
woman seated in the same restaurant with the *rapariga*. In a seizure of anxiety,
the *rapariga* inwardly constructs a miscellany of accusations against the stranger.
At first the list of complaints appears as a random babble, since the strange
woman is accused both of licentiousness and of excessive piety and prudery.
What confers unity upon the accusations is the *rapariga*'s continuing obsession
with the female role. Lithe, elegant, wearing a beautiful hat, the rival represents
a woman not yet fettered by domesticity. To counter the jealousy she feels, the
rapariga seeks to magnify the importance of her own wife-and-mother status.
The untrammeled blonde lacks these essential attributes of womanhood: "vai
ver que nem casada era (Bet you anything she isn't even married),'' "vai ver que
não era capaz de parir-lhe, ao seu homem, um filho (I'll bet she couldn't even
bear her man a child; p. 12)." She succeeds in elaborating a scheme in which all
the blonde woman's attractive features become indices of a reprehensible
deviation from the proper role.

The climax of this scene occurs when the *rapariga* appoints herself as the
voice of well-regulated womanhood and, in direct but unuttered allocution, reprimands the aberrant and incomplete female: "Bem sei o que te falta, fidalguita,
e ao teu homem amarelo! E se pensas que t' invejo e ao teu peito chato, fica a
saber que me ralo, que bem me ralo de teus chapéus. A patifas sem brio como
tu, a se fazerem de rogadas eu lhes encho de sopapos (I know what you need,
my beauty, you and your sallow boyfriend! And if you think I envy you with
your flat chest, let me assure you that I don't give a damn for you and your hats.
Shameless sluts like you are asking for a good hard slap on the face; p.
13)."

Maria Luisa Nunes, noting the directness of address in the scolding and
the absence of a mediating narrator, correlates this directness to the heroine's
extreme, overwrought state.[25] One may also say that this direct "stating her
case" shows that the *rapariga*, after wandering about amid contradictory and
half-formulated thoughts, has finally developed a point of view that she can
voice. Her defense of traditional wifely behavior is firm and programmatic,
capable of being preached to the sinful. Although this voice is assertive, few
readers will find it a satisfactory instrument for resolving the heroine's tumult.
Rather, it is a falsifying voice, another evasive displacement. Its essential
inefficacy is revealed when the heroine, lying on her bed later that night, finds
her inner turbulence still in force.

VIII

The next section, the drunken reverie of the story's title, finally breaks with
the preceding pattern of vague perturbation, attitudinal upheaval and successful

evasion of the root problem. The *rapariga* comes face to face with her domesticated persona and with her disaffection from that role. She abandons her defensive strategy of constructing authoritative-sounding statements to neutralize her puzzling new sense of existential terror.

Direct quotation from the woman's ongoing mental processes reveals a self-examination which is neither distorted by romanticizing nor by a rigid model of proper womanhood. She makes an anguished attempt to identify those features of her existence that now seem distressingly absurd: "Aborrecimento, aborrecimento, ai que chatura. Que maçada . . . Que é que se havia de fazer. Ai, è uma tal coisa que se me dà que nem bem sei dizer (Boredom . . . Such awful boredom . . . How sickening! . . . What was one to do? How can I describe this thing inside me? p. 14)." The struggle culminates in the production of a synthesizing self-description: "desiludida, resignada, empanturrada, casada, contente, a vaga náusea (disenchanted, resigned, satiated, married, content, vaguely nauseated; p. 15)." Throughout the course of the story, she has elaborated numerous self-characterizations: the belle, the fragile lily, the woman with a housekeeping problem, the sparkling conversationalist. Now, for the first time, she has worked out an image that the reader can accept as an accurate one.

Following this breakthrough, the woman has considerably greater success in dealing with her crisis. Having admitted that her household life is somewhat absurd and meaningless, she convinces herself that this status is, paradoxically, good and comforting. She refers frankly to her husband and children as the "cousas . . . nauseantes (nauseating . . . things; p. 15)" that will enable her to go on living after her crisis of insight.

Although the heroine here achieves her most authentic voice, her powers of articulation still lag considerably behind her desire for self-knowledge. She herself bewails her insufficiency, while the omniscient narrator emphasizes it by ironically "helping her along." The heroine gropes for an adequate description of her new revelations: "Ai que cousa que se me dá! (Heavens above! What *is* wrong with me?)" The narrator emerges from a period of silence to provide, in omniscient fashion, the answer: "Era a tristeza (It was unhappiness; pp. 15-16)."

The incomplete, but authentic, articulation of her life situation frees the *rapariga* from the anxiety that has plagued her up to this point. The story's ending reveals her planning a reaccommodation into her newly-conceptualized role, beginning with a massive housecleaning: a notably partial triumph.

The *rapariga*'s problem is emblematic of a more generalized difficulty affecting women. To achieve a valid and effective voice, women need more than the simple ability to make statements. Here, the heroine has cultivated a markedly feminine set of verbal skills. These capacities serve her well for such functions as socializing, flirtation, scolding, moralizing and the fabrication of a princess persona for herself.

The heroine's serious difficulties arise when she tries to apply these hyperfeminine strategies to her existential crisis. The radical self-questioning she needs to enunciate cannot find its adequate expression. The *rapariga* avoids taking a responsible look at her life situation by producing a barrage of frivolous or self-righteous verbiage. To assume a conscious hold on the issue at stake, she must find a new "voice" altogether.

The narrator reveals this struggle by withdrawing when the woman faces the possibility of speaking to her true problem. On each of these crucial occasions, the woman makes an attempt to address the issues of her life, but only at the story's end has she achieved a satisfactory statement.

IX

Compared to these housewives who formalize so little of their insight into overt utterance, the adolescent heroine of "Preciosidade (Preciousness)" presents an impressive picture of verbalization. After her crisis of self-reappraisal, she not only voices her new perception but shouts it out, albeit in solitude. Moreover, unlike the older heroines, she does not allow her circumstance to remain unchanged after her great moment of introspection. She demands a small, but figuratively important, alteration in the world's treatment of her. This novel speech act, a startling self-assertion, is successful in obtaining the desired results. Before she can effect this successful articulation, though, the heroine must emerge from a rigid and self-stifling life pattern that leaves no room for such communication.

In this story, as in the previous two, the heroine has mastered a complex set of strategies to suppress awareness of her status as human being. Instead of obsessive conformity, though, she relies on deviance as her chief protection. She conceives of herself as an exceptional being unaffected by the incompleteness and instability that afflict existents. Variously, she is "um centauro (a centaur; p. 99)," "impessoal . . . filha dos deuses (impersonal . . . the daughter of the gods; p. 103)" and "a princesa do mistério intacto (the princess of that intact mystery; p. 101)." The outward manifestation of this pretension to a special être en soi is a massive avoidance of human contact. Discourse tasks, insofar as they confirm the uniform humanity of the participants, pose a threat to her privileged status. The narrator details the girl's tactics for evading verbal transactions. For example, here is her behavior at school: "Atravessava o corredor interminável como a um silêncio de trincheira, e no seu rosto havia algo tão feroz—e soberbo também, por causa de sua sombra—que ninguém lhe dizia nada. Proibitiva, ela os impedia de pensar (She crossed the corridor, which seemed as interminable as the silence in a trench and in her expression there was something so ferocious—and proud too because of her shadow—that no one said a word to her. Prohibitive, she forbade them to think; p.98)." The intensity of her horror of verbal contact becomes even more manifest through the structuring of narrative voice. The narrator very rarely quotes directly from the girl's inner voice during the first part of the story. The two longest citations from her conscious formulations refer directly to her continual fear that others "dissessem alguma coisa (might say something [to her]; p. 96)." Here, the narrator carries the burden of explanation for the girl's rejection of human contact; she herself cannot look at her behavior and interpret it. In the narrator's analysis, the heroine dreads even the most mundane speech acts because they may call into question her specialness: "era obrigada a ser venerada (she was obliged to be venerated; p. 96)," not humanized.

When discourse cannot be suppressed, it can be frozen into a private ceremony, again reducing the possibilities of human contamination. A dominant reliance on ritual format is evident in the girl's relations with the family maid. Because the heroine's schedule is unlike that of other family members, she spends several hours each day alone in the house except for the company of the servant. These hours have their own routine. Breakfast is served in silence. Upon coming home from school, the girl initiates speech, but only to direct a unilateral verbal aggression against the maid: "gritava com a empregada que nem sequer lhe respondia (she shouted at the maid who did not even answer; p. 99)." As the maid serves lunch, the ceremony of stylized hostility becomes a reciprocal exchange:

—Magrinha, mas como devora, dizia a empregada esperta.
—Pro diabo, gritava-lhe sombria.

"Skinny, but you can eat all right," the quick-witted maid was saying.
"Go to blazes," she shouted at her sullenly. (p. 99)

Fear of human contact, though, must be weighed against the girl's equal horror of solitude. When she is not in a definable role in relation to others, she suffers intimations of nothingness. By setting herself back within the established context of conventionalized relations she can feel secure, "poder se tornar com alívio uma filha (become to her relief a daughter; p. 100)." The girl's solution to this dilemma is to cultivate a form of discourse with the maid that still maintains the necessary distance: "conversando, evitava a conversa (conversing, she avoided conversation; p. 100)."

None of this "nonconversational" conversation appears transcribed in the text. However, the narrator gives several clues to its functioning. The girl conceives the interaction as a rite in which the maid is an "antiga sacerdotisa (ancient priestess; p. 100)." The goal of the conversation is to forestall the transfer of information. The maid is the possessor of worldly knowledge with which she may try to contaminate the heroine. Again, the heroine's actions evade exposure to the more problematic aspects of the human condition. Although she cannot bear literal solitude, she cannot let the maid impinge on her spiritual solitude. As an index to the intensity of her concern, her own formulation of it appears in a direct quotation from her consciousness: referring to the worldly maid, the girl thinks "Ela imagina que na minha idade devo saber mais do que sei e é capaz de me ensinar alguma coisa (She imagines that at my age I must know more than I do, and she is capable of teaching me something; p. 100)."

X

The detailing of the girl's stratagems has an ironic edge. The most notable feature of her postures, apart from their Byzantine intricacy, is their inadequacy. The girl is troubled by a dim awareness that she is acting in bad faith, shirking her human responsibility. The signs of this awareness are the words the narrator applies to her, presumably reflecting something the heroine feels but cannot quite formalize. Displaying aloofness in the hall, the girl dreads penetration of "o seu disfarce (her disguise; p. 98)." Exhibiting scholarship in the classroom, she becomes "a grande fingida (the great pretender; p. 98)." Even as insulation, her charade is only minimally successful; one sees her barely suppressing panic.

From elements dispersed throughout the early part of the text, the reader pieces together the motives of the heroine's unease. Outstanding among these is her anxiety about her femininity and reluctance to assume the adult female role. Previous critics have pointed out the sexual turbation she suffers, but the question of role in social interactions is also salient.[26] The heroine's rejection of role manifests itself in a minimalization of her potential for "feminine charm." Already a plain girl, she exaggerates her deviance from the ideal of young ladyhood. A stiff, pseudo-military gait, unkempt physical appearance and rough manners proclaim her refusal. In a well-known pattern (e.g., the so-called Bluestockings), disquietude over "womanliness" has as its concomitant a dedication to scholarly work. The classroom offers refuge from her confusion because it is the space "onde ela era tratada como um rapaz (where she was treated like a boy; p. 98)." Her ugly, noisy shoes emerge, through repeated mention, as the paradigmatic marks of her antifemininity.

XI

Clearly, the heroine cannot maintain her guarded "preciousness" indefinitely. It is too difficult a task to deny that she is a person in relation to other persons and, specifically, a woman in relation to men. Lispector's story here makes a point that is also key to Beauvoir's analysis of the female adolescent.[27] No matter how unappealing the young girl finds socially-defined womanhood, she cannot opt out of the web of social bonds. Explicitly or implicitly, she must confront conventional expectations about womanly comportment. The confrontation may result in a passive recreation of the circumscribed womanhood the girl has seen around her. The more aware adolescent, however, begins a struggle to reaccommodate women's role to her individual needs. She agrees to acquire certain attributes of womanhood, but feels torment upon doing so. Beauvoir cites literary, essay, and documentary sources that reveal this conflict. The necessity of becoming a woman generates fear of losing one's uniqueness and sense of life's rich texture. For Beauvoir, this terror is justified, since the current arrangement abruptly curtails the girl's freedom precisely at the moment when she assumes adult status.

The heroine of "Preciosidade" experiences such a confrontation during the course of the story. The event that triggers this confrontation is, in itself, trivial. Two youths, passing the girl on the street, reach out, touch her and flee.

Narrating in *tempo lento*, the third-person relator keeps the reader fully informed on the girl's mental processes. The information is conveyed through the narrator's summary and analysis, through indirect interior monologue and through quotations from her conscious formulations. What stands out here is not the sexuality expressed in the encounter. Rather, the heroine concentrates on the meeting as a social interaction. Her concerns are those of the young woman wondering how to behave in a social situation. As the two youths approach, she must structure her own behavior so as to maintain her dignity. Questions of posture, gait, where to cast her eyes and how to maintain a composed face contribute to what sociologist Erving Goffman has called "the presentation of self in everyday life."[28] These quotidian preoccupations bring home the fact that the girl is, indeed, one of many human beings existing in interrelation. Forced to see herself through the eyes of others, she is suddenly aware of her poor performance in the female role. Her disheveled and unbathed person, her innate plainness and, above all, her clumping shoes make her a figure of social failure.

Following the encounter, the girl's voice disappears from the story temporarily. The narrator, in panoramic summary, informs us of her subsequent actions. The reason for not revealing her mental processes is explicitly given: "não tinha pensado em nada (she hadn't thought about anything; p. 106)." Dislodged from her strict life patterns, she avoids her school, shunning the one area in which she enjoys full mastery of the discourse situation. This anomalous renunciation suggests an incipient rejection of her strategems for keeping discourse, and hence life, under close restraints.

The girl's voice resurfaces at the moment she attempts to reinsert herself into her old routine. In this scene and the following one, which takes place in the school rest room, the heroine has two opposing voices. The first to be heard is her old voice, with its devices for blocking out the problematic and disturbing. The signs of the girl's crisis are patent. Yet upon being questioned by a classmate, she denies that anything is amiss. This effort at denial is not only inefficacious but absurdly counter-productive. Unable to regulate her volume, the agitated heroine startles several schoolmates with a loud "Não (No; p. 106)."

The recognition of her loss of control drives the heroine to seek refuge in the restroom. Here, in solitude, another voice asserts itself for the first time. This new voice is radically unlike her evasive speech; it proclaims the truths the other voice labors to hide: "diante do grande silêncio dos ladrilhos, gritou aguda, supersônica: Estou sòzinha no mundo! Nunca ninguém vai me ajudar, nunca ninguém vai me amar! Estou sòzinha no mundo! (before the great silence of the tiles, she cried out in a high shrill voice, 'I am all alone in the world! No one will ever help me, no one will ever love me! I am all alone in the world!; p. 107)"

The new voice, with its disquieting assertions, cannot yet supplant the girl's old voice. Rather, the reader witnesses a dialectic between the two voices within the same young woman. As the accustomed voice resumes its evasive, dehumanizing tactics, the new voice contests the validity of such procedures. The result is an episode of literal self-questioning and self-confrontation. The narrator transcribes this debate as both uttered and unuttered statements in direct citation and as indirect interior monologue. The use of reflexive verbs in this reportage (interrompeu-se: she interrupted herself; retrucou-se: she retorted to herself) emphasizes that this is self-versus-self discourse.

In warring, the two voices lay bare the principal features of the girl's conflicted state. The old voice would turn away from her new existential insights, returning to quotidian routine before change and growth can take place. The new voice refuses to allow this banalization. Here they oppose one another within the space of one quotation. The girl is missing class because of her crisis, and begins with a trivial reaction to the situation: "Não faz mal, depois copio os pontos, peço emprestado os cadernos para copiar em casa—estou sòzinha no mundo! (It doesn't matter, I'll copy the notes later, I'll borrow someone's notes and copy them later at home—I am all alone in the world!; p. 107)" The issue being disputed is what Massaud Moisés calls "abandoning . . . the mental stagnation which maintains reality intact, in order to gain the condition of being a person."[29] The second focus of contention is the old voice's harshly dismissive attitude toward the human being. This deliberate denigration of self and others is intolerable to the new voice, who says in rebuke: "Não diga isso . . . . Uma pessoa é alguma coisa (Don't say that . . . a person is something; pp. 107-108)."

During this self-encounter, the girl takes preliminary steps toward reestablishing her neglected ties with her fellow beings. Her rather wild appearance, cultivated as a barrier between herself and others, now receives a critical review and remedial action. These measures point to two radical departures from the heroine's accustomed manner of life. On the levels of sex role and sexuality, she assumes the feminine responsibility for presenting herself as physically attractive—a definitive accommodation to her socially-defined part in life. On the level of her discourse problem, she moves toward opening up the lines of communication with others, toward signaling her human "approachability."

Implicit in the girl's changed behavior is the tenet Beauvoir discussed. To participate in society, the young girl must become not only a person, but also a woman, in some generally recognizable sense of womanliness. But does the heroine have an awareness of this principle? The following scene, in which she speaks out on behalf of her new sense of personhood, suggests that she is at least partially conscious of the problem she is resolving. Here are the girl's words to her family: "Preciso de sapatos novos! Os meus fazem muito barulho, uma mulher não pode andar com salto de madeira, chama muita atenção! (I need some new shoes! Mine make a lot of noise, a woman can't walk on wooden heels, it attracts too much attention!; p. 108)" All the elements that have come together in her transformation are there: the individual's right to self-esteem and visible self-care; the link between being a fully entitled person and being a woman; the need to accommodate oneself to role expectations of femininity. However, the girl's ability to articulate these ideas lags behind her perception of them. Unskilled in the labor of expressing existential concerns, she produces an utterance that strikes her listeners as illogical. Her family, moreover, has neither the experience nor the expectation of hearing their daughter speak out on such matters. They take her words at the most literal level possible, and answer her: "Você não é uma mulher e todo salto é de madeira (You are not a woman and all shoe heels are made of wood; p. 108)."

Despite this discouraging response, the girl's statement is not a failure. The reader can perceive the fundamentally valid notions that underlie her wild-sounding formulation. In terms of her new-found acceptance of role, she is a woman. Her preoccupation with footwear makes sense as a metonymic displacement of her desire to make a favorable presentation of herself. The girl, too, knows that she is right, as evidenced by her persistence in the face of her family's incomprehension. In sum, she is voicing her demand in terms that make sense to her, and that establish to her own satisfaction her ability to assert herself.

Even as pragmatic communication, her garbled demand has a measure of efficacy. While the girl's actual words baffle her family, the intensity of her need is unmistakable. Without quite following the processes at work, her listeners grasp the link between the sudden necessity for shoes and the young girl's most essential vital mechanisms. The story ends with the emergence of a woman who can make a claim for herself and be heard. The narrator's last report on the heroine is "E ela ganhou os sapatos novos (And she got her new shoes; p. 108)."

Notes

[1]   Existential themes are discussed in Assis Brasil, *Clarice Lispector* (Rio de Janeiro: Editora Organização Simões, 1969); Benedito Nunes, *O mundo de Clarice Lispector* (Manaus: Edições, do Governo do Estado, 1966) and "O mundo imaginário de Clarice Lispector," in his *O dorso do tigre* (São Paulo: Editora Perspectiva, 1969), pp. 99-139; Rita Herman, "Existence in *Laços de família*," *Luso-Brazilian Review*, 4, 1 (1967), 67-74; Alvaro Lins, discussion of Lispector in his *Os mortos de Sobrecasaca* (Rio de Janeiro: Editôra Civilização Brasileira, 1963), pp. 186-93; Massaud Moisés, "Clarice Lispector: Fiction and Cosmic Vision," trans. Sara McCabe, *Studies in Short Fiction*, 7, 1 (1971), 268-81; Wilson Martins, "O romance brasileiro contemporâneo," *Inti*, No. 3 (1976), 27-36; Giovanni Pontiero, "The Drama of Existence in *Laços de família*, " *Studies in Short Fiction*, 7, 1 (1971), 256-67, and "Testament of Experience: Some Reflections on Clarice Lispector's Last Narrative *A hora da estrela*," *Ibero-Amerikanisches Archiv*, 10, 1 (1984), 13-22; Edilberto Coutinho, "Uma mulher chamada Clarice Lispector," in his *Criaturas de papel* (Rio de Janeiro: Civilização Brasileira, 1980), pp. 165-70; and Haroldo Bruno, "Solilóquio de Clarice Lispector sobre o ser," in his *Novos estudos de literatura brasileira* (Rio de Janeiro: José Olympio/Instituto Nacional do Livro, 1980), pp. 12-20. These themes are studied together with formal aspects of the works in Teresinha Alves Pereira, *Estudo sòbre Clarice Lispector* (Coimbra: Edições Nova Era, 1975), and "Coincidencia de la técnica narrativa de Julio Cortázar y Clarice Lispector," *Nueva narrativa hispanoamericana*, 3, 1 (1973), 103-111; Earl E. Fitz, "The Leitmotif of Darkness in Seven Novels by Clarice Lispector," *Chasqui*, 8, 2 (1977), 18-27, and "Point of View in Clarice Lispector's *A hora da estrela*," *Luso-Brazilian Review* 19, 2 (1982), 195-208; Samira Youssef Campedelli and Benjamim Abdala, Jr., in their edition with commentary *Clarice Lispector, antologia comentada* (São Paulo: Abril, 1981); Olga de Sá, *Clarice Lispector* (Petrópolis: Vozes, 1979); Naomi Lindstrom, "Clarice Lispector: Articulating Women's Experience," *Chasqui*, 8, 1 (1978), 44-52, "A Discourse Analysis of 'Preciosidade' by Clarice Lispector," *Luso-Brazilian Review*, 19, 2 (1982), 187-94, and "A Feminist Discourse Analysis of Clarice Lispector's 'Daydreams of a Drunken Woman',” *Latin American Literary Review*, 9, 19 (1982), 7-16.

[2]   María Luisa Nunes, "Narrative Modes in Clarice Lispector's *Laços de família*: The Rendering of Consciousness," *Luso-Brazilian Review*, 14, 12 (1977), 174-184. De Sá examines Lispector's varied narrative methods in "Clarice Lispector: processos criativos," *Revista Iberoamericana*, No. 126 (1984), 259-80.

[3]   Silvio Castro, *A revolução da palavra* (Petrópolis: Vozes, 1976), p. 265; his

43

44

Lispector commentary appears on pp. 263-67.

[4] Bella Jozef, "Clarice Lispector: la transgresión como acto de libertad," *Revista Iberoamericana*, Nos. 98-99 (1977), 22. See also her "Clarice Lispector: la recuperación de la palabra poética" and reviews of Lispector's posthumous fiction, *Revista Iberamericana*, No. 126 (1984), 239-57, 314-18, respectively.

[5] Owen Kellerman, *Estudios de la voz narrativa en el relato latinoamericano contemporáneo*, Diss. Arizona State University, 1975. See Lúcia Helena, "*Aprendizagem* de Clarice Lispector," *Littera*, 5, 13 (1975), 99-104.

[6] María Ester Gilio, remark made to Lispector in an interview, "Mis libros son mis cachorros," *Crisis* [Buenos Aires], No. 39 (1976), 42. The issue of feminine writing is explored in Maria Luisa Nunes, "Clarice Lispector: artista andrógina ou escritora?," *Revista Iberoamericana*, No. 126 (1984), 281-89. The rendering of a female consciousness is the theme of Fitz, "Freedom and Self-Realization: Feminist Characterization in the Fiction of Clarice Lispector," *Modern Language Studies*, 10, 3 (1980), 51-61, and *Clarice Lispector* (Boston: Twayne, 1985).

[7] Dennis Seniff, "Self Doubt in Clarice Lispector's *Lacos de família*," *Luso-Brazilian Review*, 14, 2 (1977), 162.

[8] Rosario Castellanos, "Clarice Lispector: la memoria ancestral," in her *Mujer que sabe latín...* (Mexico: SepSetentas, 1973), p. 129.

[9] Nancy T. Baden makes this point in "Clarice Lispector," in *A Dictionary of Contemporary Brazilian Authors* (Tempe: Center for Latin American Studies, 1981), p. 74.

[10] Jozef, 227.

[11] Jozef, 228.

[12] Note the many female protagonists in the existential novels of the Argentine Eduardo Mallea, especially Agata Cruz in *Todo verdor perecerá* (1941) and Gloria Bambil and Sra. de Cárdenas in *La bahia del silencio* (1940).

[13] Simone de Beauvoir, *The Second Sex*, trans. H. M. Parshley (New York: Knopf, 1953), p. 261; original 1949.

[14] Beauvoir, p. 142.

[15] Beauvoir, p. 34.

[16] Clarice Lispector, "Amor," in her *Laços de família* (Rio: José Olympio Editora, 1974), p. 19. Further page numbers in the text refer to this edition. The English translations are from Giovanni Pontiero's excellent version of the work, published by the University of Texas Press, Austin, 1972.

[17] Maria Luisa Nunes, 177-78, 179.

[18] Maria Luisa Nunes gives this description of such passages: "Grammatically, the imperfect takes the place of the perfect, the conditional that of the future and the pluperfect that of the preterite in direct discourse. There is also a transferral of pronouns from the first to the third person," 174.

[19] Robin Lakoff, *Language and Woman's Place* (New York: Harper and Row, 1975).

[20] Jozef, 229.

[21] Especially illustrative of this concern is Kate Millett, *The Prostitution Papers* (New York: Basic Books, 1971). Millett describes prostitutes who worked together to develop a mode of presenting grievances. The women move from an inability to state their case to being relatively able spokeswomen. Like the third-person narrator in "Amor," Millett steps back and offers the *ipsissima verba* of the prostitutes (or at least her editing of their recorded statements) once the women have become sufficiently articulate.

[22] Maria Luisa Nunes, 177, comments: "The fact that she is a Portuguese woman

living in Brazil is reflected by her unuttered speech and idioms, markedly Lusitanian as opposed to the colloquial speech of Brazil." For instance, one finds *cousa* rather than *coisa*. This Lusitanian speech also exerts a type of linguistic alienation effect on the story's Brazilian readers.

[23] Beauvoir, p. 478. Beauvoir's discussions of "The Married Woman," pp. 425-83, and "The Mother," pp. 484-527, present strong parallels to the representation of women characters in *Laços de família*.

[24] Beauvoir, p. 518.

[25] Maria Luisa Nunes, 177.

[26] Pontiero, 260 of above-cited article, sees in this story a "dramatic and turbulent account of adolescence, with its penetrating analysis of the dark, tortured recesses of a girl's mind during the difficult time of puberty."

[27] See Beauvoir's chapters on "The Young Girl," pp. 328-70, and "Sexual Initiation," pp. 371-403.

[28] Erving Goffman, *The Presentation of Self in Everyday Life* (Garden City: Doubleday, 1959).

[29] Moisés, above-cited article, 278.

Rosario
Castellanos

Rosario Castellanos:
Women Outside Communication

I

Chiapas, the home state of Rosario Castellanos, serves as setting for much of her writing. In her literary elaboration, the Mexican region exemplifies provincial isolation, Indian-white conflict, rigidly closed social patterns and entrenched resistance to change. These features of Chiapanecan life receive treatment in *El uso de la palabra* (*Speaking Up*, 1974) and two collections of short stories, *Ciudad Real* (1960) and *Los convidados de agosto* (*At the August Fair*, 1964). Most importantly, they figure in her two famous novels, *Balún-Canán*, 1957; English translation, *The Nine Guardians*, 1960) and the 1962 *Oficio de tinieblas* (*In Darkness*). These novels share not only the same fictional locus, but also reflect the same historical moment, the late thirties. The vigorous social reforms of President Lázaro Cárdenas make this period illustrative of social change and reactionary opposition to that change.

Both Chiapas novels are wide-ranging; neither simplifies the societal issues under examination. The diversity of the subject-matter and the complexity of its fictional organization ill suit these novels for classification as "indigenist" or "political" novels. An index of their great multiplicity is the variety of thematic and structural aspects worthy of critical discussion. For Jean Franco and John S. Brushwood, intercultural conflict is at the heart of the Chiapas novels. Franco notes that, unlike many indigenist novels, Castellanos' works avoid any Manichean distinction between good Indians and white oppressors. Rather, the mutual incomprehension and misinterpretation of the two groups is the topic of exploration. The resolution of this conflict is also satisfyingly complex. Each novel features an Indian uprising that cannot possibly result in a physical victory. However, through subtle infiltration, the cultural values of the indigenous people prevail.[1] Brushwood discovers a constituent of "optimism [that] consists of the suggestion that new and more radical approaches to the problem" may yet establish equitable relations between cultures.[2]

Castellanos' depiction of the Indian culture is the feature that draws the interest of Joseph Sommers and many others.[3] Sommers finds older indigenist writers eager to "document" the Indian from without. The reader encounters reportage on the economic and political problems, customs and other observable traits of the Indian population. Castellanos exemplifies a new strategy for giving the Indian a literary image. Myth, poetry and beliefs become the keys to understanding how the Indian goes about organizing life experiences and knowledge of the world.

A denunciatory exposé of the landed class is manifestly part of the novels. This vein, too, has won critical notice.[4] The fictional landowners react to reform legislation with an utter absence of dignity and scruples. They conspire to obstruct the implementation of reforms, to corrupt or intimidate the agents of change and to forestall any alteration in their way of life. Sexual and religious hypocrisy merit a mordantly ironic treatment.

Castellanos' self-commentary focuses on her deviation from the realist esthetic with its resultant "literatura de denuncia . . . catálogo de ignominias (literature of denunciation . . . catalog of atrocities)."[5] According to the novelist, this direct, humorless transcription of realities "no ha horadado siquiera una piedra minúscula (hasn't even worn through one tiny pebble)."[6] Her allegiance lies with a more distanced, formulaic and ironic mode of representation: hence, one more able to change public attitudes toward social ills.

Less commented-upon than the above aspects, but unmistakably a part of the works, is the fabrication of emblematic women's voices. This goal of Castellanos' literary program is most evident in several texts using exclusively or predominantly women's speech.[7] *Balún-Canán*, too, examines feminine speech. The reader frequently depends on a seven-year-old girl to tell the story. Only well into the novel does a third-person narrator appear. *Oficio de tinieblas* stands apart from such writings in that it features no dominant female voices. However, this absence by no means signals a loss of interest in the interrelation of sex role and communication: quite the contrary.

According to critical consensus, *Oficio de tinieblas* is more satisfyingly complex in the elaboration of its fictional *sujet* than is *Balún-Canán*.[8] Part of this richness is the later novel's oblique demonstration of women's communication problems. Women's silence, their unwillingness or inability to articulate urgent questions, and their lack of a listening ear, reveal this difficulty more eloquently than what women actually succeed in enunciating. Incomplete or ineffective expression is typical, to some degree, of all female characters in *Oficio*. The presence of the omniscient, editorializing third-person narrator stands as witness to this deficiency. No woman in the novel, however intimate her connection with key events, can give a proper account of them.

II

The early chapters of the novel contain, among other things, a series of tableaux centering on a woman or women within a situation of inadequate communication. The women are from both cultures and of varying age and social station. The immediate causes of their inexpressive behavior also range widely. Yet these vignettes affirm, through successive reiteration, that the women suffer a common blockage and that this impediment is profoundly rooted in the female role itself.

The first of these scenes appears in the second half of the opening chapter. The outset of this chapter offers a sweeping historical overview of the Indian community, stressing the uneasy, volatile relations with local whites. Here the narrator utilizes a ritualized form of speech, establishing an intertextuality with the *Popol-Vuh*. This formulaic, reiterative scripture is by no means a trivially folkloric element. Rather, as Sommers notes, it places the narrated events within an atemporal, universally significant, mythic context.[9] The voice then descends to a more mundane level to describe, in all its petty particulars, a domestic scene. The wife in this Indian household is Catalina Díaz Puiljá, the catalyst behind the novel's violent events. Catalina's first appearance, though, shows her before she acquires the strategies of command. Indeed, she feels herself to be at a nadir of helpless vulnerability. It is this extreme feeling of dependency and humiliation that impels her to the conquest of power.

As the narrator makes clear, Catalina's status and well-being are functions of her position as judge's wife. Her longstanding failure to produce a child could imperil her place in the world. Both partners in the marriage appear in this scene, but only Catalina's anxious thoughts become accessible to readers. Her husband's mental processes, the focus of his wife's fears, remain opaque to Catalina and those reading the novel:

> De reojo, mientras molía la ración de posol arrodillada frente al metate, Catalina observaba la figura de su marido. ¿En qué momento la obligaría a pronunciar la formula de repudio? ¿Hasta cuándo iba a consentir la afrenta de su esterilidad? Matrimonios como éste no eran válidos. Bastaría una palabra de Winiktón para que Catalina volviera al jacal de su familia, allá en Tzajal-hemel. Ya no encontraría a su padre, muerto hacía años. Ya no encontraría a su madre, muerta hacía años . . .
>
> Catalina se irguió y puso la bola de posol en el marral de bastimiento de su marido. ¿Qué lo mantenía junto a ella? ¿El miedo? ¿El amor? La cara de Winiktón guardaba bien su secreto. Sin un ademán de despedida el hombre abandonó la choza. La puerta se cerró tras él.
>
> Una decisión irrevocable petrificó las facciones de Catalina. ¡No se separaría nunca, ella no quedaría sola, no sería humillada ante la gente!

> Out of the corner of her eye, while she was kneeling at the stone to grind up a day's supply of *posol*, Catalina kept watching her husband. When would he force her to repeat the separation vows? How long would he put up with the insult of a barren wife? Marriages like this one had no validity. One word from Winiktón and Catalina would be sent back to her family's hut out in Tzajal-hemel. She would no longer find her father, who had died years ago. She would no longer find her mother, who had died years ago . . .
>
> Catalina got up and put the bundle of *posol* in with her husband's supply of provisions. Why was it he kept her around? Fear? Love? Winiktón's face gave no clue. Without so much as a gesture of good-bye the man left the hut. The door closed behind him.
>
> Catalina's features grew hard as an irrevocable resolve took hold of her. They would never separate, she would never be left alone, she would never be humiliated in front of everyone![10]

Here, Catalina's entire thoughts and behavior are determined by a conflict-ridden communicational circumstance. She would most like to know her husband's position with regard to their marriage, yet she cannot ask him about it. Indeed, she shrinks from addressing him in any manner, lest she call attention to herself and her barren condition. Her extreme strategy of self-effacement has spread to the sociolinguistic aspects of their interaction. Catalina will not risk uttering routine pleasantries as the couple prepares for the day's activities; she avoids even a formulaic good-bye; she cannot look her husband in the face, but only watches him "out of the corner of her eye."

Catalina's profound inability to ask for needed information has its exact counterpart in her husband's disinclination to give out information about himself. Despite her incessant spying, hypothesizing and rampant speculation, Catalina ends this scene with no more information about her husband's ideas than she had at the outset. She does, however, succeed in deepening her conviction that he, like her, must be preoccupied with questions of childbearing and marital status. She does not admit the possibility that Winiktón's failure to divorce her might stem from absorption in other matters. Catalina's method of divining her husband's thoughts, though superficially one of observation and informed hypothesis, is really one of almost pure solipsism.

The ironic element in the couple's relation, which later becomes patent, is only suggested here. Winiktón gives "no clue" that would permit an assessment of the validity of his wife's imaginings. Reading the novel, one must share, for the moment, Catalina's lack of confirmable information about Winiktón's thoughts.

Although this early scene takes place in an indigenous household, there is little that is exotic about it. It has the feature of instant recognizability for a Western reader. Its fundamental ingredients closely resemble those of routine domestic melodrama or farce. One sees the uncommunicative husband whose morning silence drives his wife to distraction and the self-dramatizing woman tormenting herself with imagined scenarios of disaster ("humiliated in front of everyone!"). The cross-cultural evocation of these stereotypes by no means implies support of the proposition that men are inherently stony and women hysterical. Rather, it becomes the task of the novel to lay bare the societal factors that operate to block communication between the world's Catalinas and Winiktóns.

The first of these factors is already evident in the morning scene: unequal distribution of power between the sexes, here exacerbated by the wife's barrenness. Castellanos sets forth one of the main tenets of her literary feminism: the blame does not lie with individual members of the male sex. Winiktón, though somewhat inconsiderate, is not Catalina's oppressor; indeed, he emerges as one of the novel's two emblematic justice-seekers and a thoroughly good man. Catalina does not fit the part of the pathetic victim. Her morose, brooding approach to life's difficulties makes her a less than appealing representative of subjugated womankind. Nonetheless, she is subjected to her husband's will. He could, if he cared to, deprive her of her entire wealth and community standing. Emblematic of this inequity is the imagined divorce procedure: the man may force the woman to speak words contrary to her true desires. Across such inequality of position, the couple cannot speak. The wife does not feel safe asking for information she needs; the husband does not feel under any obligation to inform his wife of his plans, even as they concern her.

A secondary socially-determined barrier between the two becomes evident in the next scene. As the husband comes home from his day's labors, the narrator begins to move back and forth between telling us the husband's thoughts and his wife's, along with her own commentary upon those thoughts. In this scene, the couple does speak, but their conversation is minimal. Catalina has brought a strange girl into the household, but Winiktón initially fails to respond even to this circumstance. Only the information that "un caxlán abusó de ella (a white man raped her; p. 29)" elicits an intense reaction from the husband. Here the reader follows the workings of Winiktón's mind as he struggles to organize, from inchoate experience, the concept of justice.

Catalina, however, remains wholly outside her husband's mind. Her only clues to his inward ferment are his failure to notice that she has cooked and served dinner, and upon being pressed, his wordless rejection of the food. Now the reader begins to view Catalina's struggle to reconstruct, from the evidence she has, Winiktón's probable mental operations.

This shift places the reader in a position of privilege. It comes directly after a detailed and trustworthy account of the husband's mental processes from the narrator. Thus, it is possible to hold up Catalina's imaginative recreation of those processes to this reliable model, identifying the significant areas of discrepancy.

What stands out is Catalina's inability to guess correctly any but the most patent features of her husband's state. She notes that habitually "el mutismo era su modo de concentrarse más profundamente en lo que le rodeaba. Pero esta vez Pedro no atendía. Estaba distraído, ausente (he retreated into silence to pay closer attention to what was going on around him. Only now he wasn't paying attention. His mind was somewhere else; p. 32)." From this observation, her speculations go wildly astray. Once more she places her sterility in the foreground of her husband's mind. In her representation, the man is intensely concerned with concrete matters of household management—for example, the cost of maintaining the rape victim versus her value as a domestic servant. By placing these preoccupations in her husband's mind, she deduces the basis of his disquiet: "¿Con qué derecho una mujer estéril como ella trataba de eludir lo penoso de sus obligaciones? Al contrario: debería compensar esta falta suya aventajando a las demás en abnegación (What right did a barren woman like her have trying to get out of unpleasant chores? Just the opposite: she should make up for her failing by being the most self-sacrificing of women; p. 32)."

Shortly afterwards, Catalina, still spying on her husband, formulates this assessment of the man's state: "Ya no piensa en nada; ya no piensa en nadie (Now he's not thinking about anyone; now he's not thinking about anything; p. 33)." The narrator transcribes her thought as a direct citation, then steps back to comment: "Y esta certidumbre la apaciguó (And she found it a comfort to know for sure)." The seemingly banal remark is really the prelude to a structural device of great ironic impact. Turning again to the exploration of Winiktón's mind, the narrator reveals the man's struggle to correlate disparate information and experiences into a synthetic concept of justice/injustice. He reviews vast portions of his past, searching for significant uniformities of experience.

What emerges from these alternations between Catalina's mind and Winik-tón's is an exposition of the ways in which they organize their perceptions. Again, the reference to male and female stereotypes is evident and purposeful. The woman views the world in its particulars, especially insofar as they relate to her home circumstance. Kinship, marriage and household economics are the axes around which she arranges new data. The man, on the other hand, looks beyond the walls of his own home. While his skill in day-to-day human relations may be less than his wife's, he is more able to achieve a total vision of human phenomena.

The disjuncture between the two becomes most patent when each considers the same issue. For instance, Catalina sees the rape as a potential element in her strategy to remedy the confused state of her family affairs. On a short-term basis, the girl is "una boca más (another mouth to feed)" but also "quien le ayudase en las faenas más rudas (someone to help out with the heavy chores; p. 32)." Winiktón identifies her as a typical victim of the established order, hardly more than a token of exploited Indian womanhood. Sterility, the key topic for Catalina, never becomes the explicit topic of Winiktón's considerations. It appears only at several removes. The omniscient narrator, providing a pano-ramic overview of the man's attitudinal formation, mentions as one of many factors "el hecho de que en él acabara su linaje (the fact that he was the last of his line; p. 32)." Winiktón may not even be consciously aware that this circumstance is part of the structure of his formative experience. At any rate, its personal implications (for example, the possible invalidation of his marriage) are not what affect him. Rather, his anomalous position and increased solitude leave him more open to radicalizing influences.

From this point on, each successive representation of the couple reiterates this disparity between them. For instance, Winiktón ends the evening scene by literally, as well as attitudinally, stepping outside the confines of his all-too-personal home. As he stands outside, considering the workings of society and the cosmos, his wife remains in bed, dreaming about her brother and incubating household power ploys.

The next chapter shows Winiktón looking on while Catalina haggles with the rape victim's mother. Again, women belong to the realm of concrete observables. Bargaining over the question of bride-price, the two women speak in the most material specifics. Their conversation is full of references to prosaic reality. The mother demands five fat rams, three jugs of liquor, and a large store of corn; Catalina counters that the bride has no maidenhead and cannot be sold. Winiktón, the man of abstractions, stands back to examine the women's behavior and the values represented therein. "Winiktón se avergonzó de que una madre preguntara el precio antes que ninguna otra cosa. La quiere vender como un animal, pensó (Winiktón found it shameful that a mother should ask the price first thing. She wants to sell her like an animal, he thought; p. 39)." The man takes little part in the proceedings. When he does, his role is not that of "marido de Catalina Díaz Puiljá (the husband of Catalina Díaz Puiljá)" but "juez, pesador de las acciones de los hombres (judge, weigher of the actions of men; p. 40)." While the wife emerges with a financial victory, the husband leaves the encounter having made further progress toward a fully aware articul-ation of the word "justice."

Through repeated demonstrations, the disjuncture of the two acquires a comic dimension. On page 188, for example, eleven years have gone by and Catalina is still puzzling over her husband's failure to divorce her. She is certain that his handling of this matter must bear some relation to his current long absences from home, her sterility being the key factor in both questions. Winiktón, meanwhile, has become active in the promulgation of agrarian reform.

The reader and narrator together have followed Winiktón through a succession of transforming experiences. From his initial insight that there is something amiss in the social order, he has come to take an active responsibility for changing that order. Major episodes in his education include learning to read, grasping "company store" exploitation, hearing Lázaro Cárdenas speak, witnessing the failure of superficial reforms, acquiring a government sponsor and training an apprentice. The events mark him profoundly. Yet, in years of focusing obsessively on Winiktón, Catalina has remained unaware of the process and unable to understand why it is important.

III

The depiction of this couple represents a major departure from the literary feminism exemplified by Kate Millett. For Millett, one of the worst offenses of literature is its collusion in perpetuating the "two-spheres doctrine," that is, the notion that men and women have few common features and concerns.[11] Women, according to this dogma, center their attention on self, home and kin while men master the affairs of state and the arts and sciences. In its fully enunciated form, as a nineteenth-century social philosophy, the doctrine overtly asserts that this separation is a natural and a desirable state of affairs, appropriate to the constitution of the two sexes.

The literary manifestation of these same notions appears, according to Millett, in works that assign female characters such traits as domesticity, self-absorption, strong family ties and an inability to formalize significant generalizations from acquired knowledge. The same binary scheme gives male characters such attributes as altruism, broad-mindedness and abstract reasoning capacity.

In her application of this analysis, Millett does not set up a distinction between works that favor the dichotomy of roles and those that offer it only as a faithful reflection of real-world circumstances. Her assumption is that an author who, without comment, differentiates males and females according to the stereotyped pattern, gives silent consent to the two-spheres doctrine. The effect of such work is to reinforce the reader's conviction that men and women are unlike and unequal.

Two alternatives to the perpetuation of stereotypes appear in Millett's writings. In *Sexual Politics*, she praises Genet for his hyperbolic, conceitful burlesque of "male" and "female" behavioral traits. The reader encounters a system of ironic relations designed to expose the oppressive, arbitrary character of sex roles. "Masculinity" and "femininity" are constantly in the foreground, subject to questioning and ridicule.

56

The second alternative is not present programmatically in *Sexual Politics*, but rather implicitly in Millett's autobiographical-documentary-creative writings (*The Prostitution Papers*, 1971; *Flying*, 1974; *Sita*, 1977). These texts distribute "male" and "female" personality characteristics among the figures represented without much regard for their biological sex. An especially clear example of this procedure is *The Prostitution Papers*. This volume consists principally of Millett's transcriptions of interviews with prostitutes she was counseling. Even without being notably sexist, one might expect prostitutes to exhibit certain unpleasant features frequently considered typical of women. For example, one might imagine them to show an over-absorption in self and a narrow interest in immediate associates to the exclusion of larger concerns. In Millett's presentation, however, the women relate their specific problems to general questions of morality, social administration and, of course, sex roles. The author does not claim that prostitutes would ordinarily be found speaking in these terms. Rather, she hopes to demonstrate that the women possess the capacity to become articulate about social problems if they receive support and encouragement.

Castellanos follows neither of these tactics. Unlike Genet, she does not make a specific, mannered presentation of sex roles or engage in extravagant inversions. Her delineations of male and female are within the bounds of verisimilitude. Nor has she "corrected" the imbalance between male and female images, as is Millett's practice. Yet the reader can see that, within Castellanos' fictional world, the "two-spheres doctrine" is a pernicious force. Its devastating effect on Catalina's marriage and on her ability to sustain effective communication is patent.

Objecting to the literary representation of sex roles in conventional terms, Millett expresses a specific fear. If the conventional scheme is unfavorable to women, assigning them more debilities than assets, then literature that reflects that scheme will show women as less worthy than men. Applying Millett's idea to Castellanos' novel, one may ask whether Castellanos has not done women a disservice by portraying an hysterical, scheming female and her socially-aware mate. Such a question is especially relevant to the second half of *Oficio*, where Catalina becomes a grotesque Delphic priestess. She writhes on the ground, foams at the mouth, and retreats into near catatonic states. Her frenzied leadership turns the Indian protest movement into a fanatical, chaotic crusade. In a final attempt to retain her vatic stature, she offers up her foster son as a human sacrifice on Good Friday. Might not this depiction reinforce, for instance, the conviction that women are too emotional to be leaders?

The first argument against any such antifeminism is the novel's insistence on the social causation of Catalina's malaise. Signaling a structural defect common to the Indian community and Western civilization, the narrator stresses that Catalina's "posición de mujer sin hijos era tan precaria (position as a childless woman was so precarious; p. 44)." Other women continually draw attention to her failure to live up to role expectations. Given this strong social stimulus, it is understandable that the deviant should become obsessed with reproduction, status and power. Moreover, when the ill effects on Catalina's personality manifest themselves, the community offers her no support. Afraid of Catalina's aberrance, "las mujeres se apartaban de ella con temor y, a distancia, espiaban sus intenciones (the women drew away from her in fear and, from a distance, kept a wary eye on her; p. 192)." Though critics have stressed Castellanos' psychological representation of unique individual Indians, Catalina must not be seen only in these terms.[12] Seeing her as a psychological case study could imply a serious displacement of guilt from society to the individual.

Indeed, all through the novel, one notes society's determination to define women in terms of their reproductive capacities. Indian and *ladino* alike exhibit irrational thinking about childbearing. For example, Isabel Zebadúa is convinced that God has shown disapproval of her second marriage by striking her barren. Fernando Ulloa, an educated urban liberal, is not exempt from such notions. Fernando is willing to attribute the unprincipled behavior of his common-law wife to "una frivolidad natural en su sexo (a frivolity natural to her sex; p. 10)." He considers that childbearing and childrearing constitute a natural check on the instability of women. Lacking this stabilizing factor, his wife cannot be expected to keep her actions within ethical bounds. Here one sees the attitudes that Castellanos mocked in her essayistic writings:

> Mas, de una manera tácita o expresa, se le ofrece [a la mujer] así la oportunidad de traspasar sus límites en un fenómeno que si no borra al menos atenúa los signos negativos con los que estaba marcada; que colma sus carencias; que la incorpora, con carta de ciudadanía en toda regla, a los núcleos humanos. Ese fenómeno es la maternidad.

> But, either tacitly or overtly, woman is offered the chance to transcend her shortcomings through a phenomenon that, even if it can't eradicate them totally, at least mitigates the negative features she was marked with; that helps make up for her defects; that makes her a card-carrying member of the human race. That phenomenon is maternity.[13]

Even if Catalina is society's victim, the fact remains that she is less appealing than Winiktón. She withdraws into brooding obsession, but he expands his horizons: "Como para descargarse del peso de sus preocupaciones, Winiktón salía a buscar con quien compartirlas (As if to relieve the weight of his concerns, Winiktón went out looking for someone to share them with; p. 190)." To see how Castellanos' utilization of stereotypes is corrective rather than reinforcing, one must look at the secondary characters. Appearing in humorous vignettes, these Indians and *ladinos* support, through reiteration and variation, the proposition that women's role discourages communication.

IV

The first *ladina* whose consciousness is revealed is Mercedes Solórzano. Like Catalina, she is a deviant female in a precarious and isolated position. Mercedes has saved herself from life on the streets by serving as procuress to the town's most powerful man. Unlike Catalina, Mercedes does not abstain from speech lest she jeopardize her standing. Her strategy is an overabundance of speech designed to create an illusory or fallacious appearance of communication.

One first encounters Mercedes conducting a most tortured and Byzantine conversation. Having summoned an Indian vendor, ostensibly for a bargaining session, Mercedes deviates from the conventions governing such encounters. In that town, *ladinos* are rude and distant to Indian vendors. Mercedes, however addresses the girl in indigenous language and offers her a seat. leaving her "confundida por la amabilidad (confused by her friendliness; p. 18)." After a few perfunctory remarks in her "buyer" role, Mercedes breaks with this role and speaks on topics inappropriate to the apparent situation. She reminisces about her youthful vigor and asks intrusive questions about the girl's marital status and prospects. When the "buyer" returns to the bargaining theme, her rupture with expected behavior is still uppermost. Rather than reply to the asking price with a conventional protest, the buyer mocks the seller for demanding too little. The whole discourse is moved further into the realm of strangeness by her insistence that the Indian address her by her first name. Moreover, both supposed bargainers occupy a "store" that is patently lacking in saleable goods.

Mercedes' disorienting conversation is her linguistic strategy for disarming and baffling the girl, who is being set up as the rich man's rape victim. In addition, she must determine the girl's virginity without recourse to direct inquiry. Here. the procuress makes use of language to baffle and disconcert her victim and to disguise the true nature of the encounter. But when the woman remains alone, it becomes clear that she cannot halt her treacherous, confusing speech even when it serves no pragmatic end.

The ironic narrator, characteristically provides a "distancing" preface before plunging the reader into the flow of a character's thoughts. An "explanation" of the procuress' habit of soliloquizing is proffered: "El temperamento de doña Mercedes era comunicativo (Doña Mercedes was naturally communicative; p. 20)." The manifest cynicism of the remark, which immediately follows Mercedes' display of verbal guile and obfuscation, places everything she is about to say under suspicion. The narrator also alerts one to the nature of Mercedes' speech act. Rather than speak to herself. she addresses a being of her own invention, "imaginando un impreciso auditorio (imagining some vague listener; p. 20)."

The fictional listener may be vague, but Mercedes implicitly assigns him certain attributes. As her form of address, she uses the regional and familiar *vos*. The novel uses this form principally for Spanish-language representations of conversation in the Indian language; an Indian who speaks in Spanish also uses the *vos*. For the *ladinos*, the *vos* would seem to be contaminated with associations of provincialism, low status, and lack of education. No Mexican Spanish speaker with serious pretensions to respectability deviates from the standard form, *tú*. Only the lax and "fallen" Mercedes flaunts the nonstandard form. She exploits it to create the illusion of intimacy outside the narrow primness of proper society, "como si fuéramos de confianza (as if we were old friends; p. 21)." Here she casts her listener in the role of (male) crony, emphasized by her addressing him brassily as "compadre (buddy; p. 20)."

Mercedes' goal in constructing this being and drawing him into collusion is to make him accept a favorable, if inconsistent, account of herself. Her first tactic is to displace the listener's disgust from her own recruitment practices to her employer's "unclean" desire for Indian girls. She virtuously intervenes to mitigate the impropriety. Through her vigilance, she saves her undiscriminating employer from enjoying the more evidently unhygienic girls he might unthinkingly accept.

Next, Mercedes presents herself as a basically sensitive and noble individual to whom "da remordimiento hacer estas cosas (it is shameful to do these things; p. 20)." All consideration of verisimilitude is abandoned as the procuress states: "en la honra nadie me ha puesto nunca un pie adelante. Las señoras bien se pueden mirar en mí, que soy un espejo de cuerpo entero (as for maintaining your honor, nobody's ahead of me on that score. If those fancy ladies take a good look, they'll see I'm every bit as good as them; p. 21)."

The third positive trait Mercedes claims for herself is charity, demonstrated in her story of a great favor she once did her employer. When he appeared as a terrified virgin in her brothel, Mercedes befriended him and eased his fright at this rite of initiation.

Clearly, no one woman can police the selection of rape victims, maintain her honor and also embody the "prostitute with a heart of gold." However, Mercedes' listener cannot raise these objections because she has not endowed him with any capacity for critical judgment. To be successful, a hypocrite must learn careful limits to untruthfulness, lest an excessive statement destroy credibility entirely. Mercedes' phantom listener is the hypocrite's ideal audience because he "will swallow anything."

The final irony is that this soliloquy, even with all the distortions and ramshackle arguments, makes two valid points. Mercedes recognizes that part of her problem is the lack of acceptable options open to women without wealth or male protectors. Without her employer's aegis, she observes, "¿adónde hubiera yo ido a parar? Estaría yo de atajadora, como tantas infelices que no tienen donde les haga maroma un piojo. O de custitalera, o de placera . . . a saber (what would have become of me? I'd be out robbing from the Indians, like so many poor women who can hardly keep body and soul together. Or I'd be living out practically in the same place as the Indians to try to sell them stuff, or out in the plaza . . . who knows; p. 21)." Mercedes also dimly realizes that too much depends on remaining in the good graces of her employer. The importance of this fact becomes increasingly clear throughout the novel as the unscrupulous boss repeatedly punishes those who offend him and rewards those who please him. He incarnates a male stereotype at least as negative as any of the female types who appear throughout the novel. The narrator is explicit about the relation between sex role and the man's reprehensible behavior, speaking on one occasion of "la insensibilidad de Leonardo, con ese orgullo del macho que no está acostumbrado a recibir dones sino tributos (the insensitivity of Leonardo, with that pride of a macho who's used to receiving tributes, not gifts; p. 97)."

Though able to glimpse the limitation of female roles and the problem of exaggerated *macho* dominance, Mercedes cannot relate these issues to her devious communicational style. When the reader places the two together, the result is essentially a sex-role analysis of female hypocrisy. Mercedes is another figure who provides pseudo-documentary validation of a common stereotype while exposing the social pressures that force women into stereotyped behavior. To quote again from Castellanos' cultural criticism:

> Se ha acusado a las mujeres de hipócritas y la acusación no es infundada. Pero la hipocresía es la respuesta que a sus opresores da el oprimido, que a los fuertes contestan los débiles, que los subordinados devuelven al amo. La hipocresía es la consecuencia de una situación, es un reflejo condicionado de defensa—como el cambio de color en un camaleón—cuando los peligros son muchos y las opciones son pocas.

> Women have been accused of being hypocrites and there's some truth to the accusation. But hypocrisy is the way that the oppressed reply to the oppressors, that the weak answer back to the strong, that subordinates respond to their master. Hypocrisy is the consequence of a situation, a conditioned defensive reflex—like a chameleon's change of coloration—when the dangers are many and the options are few.[14]

Nonetheless, Mercedes is an oppressor as well as one of the oppressed, and cannot be easily placed as a simple victim of the Establishment. Unlike the pathetically appealing victim-prostitutes of sentimental-realist fiction (for example, Manuel Gálvez' 1919 *Nacha Regules*, Argentina; the 1903 *Santa* by Federico Gamboa, Mexico), Mercedes is repellent in her behavior and appearance: "cuarentona, obesa, con los dientes refulgiendo en groseras incrustaciones de oro (fortyish, obese, her teeth aglitter with tacky gold incrustations; p. 17)." The narrator of *Santa* is characteristic in his unabashed sentimentalizing of the heroine's plight. The sardonic narrator of *Oficio*, though, alienates the reader from Mercedes' potential pathos by noting the laxity and indolence that facilitate her degradation: "Sus dos manos, acostumbradas al ocio, descansaban sobre el regazo (She kept her hands, which were used to lying idle, in her lap; p. 21)."

V

The ambiguity of the woman who may be guilty of complicity in her own subjugation is a constant theme of Castellanos' fiction. As Raúl Ortiz notes, she "apunta con idioma ágil, jocoso y dúctil, contra la hipócrita complicidad de hombres y mujeres que se arrellanan en un status quo del que ambos sexos pretenden obtener ventajas y provechos (takes aim with her agile, witty and flexible language against the hypocritical complicity of men and women who find a cozy niche in a status quo which both sexes try to turn to their advantage)."[15] This troubling issue receives special attention in the juxtaposed fictional cases of Marcela and Idolina. Each is an adolescent repelled by what she has seen of adult male-female relations. Each rejects adulthood by withdrawing into morose silence and childish helplessness—in a sense, an exaggeration of the normal female role. However, their parallelism breaks down when one looks at the above-discussed feature of "victimization" with its complicating factor, "complicity."

Marcela, the Indian girl Mercedes recruits for rape, is the most uncomplicated example of oppression in the novel. In swift succession, she suffers entrapment and betrayal by Mercedes, rape by Leonardo, a beating from her mother and expropriation by Catalina, who simply takes over the running of the girl's life. The narrator reports Catalina's assessment of Marcela: "esta muchacha insignificante y estúpida que ella usaba como un simple instrumento de sus propósitos (that insignificant, stupid girl she was using as a simple pawn in her game; p. 46)." The older woman inflicts her idiot brother on Marcela as a husband and then forces her to bear the child that the older woman could not produce.

More interesting than these distressing events are Marcela's reactions to them. Does she possess the capacity to protest, to demand a voice in the disposition of her fate? This question is put to the reader as the narrator affords a series of brief glimpses of Marcela responding to crucial life situations. The first of these is the conversation with Mercedes in which the Indian girl emerges as the loser. Ignorance, confusion and shyness maintain her in a state of perfect passivity. Upon reencountering the procuress after the rape, Marcela abandons this behavior. When the procuress attempts to reestablish the false game of seller and buyer, Marcela throws the "payment" at Mercedes and smashes her wares against every available surface. This assertion of self is notable not only for its vigor but for its utter inefficacy. The procuress and rapist have deprived Marcela of dignity and honor, while she has merely succeeded in causing a minor inconvenience. The same pattern of inarticulate and inefficacious rebellion recurs shortly afterwards when Marcela refuses an offering of alms.

Given the failure of her self-expression, it is understandable that Marcela should pass mutely through the next several events that befall her. During this period, the narrator also reveals a key factor underlying the girl's expressive deficiency. Listening to other persons discussing her case, Marcela has this reaction:

> Repitió mentalmente la frase, saboreándola: "un caxlán abusó de ella." Esto era lo que había sucedido. Algo que podía decirse, que los demás podían escuchar y entender. No el vértigo, no la locura. Suspiró aliviada.

> She repeated the sentence to herself, savoring it: "a white man raped her." That was what had happened. Something that you could say out loud and other people would listen and understand. Not a fall into dizziness or madness. She breathed a sigh of relief (p. 29).

One becomes aware of a profound lack in the girl's formation beyond a mere absence of information on sexuality. She had not realized that this area of human experience could be grasped through linguistic structures, and, through this same ordering system, communicated to other people. Here one sees an implicit plea for the open, rationalistic discussion of sexual topics as part of a young girl's formation. An articulate awareness might have enabled Marcela to avoid rape. At any rate, the realization that her bewildering, inchoate experience can be patterned by a sentence marks a move toward rational living. The universality of linguistic expression impresses upon the rape victim that her experience is not unique and eases her isolation.

Despite her insight into the possibilities for communication, Marcela finds no opportunity to speak out. She is next presented registering a series of wordless protests against her pregnancy and giving birth. She bases her actions upon a poor understanding of the largely involuntary nature of these functions. This confusion is patent not only to the reader and narrator but to Catalina. Catalina is impressive in her successive refusals to enlighten her ward about the physiological processes that terrify the girl. Bitterly jealous, the woman long avoids mention of pregnancy. Finally, she screams at her: "¡Vas a tener un hijo You're going to have a baby! p. 46)." This delivered, the news sends the previously unaware Marcela into a panic. The narrator draws attention to Catalina's angry, aggressive withholding of communication: "calló (she was silent)," "enmudecía (she wouldn't say anything; p. 46), " "dejaba sola a Marcela (she left Marcela alone)," "desde afuera la miraba (she looked at her from without; p. 47)." Along with the call for informative and supportive discourse, one finds a laying-bare of yet another stereotypic notion: that women are jealously cruel to one another. Here, the implement of cruelty is silence.

Marcela's subsequent near-autistic behavior is unattractive, but the narrator manifestly absolves her of responsibility for it: "Marcela, a quien la adversidad había reblandecido los tuétanos, ya no protestaba (Life had beaten Marcela down to a pulp, and she gave up protesting; p. 47)."

Idolina appears in a very brief vignette attached to the end of the chapter on Marcela's rape. After being connected to Marcela in this enigmatic fashion, the *ladina* girl disappears from the narration for several chapters. Idolina first appears to the reader almost exactly as she hopes to appear. The girl lies in bed, apparently paralyzed, while her mother kneels by her bedside bewailing their unhappy fortunes. This scene, following Marcela's victimization, would seem another illustration of suffering womankind. However, the narrator implants in the melodramatic scenario an element of doubt: "Idolina no hizo ningún movimiento que delatara su vigilia (Idolina took care not to let on she was awake; p. 23)." Once more, the distancing alerts the reader to the devious nature of human beings, placing the characters under suspicion.

The hint of guile receives no further elaboration for some time. Idolina occurs next as a topic in a bitter argument between her stepfather (Leonardo) and mother. From the violent exchange, one pieces together the family history, quite a Gothic tale of adultery, betrayal and murder. In this version, Idolina is apparently the victim of an hysterical paralysis. One then finds a second version of the same events by the trustworthy narrator. The second presentation eliminates the melodramatic rhetoric of the first, sets events in chronological order and comments drily upon the proceedings. The salient factual discrepancy between the two is the nature of Idolina's deterioration. The narrator introduces a strong element of willful manipulation on the invalid's part: she was "terca en su voluntad de dejarse consumir (stubbornly determined to waste away; p. 77)." Especially impressive is her ability to predict the effect her ailment will have upon her hated elders, deliberately exacerbating their chaotic situation.

The next chapter reveals Idolina's exceptional communicational circumstance. She effectively cuts off all those whom convention would allow as her conversational partners. Instead, her sole reciprocal relation is with an Indian nurse, a woman as alienated from indigenous society as Idolina is from white society. As in Mercedes' pseudo-intimate speech, the two use *vos* to establish a special collusion outside the rigid strictures of small-town propriety.[16] Intimacy and sharing, however, are not the true basis of their extravagantly private communication system. Their real purpose is to exclude other people. The manner in which their dialogue is presented stresses its private and cryptic character. Nearly every utterance must be decoded by the commenting narrator, often with a lengthy explanation, before the reader can grasp its significance.

Two elements stand out in this conspirators' exchange. One is its reliance on myth and ritual and, indeed, the ritual character of the interaction. The opening line of the dialogue is literally a formula, the fixed first line of an Indian legend. The nurse twice invokes the formula and is twice rebuffed by the girl, who aborts the proffered story-telling session. The pattern of advance and rejection then turns out to be another ritual, a private ceremony between the two initiates. Throughout, one finds taunts and reproaches that appear to be fossilized into an invariable form, for example, "Que te compre el que no te conozca (Someone should buy you who doesn't know what he's getting into; p. 81)" as a formula of chiding. These stylized expressions of hostility give way to equally fixed conciliatory phrases. As the narrator explains, "Su relación era un juego de concesiones e imposiciones recíprocas cuyo mecanismo había perfeccionado una intimidad exclusiva (Their relations were a set of reciprocal concessions and impositions whose give-and-take had been worked out through their exclusive intimacy; p. 81)." Of the various intimate ceremonies, the most ritually powerful is the nurse's prophetic reading of the ashes in the grate. The future promise of vengeance and triumph for the two creates a virtual cult between them. Apart from these magic and cultist features, the pair's relationship rests on a very concrete piece of privileged information. Idolina is feigning paralysis; the nurse seconds the deception in order to enjoy the benefits of their dual withdrawal.

At this point, Idolina appears skilled in the exercise of deceit and manipulation. The narrator emphasizes her precocious intelligence and strong will, features that set her apart from the ovine Marcela. Idolina continues to exhibit an extraordinary superficial sophistication in worldly matters. An illustration of her facility occurs when, finally forced to abandon her false paralysis, she takes one of her first walks through town. Nobody greets Idolina or the woman with her, a circumstance the girl recognizes as signaling some grave disturbance. Despite the companion's pseudo-explanation, Idolina works out a way of accounting for the facts: "No nos saludan porque nos desprecian. A ella por perdida y a mí por consentidora. Lo que se dice de Julia y de mi padrastro es verdad (They don't greet us because they look down on us. They think she's a loose woman and I'm going along with her. What they say about Julia and my stepfather is right; p. 203)." Through observation and analysis, the girl accumulates a trove of damaging information about her fellow townsmen, hoping to put it to use.

However, in the final chapters, Idolina moves back toward being a victim. One discovers that her sophistication is less than it appears to be. The narrator discloses that, despite her extensive knowledge of the town's network of illicit liaisons, the girl does not know what censurable activity is involved. The attitude of others toward the participants is all that allows her to grasp the pattern of sexual alliances. Again, one finds Castellanos' tenet that maintaining young girls in ignorance is a great wrong. Lacking valid information, Idolina remains in a "pureza malherida . . . inocencia corrupta (mangled purity . . . corrupt innocence; p. 201)."

Idolina's final defeat results largely from her isolation from central patterns of communication and information exchange. Her reliance on spying, gossip and private speculation to envision the world proves inadequate. An incomplete grasp of sexual and political matters ruins her campaign to discredit her stepfather. The denunciatory strategy is so poorly constructed that it paradoxically helps the man to consolidate his hegemony. Moreover, her association with the stepfather's mistress turns to her disadvantage—a factor that, from her marginal position, she failed to see. The final chapter reveals the defeated Idolina back in her bed, staring at the wall.

This same chapter shows the stepfather enjoying the success of his own schemes. His triumph has much to do with his careful observation and assessment of local events. His information proves superior to Idolina's because it comes from an intimate contact with reality: caucases, interrogation of witnesses, visiting the sites of events, dispatching spies and meeting with officials. Clearly, these methods of information-gathering are open only to a male in a position of some importance. A woman, unable to circulate freely and ask questions, barred from political bargaining and plotting, must use methods resembling Idolina's. In this sense, the battle between the scheming stepdaughter and her equally scheming stepfather signals a fundamental injustice in sex roles. The communicational circumstance of a well-placed male gives him a political advantage of significant proportions.

VI

Among the numerous other females who populate the work, one finds many exemplars of withdrawn, self-centered, hypocritical and subjugated womanhood. The respective mothers of Marcela and Idolina are two tokens of the "martyr" type frequently associated with Latin society. The novel's cross-cultural representation of the type removes its "Latinity" to reveal it as one response to a confining role. The narrator is explicit in letting the reader know that self-advertised martyrdom is one outgrowth of women's problems.

Marcela's mother, Felipa, first appears at the moment of reencountering her raped and exhausted daughter. She executes a displacement of sympathy from the daughter to herself, loudly proclaiming the anguish the girl has put her through that day. This evasive tactic allows her to avoid knowing what has really happened to the girl and to indulge in public self-dramatization. After a lengthy transcription of the woman's complaints, the narrator unsympathetically refers to them as "aquella catarata de lamentaciones (that great gush of lamentations; p. 27)."

In the previously mentioned bargaining episode, Felipa appears in an equally unfavorable light. At first, she is uncertain why Catalina and Winiktón have come to call. The narrator reveals her thoughts at this juncture. This shows her entire attention to be focused on preparing the complaints she can employ in the ensuing conversation: "Todo lo que gano ¡y es tan poco! se lo comen mis hijos. Ay, parecen sanguijuelas, nada les basta, nada los deja contentos . . . . A mí me está secando la tristeza (Everything I earn—and it's hardly anything!—my children eat it right up. They're like little bloodsuckers. Nothing is ever enough for them, there's no pleasing them . . . With all the trouble I've got, there'll be nothing left of me; p. 39)." During the conversation, Catalina manages to establish that Marcela has been raped and is about to be married to an idiot. Felipa continues resolutely to lament her own problems, now exacerbated by recent events in her daughter's life. This pattern of displacement reaches a final point of absurdity when Felipa's last words in the chapter are "Me duelen mucho mis pies (My feet are killing me; p. 42)."

What is shown of this woman might represent her as simply one obnoxious individual. But, once more, the narrator intervenes with direct commentary to modify the picture. The goal is to move the reader toward considering all the complexities of the character's situation. It is stressed that Felipa has fallen into an especially difficult role since her husband, who ought to speak for her, has become a drunk. While emphasizing the role-related character of Felipa's problem, the narrator is also frank in voicing disapproval of her tactics for dealing with the world: "Y en cuanto a Felipa las costumbres no la autorizaban a tener voz propia. Y aun cuando la hubiese tenido no habría hablado jamás eficazmente en favor de su hija, no habría acertado a salvarla. Le gustaba gemir y lamentarse. Le gustaba sufrir (And as for Felipa, custom did not allow her to have a voice of her own. And even if she had had one, she would never have spoken up effectively on behalf of her daughter, she would never have worked out a way to save her. She liked to moan and wail. She liked to suffer; p. 44)."

Idolina's mother also first appears in a moment of lamentation. Her case, however, is more complex. Her daughter's plight enters into her considerations, complicating her self-pity with guilt. Moreover, lamentation is essentially a private activity which she practices in solitude. When others are present, she relies on silence to advertise her sufferings. The narrator describes in detail the Byzantine arrangements of the household which permit this woman to avoid even ordinary verbal interchanges. These strategies range from the location of the various members of the household, minimizing contact, to a systematic failure to register what others are saying. For example, here is the description of dinner-table conversation: "A la hora de comer—única en que el matrimonio se reunía—las frecuentes interrupciones de Leonardo, que aludían siempre a la fiesta, no desviaban a Isabel de la tranquila y rutinaria línea de su conversación (At dinner time—the only time the couple got together—the frequent interruptions of Leonardo, which always had to do with the party, failed to deflect Isabel from following the usual calm routine of her conversation; p. 67)." Communication is so effectively muted that Leonardo announces at one point, "supongo que ya te habrás enterado de que esta noche doy una fiesta en mi casa (I imagine you've probably heard that I'm giving a party at my house tonight; p. 68)."

Perversely, Isabel ends up deriving a good deal of satisfaction from this scheme. When her husband's behavior brings a scandal, Isabel basks in public recognition of her long-suffering silence: "Su conducta imperturable llenaba de elogios las murmuraciones de Ciudad Real. Una santa Rita de Casia, ¡ ni que ver! (Her imperturbability won her the praise of the town gossips. Saint Rita of Cassia herself couldn't have done better! p. 200)." Both spouses benefit from this widespread notion of their marriage. The picture of the wealthy philanderer and his patient wife is easy to grasp and favorable. It serves as an acceptable substitute for the real story of Leonardo and Isabel, with its troubling ambiguities and guilt. By the end of the novel, the couple has normalized its relations with the community and each other. Isabel's bitter silence has brought concrete rewards. Here, one sees gossip, superficially a malicious form of discourse, aiding to bring an anomalous and unwieldy situation within the bounds of the expected. One may even say that Isabel and Leonardo learn from the gossip about them how they may best fit into the town's social structure.

VII

Isabel's passivity stands in opposition to the utter deviance of her rival, La Alazana. The latter lives in a situation of irremediable marginality. The townspeople mark the visible signs of her condition: she is from the capital, she lives with a land-reform agent, she may be unmarried; she has no children or kin. The narrator reveals the hidden aspects: the woman is illegitimate, a concubine, a school dropout and profoundly alienated from her family of origin and her common-law husband.

What is interesting about this outsider is her wildly vacillating statements about her exceptional status. On the one hand, she communicates a fervent desire to be like the town's most respectable ladies. By manifesting this wish, she makes herself vulnerable to the assaults of those women, who are resolved to maintain a closed circle. For example, Isabel is able to wound her rival by disclosing to her the nickname that has been attached to her. "La Alazana" (The Roan Mare) points to the woman's red hair, by convention a sign of marginality, and to her habit of roaming about freely, unlike the cloistered ladies of the town.

La Alazana's second, and more successful tactic is to convey her pride in being unlike other women. She puts this point across partly through such gestures as wearing her hair loose, laughing in an unrestrained manner, walking wherever she cares to walk, and appearing unaccompanied in public. In her speech, too, she shows a freedom which is unheard of for women, remarking: "Yo tampoco quería a mi padre. Era borracho (I didn't love my father, either. He was a drunk: p. 95)." Implicit in these statements is the notion that women's role need not be one of continual self-suppression. La Alazana provides a demonstration of this tenet by literally obliging Idolina to leave her bed and join the rebellious older woman on her lengthy walks. The subversion of La Alazana's message does not escape the vigilance of the town's reactionary leader. He suggests ejecting the woman from the community before she provokes a widespread questioning of the restrictions women accept: "Ah, cómo la envidian estas encerradas, cómo quisieran tener su desvergüenza (How those women envy her, after being shut up all their lives, how they'd like to have her free-and-easy ways; p. 101)."

Despite the alarm she generates, La Alazana can hardly figure as the voice of feminism or even a serious threat to the prevailing social arrangement. Her words and actions touch on issues central to women's problems, but she herself is unaware of these issues. For example, she draws a significant generalization from her transformation of Idolina, but it is only significant to two persons. Turning to the girl's mother, she says "¿Lo ves? . . . Mi voluntad es más poderosa que la tuya. Yo he sido la más fuerte (See?... My will is stronger than yours. I came out on top; p. 135)." In her relation with Leonardo, La Alazana takes care not to assume a subjugated role. Her goal, though, is not an improvement of women's place, but a simple drive for one-upmanship.

La Alazana reiterates one of Catalina's key communicational problems: an inability to identify and comment upon the larger implications of events. The deterioration in her common-law marriage matches that of the Catalina-Winiktón bond. Again, the woman is unable to see the point of the social reforms her husband pursues. She reduces his crusading actions to their immediate effects within a limited circle. In so doing, she deprives the man's justice-seeking of any meaning. The husband directs his educational efforts to other men, accepting his wife's narrow outlook as natural to her sex.

La Alazana is unlike other women in the novel in her relatively sophisticated background. She has been affiliated with university radicals and, over the years, come into contact with a variety of reformist notions. Given her experiences, her refusal to think critically or accept responsibility seems especially grievous. Again, the narrator intervenes to prevent too much of the guilt for the woman's conduct from resting on the individual. This intervention takes the form of a long passage inserted into a chapter that shows La Alazana at her worst. Here the narrator assumes a ritual voice synthesizing all social factors impinging upon women. This collective-societal voice apostrophizes a composite figure of women only partially identified with La Alazana:

> El cuerpo que padeces ahora te va a ser revelado por un hombre. Madurarás en la entrega, adquirirás tu forma definitiva gracias a las caricias.
> El esposo es el colmador. El guarda, para tus ansias, placer; para tus vacíos, fecundidad. El va a colocarte en el rango para el que estás predestinada.
> Si el esposo no llega, niñl quedada, resígnate. Cierra el escote, baja los párpados, calla . . .

> The body you suffer now will be revealed to you by a man. You will mature by surrendering it to him, you will acquire your definitive form through caresses.
> The husband is the one who completes you. For your eager longings, he brings pleasure; for your emptiness, fecundity. He will place you in the spot you were predestined to occupy.
> If the husband doesn't appear, leftover girl, then give up hope. Button up your blouse, cast your eyes to the ground, fall silent . . . (p. 287)

After this lengthy, ceremonial presentation, one is plunged back into the ordinary narration of La Alazana's actions. Her petty behavior and that of the women around her now appear contextualized within the larger picture of society's deformation of women. This passage stands as the novel's most visible attempt to avoid the unfavorable depiction of women that Millett so fears.

The length of the passage and its highly foregrounded *écriture* are important in another way. No townsperson actually speaks in such an elaborate manner. Yet, what the townspeople tell their female children is what the ritualistic narrator tells the abstract avatar of all womanhood. By putting these submerged and implicit messages in the most attention-claiming form, the novel points out just how hard to perceive they ordinarily are. As well as making a point about La Alazana and her rivals, here Castellanos provides justification for the way the novel is constructed and for its having been written at all. The editorializing narrator, constantly breaking in with commentary, makes sense because it is so hard to see the factors at work in social intercourse. The narrator emphasizes this hidden quality by pointing out what remained submerged during a particular episode. An ironic, sophisticated narrator is one device for making these occult mechanisms visible and asserting their occult nature, but so is the act of writing a social novel.

The narrator also provides a model of how one should regard the behavior of real-life women. In the context of ordinary life, individual women may seem merely sly, whiny, withdrawn or spiteful. What is needed is to see, as the narrator sees, that this unpleasant verbal behavior grows out of an inability to achieve an effective voice. Resolutely antisentimental, the narrator refuses to disguise or soften the appalling behavior of the female characters. The rejection of specific manifestations of women's communicational problem leads to an affirmation that they point to a deep-seated problem. Through an overt commentary, the narrator signals the task ahead of us: to examine the blockage, recognize its societal roots and take measures to open up the lines of communication for women.

Notes

[1] Jean Franco, *Introducción a la literatura hispanoamericana*, trans. Francisco Rivera (Caracas: Monte Avila, 1970), p. 261; *The Modern Culture of Latin America*, rev. ed. (Middlesex, England: Penguin, 1970), pp. 124-125; *Spanish American Literature Since Independence* (New York: Barnes and Noble, 1973), p. 166.

[2] John S. Brushwood, *The Spanish American Novel: A Twentieth Century Survey* (Austin: University of Texas Press, 1975), pp. 237-38; *Mexico in its Novel: A Nation's Search for Identity* (Austin: University of Texas Press, 1966), p. 36.

[3] Joseph Sommers' interest in Rosario Castellanos' depiction of the Indian is typical of the bulk of commentary on the novelist. See Sommers, "Changing Views of the Indian in Mexican Literature," *Hispania*, 47 (1964), 47-55; "El ciclo de Chiapas: nueva corriente literaria," *Cuadernos Americanos*, 133 (1964), 246-61; "The Indian-oriented Novel in Latin America: New Spirit, New Forms, New Scope," *Journal of Inter-American Studies*, 6 (1964), 249-65; "Rosario Castellanos: nuevo enfoque del indio mexicano," *La Palabra y el Hombre* (Xalapa, Veracruz),

29 (1964), 83-88; and *After the Storm: Landmarks of the Modern Mexican Novel* (Albuquerque: University of New Mexico Press, 1968), 83-88. Other discussions of this theme include Emmanuel Carballo, "Rosario Castellanos," in his *Diecinueve protagonistas de la literatura mexicana del siglo XX* (México: Empresas Editoriales, 1965), pp. 409-24; Walter M. Langford, "Rosario Castellanos," in his *The Mexican Novel Comes of Age* (Notre Dame: University of Notre Dame Press, 1971), pp. 182-85; Günter Lorenz, "Rosario Castellanos," in his *Diálogos con América Latina* (Santiago de Chile: Editorial Pomaire, 1972), pp. 185-211; and César Rodríguez Chicharro, "Rosario Castellanos: *Balún-Canán*," *La Palabra y el Hombre*, 9 (1959), 61-67. Shorter journalistic or descriptive notes on Castellanos also tend to emphasize this feature of her work. It is clear from the above-described consensus that Castellanos' portrait of Indian culture "from within the Indian" is her most widely-recognized and impact-producing novelistic achievement.

4   Protest, as expressed through novelistic language, is the element that interests Alfonso González in "Lenguaje y protesta en *Oficio de tinieblas*," *Revista de Estudios Hispánicos* [University, Alabama], 8, 3 (1974), 413-17. Rhoda Dybvig's master's thesis, published by the Universidad Nacional Autónoma de México in 1965, focuses on the element of denunciation in the author's works. See, in particular, pp. 71-72. Castellanos' critically questioning attitude toward Mexican history, and particularly the faulty implementation of reform measures, is the focus of Beth Miller, "Historia y ficción en *Oficio de tinieblas* de Rosario Castellanos," *Texto Crítico*, No. 28 (1984), 131-42, and Sommers, "Forma e ideología en *Oficio de tinieblas* de Rosario Castellanos," *Revista de Crítica Literaria Latino-americana*, 7-8 (1978), 73-91.

Commentary that considers both Castellanos' feminism and the author's literary ideas and expression include Gabriella de Beer, "Feminismo en la obra poética de Rosario Castellanos," *Revista de Crítica Literaria Latinoamericana*, No. 13 (1981), 105-112; Lucía Fox-Lockert, "El feminismo en la obra de Rosario Castellanos," *Letras Femeninas*, 5, 2 (1979), 48-56; Naomi Lindstrom, "Rosario Castellanos: Representing Women's Voice," *Letras Femininas*, 5, 2 (1979), 29-47, and "Narrative Technique and Women's Expression in a Novel by Rosario Castellanos," *Modern Language Studies*, 8, 3 (1983), 71-80; Phyllis Rodríguez-Peralta, "Images of Women in Rosario Castellanos' Prose," *Latin American Literary Review*, 6, 11 (1977), 68-80; and Stacy Schlau, "Conformity and Resistance to Enclosure: Female Voices in Rosario Castellanos' *Oficio de tinieblas* [*The Dark Service*]," *Latin American Literary Review*, 7, 24 (1984), 45-57.

5   Rosario Castellanos, "Notas al margen: nunca en pantuflas," in her *Mujer que sabe latín...* (México: SepSetentas, 1973), p. 185. The author explains her objections to realism on pp. 180-85, along with her suggestions for a more effective means of expressing social problems in literature.

6   *Ibid.*

7   Especially notable in this regard are Castellanos' plays and dramatic poems: *Tablero de damas* (México: Revista América, 1952), "Lamentación de Dido," in her *Poemas 1953-55* (México: Colección Metáfora, 1957), *Salomé y Judith* (México: Editorial Jus, 1959), and *El eterno femenino* (México: Fondo de Cultura Económica, 1975).

8   Brushwood, *Mexico in its Novel*, p. 36. Brushwood is like many critics in preferring the second novel, though the earlier *Balún-Canán* continues to be better known.

9   Sommers, *After the Storm*, p. 160.

10 Castellanos, *Oficio de tinieblas* (México: Joaquín Mortiz, 1962), p. 13. Subsequent page numbers for this novel refer to this edition.

[11] For an application of this analysis to a literary work, see the discussion of Alfred, Lord Tennyson's *The Idylls of the King* in Kate Millett, *Sexual Politics* (Garden City: Doubleday, 1970), p. 148.

[12] Dybvig, p. 60, says of Catalina, "Se hunde en su propio problema sicológico." Brushwood stresses that Castellanos' "indigenism" emphasized psychological elements over sociological ones; see, especially, his remarks in *Mexico in its Novel*. p. 36.

[13] Castellanos, "La mujer y su imagen," in her *Mujer que sabe latín...*, p. 25.

[14] Castellanos, "La participación de la mujer mexicana en la educación formal," in her *Mujer que sabe latín...*, p. 25.

[15] Raúl Ortiz, preface to Castellanos, *El eterno femenino*, p. 6.

[16] Of course, the *vos* may also signal a representation in Spanish of a conversation in the indigenous language; in any case, the linguistic circumstance sets the two conversationalists apart from the rest of local society and closer to one another.

Marta
Lynch

Marta Lynch:
The Mechanisms of Inefficacy

I

The outstanding characteristic of the literary career of Marta Lynch was undoubtedly her ability to arouse controversy. Lynch herself noted with satisfaction that her writings retained their power to baffle and disconcert long after their publication. For Lynch, it was important that her work provoke strong reactions from a wide spectrum of readers, rather than appear as the expression of one predictable political or social stance. In her analysis, her work is successful insofar as it disrupts the reader's convenient notions of how national or human affairs operate.[1] Lynch's fellow novelist Eduardo Gudiño Kieffer recognizes the validity of this approach. He identifies Lynch's great virtue as that of being "polémica y controvertida (polemical and the focus of controversy)." While Gudiño Kieffer faults Lynch for occasionally becoming merely "farragosa (windy)," he sees her tactics for exciting debate as a positive social and literary achievement.[2]

Examining Lynch's work and reaction to it, one sees several highly sensitive areas upon which she repeatedly concentrates. One of these is the longstanding debate, a highly productive one in Argentine letters, over the appropriate cultural identity of the Argentine citizen. Implicit commentary on this matter appears throughout her fiction. More overt statements appear in her interviews and journalistic essays. Here, she insists that her own sometimes disorienting attempt to establish an identity and values typifies the recent experience of Argentina as a whole. Her remarks have often elicited heated response. For example in 1971, Lynch was severely criticized by David Vinas[3], who objected to her contention that Argentines, in constructing a national culture, could still benefit from European models.[4]

A second Lynch concern is the portrayal of persons involved in socio-political happenings. Her first two novels, *La alfombra roja* (*The Red Carpet*, 1962) and *Al vencedor* (*To the Victor*, 1965) offer criticism of specific shortcomings of Argentine society. The two works fit a recognizable pattern: the novelistic denunciation of identifiable social ills (dehumanizing power politics and lack of economic opportunity). In subsequent novels, the social criticism is

73

more diffuse; blame is less easily assigned. *La señora Ordóñez* (*Mrs. Ordóñez*, (1967), *El cruce del rio* (*The River Crossing*), 1972), *Un árbol lleno de manzanas* (*A Tree Full of Apples*, 1974) and *La penúltima versión de la Colorada Villanueva* (*The Penultimate Version of Colorada Villanueva*, 1978), and *Informe bajo llave* (*Top Secret Report*, 1983), as well as the short stories in *Los años de fuego* (*The Years of Fire*, 1981) and *No te duermas, no me dejes* (*Don't Go to Sleep, Don't Leave Me*, 1985), all contain varying proportions of political and social commentary together with narration of intimate experience. Events occurring in national and world politics frequently appear in the fiction, but they are always shown as they affect the characters personally.

Lynch has created characters committed to a very wide range of political positions, from revolution to defense of the status quo. The delineation of these characters and their activities has two impressive features. One is the generally favorable treatment accorded the figure of the militant. Indeed, the 1972 novel not only gives a sympathetic rendering of the actions and death of a guerrilla fighter but also bears a dedication to the author's late brother, explicitly identified as a militant. The other is the highly personalized and particularized portrayal of politically-involved persons. This procedure has given rise to complaints that Lynch suppresses the ideological basis of these characters' behavior. Ernesto Goldar, to cite one such polemicist, grudgingly praises Lynch's complex and informed novelization of Peronist youth activities in *La señora Ordóñez*. For Goldar, however, this complexity is suspect. He accuses the author of subtle literary-rhetorical strategies to banalize and trivialize the political endeavors represented, reducing them to the level of local color or focusing exclusively on the affective responses of participants.[5] There has also been a widespread enthusiastic response to Lynch's interest in politics as reflected in the individual's unique human experience.[6]

Given her longstanding attraction to controversies, it is almost inevitable that Lynch should participate in the current debate over the assigning of sex roles. In this area, too, her activity has ranged from express public declarations to the literary working-out of essentially feminist notions. Sex role analysis is an implicit constituent of her short stories, beginning with the 1967 *Los cuentos tristes* (*Sad Stories*). This collection has earned critical attention for its emblematic figures of marginal women.[7] *Cuentos de colores* (*Colored Stories*, 1970) and *Los dedos de la mano* (*The Fingers of the Hand*, 1976) apply a similar type of literary examination to representative middle-class female characters. Commentators have also discerned a critical assessment of women's status in *El cruce del rio* and *Un árbol lleno de manzanas*.[8]

However, critical consensus situates *La señora Ordóñez* as the foremost example of Lynch's literary feminism. H. Ernest Lewald has shown the strong affinities between this work and the writings of prominent Argentine social critics. He attributes the novel's great impact to its accurate identification of the most troubling features of sexuality and the question of women's status.[9] In effect, the 1967 novel produced such a notable reaction that Lynch subsequently complained that its success obscured her other writings.[10]

La señora Ordóñez merits study here not only for its demonstrated "relevance," but also for its satisfyingly complex construction. It represents the author's departure from the largely realist *écriture* manifest in her early work. In *La señora Ordóñez*, one finds a more formulaic, artful mode of novelistic representation; the formal issues of fictional elaboration are more visible and handled in a more innovative fashion. The willingness to experiment extends to the treatment of features that interest us here. The disposition of narrative voice, dialogue between characters, the heroine's difficulties in being honest with herself and in arriving at an adequate self-characterization, her efforts toward self-assertion: all these elements serve to address questions of discourse and women's voice, Blanca Ordóñez is paradigmatic of a woman attempting, in middle life, a massive self-questioning and some means of self-expression. The successive failures of endeavors cannot really be said to educate or to form Blanca, who is as mute and confused at the novel's end as at its outset. Rather, the reader is the one who, through the fictional structuring of Blanca's inarticulate disorientation, gains a clearer understanding of the social forces at work. The disparity between the reader's learning about Blanca and her own failure to learn is significant. It brings home a basic tenet of Lynch's novelistic feminism. The individual woman cannot be expected to enunciate clearly her current status and proximate needs simply by her own willful striving. The necessary condition for this successful verbalization is the articulation, at a societal level, of problems inherent in the present sex-role arrangement. Lynch's novel, then, stands as part of this dialogue that society must undertake.

II

The most immediately notable structural feature of *La señora Ordóñez* is the alternation between first and third-person narration. The novel is divided into blocks of text, each block being narrated entirely by Blanca Ordóñez or entirely by the omniscient narrator. Apart from the obvious transfer of pronouns from first to third person, the differentiating features of the two voices are relatively subtle. Indeed, strong uniformities present themselves. Both Blanca and the third-person narrator recount past events and relay, using the present tense, events still in progress at the time of narration. Both focus principally upon Blanca's behavior and reactions. Both convey the thoughts of secondary characters, the narrator through an omniscient revelation of consciousness and Blanca through elaborate conjecture proffered with pseudo-omniscient certainty. The heroine's accounts of herself are not inchoate, precognitive stream of consciousness. Her thoughts are, at least superficially, as fully-articulated and considered as those of the narrator; one cannot help but note her ostensible frankness and displays of insight. Given these strong similarities, the reader may wonder why this double system of narration is necessary to convey the peculiarities of Blanca's distress. Only gradually do the discrepancies between the two voices become visible and significant.

The first block of narration belongs to the third-person narrator. This passage won some notoriety for its harsh bluntness in the depiction of conjugal relations. This feature is especially noteworthy in the Argentine novel, where considerations of decorum have, until quite recently, exercised a muting effect upon the artistic representation of sexual activities.[11]

From the point of view of this study, the narrator's intimate exposure of Blanca has a special interest. While startling the reader, the narrator is also emitting an implicit warning about Blanca and what Wayne Booth would call her "reliability" as speaker.[12] This scene makes manifest the strong irrational vein that runs through the woman's attitudes and actions. Throughout the episode, Blanca registers strong feelings of aversion and uncleanliness. Her disgust leads her to perceive her own body as "impúdico y feo (indecent and ugly)"[13] and to submit it to a frenzied ritual of cleansing, amid hysterical weeping. The narrator also points out how little immediate cause underlies these extreme reactions; Blanca's husband is a gentle and tactful lover. Moreover, the analysis of the heroine's emotions is not favorable to her; for example, "no había piedad hacia su marido sino piedad por ella (she didn't feel any sympathy for him, only self-pity; p. 14)."

This disproportion between Blanca's visible circumstance and her inappropriate, melodramatic reaction suggests a profound disturbance in her ability to register experience. Before Blanca's own words appear, the narrator already has her "under suspicion." The reader suspects the heroine of a tendency toward self-dramatization, self-pity and a history of instability. The initial planting of doubt is important because her statements so successfully mimic those of a truly lucid and insightful individual.

Blanca's first block of text is an unuttered commentary upon a conversation in which she is also a participant. Her words here have two rhetorical goals. One is the ironic denunciation of a highly convention-bound and socialized form of discourse. The heroine mocks the banality and artifice of the remarks exchanged and the elaborate rites of recognition and greeting in a pretentious resort hotel. Her basic complaint, however, is not the ridiculous character of this gala display, but rather the exclusion of any more meaningful verbal transaction: "hablan de sus hijos y de sus casas estupendas sin ceder en cuanto a la absoluta imposibilidad que tenemos de intercambiar otra cosa que no sea hipocresía, tedio o tristeza (they talk about their children and their fantastic houses, keeping things fixed so we can never exchange anything but hypocrisy, tedium and sadness: p. 15)."

Blanca is also eager to establish her own alienated, and therefore privileged, consciousness of this deplorable discourse. While the others are implicated participants, she sets herself apart: "Soy una presencia o un testigo que no puede asimilarse a los demás (I am a presence or a witness who can't fit in with the others; p. 19)."

The woman's claim to otherness is justified, to some extent, by her trenchantly critical irony. She also adduces as proof of her separateness her willingness to invite a flamboyant homosexual to the table. This individual, with his blatant deviation from role, his shrill exclamations and disturbing remarks, succeeds in causing discomfort among the staid conversationalists. For Blanca, his inclusion is a rebellious rupture with the code that stultifies discourse at the resort.

Other of the heroine's actions and thoughts, however, cast doubt upon her supposed spiritual distance. In an elaborate display of conversational "one-upmanship," she feigns a speaking acquaintance with a member of a prominent family. This duplicity requires considerable concentration and expertise on her part. Yet, she claims it is no more than a resigned concession to her husband's notions of proper wifely comportment. The heroine's unspoken thoughts also seem suspiciously close to the general tenor of the conversation. She worries obsessively about the effects of the late hour upon her physical appearance. Comparing herself with the other women present, she is frankly delighted to note the marks of aging on their faces. When not preoccupied with cosmetic questions, she frequently engages in gossipy speculation about the other members of her party. In short, rather than be an alternative to the superficial and malicious spoken conversation, her inner discourse is often a mirror of it. It remains uncertain whether the heroine could truly generate a richer and more authentic discourse. She lays the blame for her trivialization squarely upon those around her; the reader wonders if much of the problem is not internalized within the woman herself.

III

The problems found in the resort scene receive further exploration in a series of segments concerning Blanca's childhood. All of these segments are in the words of the narrator, who not only relates events but also provides a synthetic summation and judgmental opinion. Here, Blanca has not yet been touched by the masque and artifice of pseudo-elegant society. However, she by no means enjoys a situation of free and authentic communication. Rather, she is firmly situated as the younger of two daughters in a lower middle-class home. This context, too, is rife with rigid expectations about what constitutes proper discourse.

The most notable feature of conversation pattern in the household is the tyranny exercised by the father, a paradigmatic *machista*. His domination focuses on two issues: the expression of sexuality and the production of discourse. The latter is controlled through a system of tacit assumptions concerning the obligations and rights of various speakers. These are the type of binding agreements one discourse analyst characterizes as "contracts."[14] For example, Blanca and her sister have learned that engaging in dinner-table chitchat entails a risk. Should they do so, they entitle their father to practice "la gran violencia familiar de modo que la charla podía caer en el vacío o desatar una furiosa tempestad coronada con imprecaciones y portazos (the great family violence so the conversation might sink like a stone or unleash a furious storm with a grand finale of shouting and door-slamming; p. 23)." The mother is obliged to produce displays of concern for the father's well-being and to arrange all matters to his liking. As recompense for these verbal acts of submission, she is allowed to emit pathetic sighs, audible signs of her martyred condition. The result of these reciprocal arrangements is a close programming of daily inter-actions. The narrator summarizes the total behavior of one family member: "tomaba parte en la comedia (she played out her role in the farce; p. 22)."

Apart from this Byzantine code of ritual, one notes a second unfortunate feature of the family's discourse. This is the fact that many of their modes of expression come to them preformulated, secondhand, imposed by mass media and religious schooling. The narrator is overt about pointing out this prefabricated language and its sources. The mother, for example, is characterized by her "extraña manera de mezclar manías conyugales y refranes de revistas (strange practice of mixing up her conjugal preoccupations with bits of magazine phraseology; p. 65)." These linguistic "hand-me-downs" become the object of explicit denunciation. The narrator deplores these forms of expression because they fail to correspond to the actual life experiences of the characters. Blanca and her sister, growing up amid this verbiage, "se preparaban para lo que hubiera de venir con un escuálido arsenal de nociones falsas y lugares comunes (were prepared for whatever might happen in the future with a squalid arsenal of false notions and clichés; p. 22)."

Several brief vignettes give an indication of the divorce between real experience and imposed, alienated language. The father interrupts his rude behavior to the three females to give an account of his courtship. Here, his language is virtually that of courtly love. The narrator transcribes and mocks his "frases encandiladas (ardent phrases; p. 21)," juxtaposing them with more illustrations of his unchivalrous comportment. A similar treatment is extended to the relations between Blanca's sister and the sister's fiancé. Although the man gives every sign of being dull, impassive and hopelessly military-minded, the omniscient narrator ironically applies to him the same descriptive adjective that his girlfriend uses: "delicioso (delicious; p. 84)," clearly the residue of an immersion in mass-media language.

The most grotesque scene involving "magazine" language is one in which Blanca's parents compare their two daughters. The entire comparison rests upon popularized notions of what constitutes femininity, a quality that only the other sister is deemed to possess. Here one finds the mother pronouncing this judgment: "Teresa tiene buenas caderas para madre . . . es de una belleza clásica, suave y mórbida (Teresa has good hips for having babies . . . her type of beauty is classical, gentle and soft; p. 65)." The denunciation of this manner of viewing young women is unmistakable when Blanca is shown later, nursing her intense shame over her failure to meet official standards of feminine grace.

A more diffuse denunciatory tactic involves Blanca's life as a child and as an adult. One learns that much of her childhood was spent absorbing various warnings about courtship, marriage, and sexuality. The narrator specifies the predominance of these themes in the father's conversation; moreover, Blanca receives her early schooling from nuns. Little of this moralistic discourse is transcribed in the novel, an omission that serves to underline its utter predictability. The girl encounters further "instruction" on these issues from her frequent visits to the cinema, exposure to popular song lyrics and other mass-culture sources. Yet, none of this massive education proves applicable to Blanca's situation as a mature woman. Despite her hours spent "learning" about the management of sexual-amorous relations, it is in this area that she is most at sea, continually bringing chaos into her life and those of her husbands and lovers.

Blanca's early immersion in mass-marketed language has effects that continue well into her adult life. Phrases leap to her consciousness at the most unexpected moments, even after she has grown too sophisticated to accept them as valid. In the midst of a hopelessly complicated situation with a lover, she cannot help but think of this scrap of women's magazine advice: "Interesa al hombre hablándole de lo que a él le interesa (To make a man interested in you, talk to him about what he's interested in; p. 92)." Pondering why she considers herself old, she realizes who her authorities are: "los artículos milagrosos de belleza, las novelas (articles on miracle beauty treatments, novels; p. 73)." Blanca, longing for self-determination, is aghast to discover how thoroughly she has internalized these alienating models.

This entire problem reaches a crisis when the heroine embarks on an affair with a much younger man. The event unleashes within her mind a massive amount of ready-made descriptions of such circumstances. Involuntarily, she finds herself calling herself a *jovata*, a cruel reference to her vanishing youth. The moralistic fulminations of her father and sister, long discarded as absurd, come back to haunt her. During a meeting with her lover, Blanca suffers a virtual attack of this stored-up language: "Otras palabras trágicas se mechaban a la tarde sin igual. Jamona, edad madura, vieja ramera. Recordaba horribles letras de tango: —¡Y pensar que hace diez años fue mi locura! (Other tragic words comingled with the splendid afternoon. Fatty, she's not getting any younger, an old whore. I kept remembering horrible tango lyrics: 'And to think that ten years ago I was nuts about her!'; p. 220)." It is notable that in the earlier portions of the novel the narrator possesses insight into Blanca's problem, but the woman seems not to. As the work progresses, Blanca moves away from blaming her immediate context for the banality or inappropriateness of discourse. She learns to see that the fossilized forms are coming from within herself and she is often successful at identifying the original models—although not at overcoming their deleterious effects. Her affair with the young man produces a sharp rise in her level of awareness of these socialized patterns. After this experience, Blanca comes to agree substantially with a point the narrator has long been making: that it was the influence of her early home environment that socialized Blanca into false modes of expression (p. 23).

There is, however, one aspect of Blanca's patterning that she never manages to confront. This is her continual formulation of statements about her physical appearance, one of the most distressing features of her discourse. Both in Blanca's segments of narration and in the narrator's, vast amounts of space go to detailed evaluations of her body. The topic expands to include the appearances of other women, whom Blanca assesses at length in a spirit of rivalry. While the woman's remarks on this theme occasionally have a component of mild self-mockery, this ironic edge cannot be a coherent instrument of social criticism. Blanca never seriously questions the necessity of spending hours of her time in the assessment of her complexion.

Two models are given for this type of obsessive behavior. One appears in the narrator's accounts of Blanca's childhood environment. Here one finds a system of folk beliefs about the body that correspond roughly to such pseudo-sciences as physiognomy. Blanca's parents "read" the appearance of their daughters and other persons as indices to inner qualities. For example, the mother rejects the elder daughter's fiancé, not for his stodgy behavior, but for his bodily characteristics. She is convinced that abundant hair and a low forehead are signs of intellectual and spiritual mediocrity. This set of beliefs is intimately involved with the issue of sex role. Blanca's prominent chin is diagnosed as a mark of deviation from model femininity. The anomaly casts doubt upon her ability to function in courtship, marriage and motherhood.

This family discourse is certain to strike the reader as superstitious and ignorant. Indeed, the presentation of these remarks superficially resembles the depiction of a quaint, folkloric scene. However, even after Blanca has rejected these folk notions, her inner and outer discourse remains focused upon physical appearances. As a sophisticated doctor's wife, she can hardly expect to gauge a woman's femininity by the size of her hands. Nonetheless, she retains the principle that people may be judged on the basis of their physical features. As in Blanca's parental home, the presentation of self is assigned moral weight. As she rises socially, Blanca makes the correlation between outer and inner self in more subtle ways.

These habits of mind are most apparent in the woman's unuttered discourse, where she is less inhibited by considerations of propriety. For example, Blanca is reproved at one point for a number of instances of misbehavior. To restore her self-esteem, she inwardly formulates the following statement: "La verdad es que siempre tuve un vientre admirable (The truth is I always had an admirable tummy; p. 71)." On another occasion, she must terminate a difficult affair with a married man; however, she finds it too painful to think through the causes of their mutual disenchantment. Through an evasive displacement, she focuses her dissatisfaction upon a physiological feature, the man's light pigmentation. This trait takes on characterological significance as she inwardly reviles her lover for being a repellent "albino (p. 96)." A similar strategy is evident in Blanca's statements about her intellectual friend, Berta. Berta troubles Blanca's conscience, rebuking her for frivolity, dilettantism, promiscuity and failure to pursue her artistic career. To neutralize Berta's commentary, Blanca elaborates descriptions of her friend's appearance. Berta is characterized as "secándose pronto y mal (withering up early and badly; p. 288)," as a plain woman who cannot presume to judge the pretty Blanca. Again, the discussion of the physical self substitutes for the evaluation of urgent issues.

Clearly, Blanca's behavior must have a model other than the one provided by her parents. This model is revealed in her interaction with other wealthy wives. While none of these women would comment upon appearances with the crudity of Blanca's parents, the topic is nonetheless central to their discourse. They share a culture in which expensive elegance, grooming and the apparent preservation of youth confer status.

Two cases illustrate this principle. Rosa, one of the circle, is rapidly losing her attractiveness. In consequence, she is invited to join in conversation only as an act of charity. When Rosa attempts to speak on intellectual issues, her discourse is taken for a pathetic attempt to compensate for her lost beauty. Although the woman's unattractiveness cannot become an explicit topic of conversation, it governs her discourse situation.

Alicia enjoys a position that is the exact opposite of Rosa's; she is an ostensibly "well-preserved" woman. Even Blanca, who considers Alicia her intellectual inferior, must be impressed by this achievement. Alicia's privileged status is visible in a conversation she sustains with Blanca. Blanca confesses to feeling unhappy over the discovery of wrinkles in her facial skin. Alicia takes advantage of this admission to deliver a lecture on the proper measures for delaying the aging process. However, this apparent offering of aid is, in fact, another display of superiority. As Blanca points out, Alicia knows that her friend cannot afford the expensive youth-preserving treatment under discussion. In short, Alicia's status is not only the result of her splendid appearance. She must also know how to speak about questions of physical appearance in such a way as to highlight her own special accomplishments and the deficiencies of other women.

The same duplicitous displacement is employed to neutralize another painful issue: Blanca's influence on her two daughters. The two girls are manifestly troubled by the unstable model of adult womanhood that Blanca provides. As the novel progresses, one sees increasing evidence that the daughters have begun to follow her most destructive behavioral patterns. Notably, the elder daughter becomes involved in a disturbing love affair that is a virtual mirror image of her mother's current liaison. Yet, these issues of influence are not discussed. Rather, mother and daughters focus upon the transmission of praiseworthy or deplorable bodily traits. The daughters reproach Blanca: "mamá, he heredado tus caderas (Mama, I've inherited your hips; p. 61)." The mother, considering her contributions to her daughters' formation, concludes "que me agradezca la desgraciadita [de mi hija] el vientre heredado de mamá y aún mucho más hermoso (I just hope that little wretch [my daughter] is thankful for the firm tummy she got from Mama and hers is even nicer; p. 71)."

The implicit analysis that arises from Lynch's fiction parallels the explicitly critical discussion found in Roland Barthes' 1966 *Système de la mode* (*The System of Fashion*). In his work, Barthes looks at the same social group—appearance-conscious, well-off middle-class women, through the writing employed in fashion magazines. He finds that these publications often touch upon potentially significant and threatening topics: politics, the status of women, the human need for productive activity. However, these topics are invariably treated in such a way as to banalize their disturbing implications. The key strategy is to focus attention upon the cosmetic aspects of any situation. For example, the question of careers for women with families becomes the question of how married career women may maintain their standards of grooming and dress. The result is a form of discourse that, while soothing to read, effectively blocks women from perceiving the larger social implications of phenomena. Like Lynch, Barthes makes it clear that the obfuscation of social issues through a trivializing, "cosmeticizing" discourse does not prevent these problems from affecting the lives of women. Lack of social vision can only compound the contradictions inherent in their lives.[15]

IV

Male-female relations are a prominent component of the novel's subject matter, with emphasis on the distorting effects of socially-defined sex roles. Nowhere is this deformation more visible than in the conversations and arguments between Blanca and her husband, Raúl. Their discourse reveals two especially troubling features: the grotesque character of sex-role stereotyping and the amount of material that cannot be discussed between husband and wife.

The first substantial interchange between the couple takes the form of an aborted quarrel. This dispute is narrated by Blanca, who, despite her involvement, comments upon the episode with ironic distance. Here the reader first encounters Raúl's preferred strategy for dominating his wife. Utilizing a convenient stereotype, Raúl casts himself in the role of long-suffering husband of an irrational wife. His characteristic ploy is to reproach his wife for poor judgment only after the results of her decisions are irremediable. In this way, he can maintain his status as the aggrieved party even should she agree with his statements.

Blanca at first handles his complaints badly. She takes his "¿Por qué lo hiciste? (Why did you do it?; p. 47)" at face value, as a literal invitation to rational discourse. Her attempts to provide reasonable explanations are clearly inadequate to the demands of the situation. Moreover, she is handicapped in her oral reasoning by the need to disguise her extramarital affair, the true reason behind much of her behavior.

The deteriorating encounter leads Blanca to realize that her husband is not asking her to reason with him, but merely to display submission. Consequently, she alters her tactics to exercise her "feminine wiles." She switches from her adult voice to a feigned "sonido de una vocecita adolescente (sound of a little adolescent voice; p. 48)." Now her address to her husband is in a language resembling baby talk. This ostentatious femininity succeeds in placating her husband's irritation; abandoning the quarrel, he falls into a satisfied sleep.

Blanca's "wiles" are ineffective in forestalling her husband's next effort to air his grievances. In this episode, too, the wife doubles as flustered participant and detached, sardonic narrator-commentator. The scene is outstanding for both partners' use of hyperbolic, theatrical devices to impress and disarm one another. The first of these is the husband's peculiar mode of opening the lines of communication. Having gone to his office, he telephones his wife at home to initiate a domestic discussion. Blanca immediately perceives the purpose of this novelty: "como si a fuerza de estar juntos nuestra capacidad de comunicación se hubiera disminuido hasta desaparecer (it's as if so much being together had made our ability to communicate completely wither away; p. 70)." The husband's stagy opening fails to add fresh significance to his reproaches, for his wife soon notes that he has no new message to convey.

During the exchange, husband and wife seek to gain advantage from an exaggeration of their sex-role traits. Playing the "poor helpless female," Blanca evades responsibility for her actions. She shifts the blame to the effects of hot weather on her organism, some vague ailment and an innate debility of will and character. Her husband, on the other hand, adopts a pose of chivalry. He repeatedly announces his willingness to rescue Blanca from her inner torment

His gallantry, far from winning his wife's sympathy, elicits her unuttered derision. Her inward commentary on the encounter becomes a parodic paraphrase of his pseudo-courtly discourse: "Hará cualquier sacrificio, se allanará a lo que le proponga, sea lo que fuese, él está dispuesto—y vaya si lo está—a ser mi Caballero y mi Brazo Armado (No sacrifice is too great for him, my wish is his command, he's at my beck and call, he's willing—and how—to be my Knight in Shining Armor; p. 72)." Blanca is insightful enough to make a fine, sardonic analysis of the strategies at work in the discussion. However, she has no ability to break out of these stereotypic patterns. Once more, she can only terminate the transaction by exhibiting her willingness to conform to Raúl's expectations concerning womanly behavior. On this occasion, she expresses a conventional wifely wish: that her husband should "take her out."

Blanca's secret commentary upon this scene is interesting partly because it reveals how much relevant material is routinely suppressed when the two speak to one another. Blanca notes that she has never spoken to Raúl about her notions concerning love—notions which underlie many of her actions. Their silence on this topic causes her feelings of isolation: "el amor del que uno no habla acaba por esfumarse como el placer del onanista, sin reflejarse en otro, sin perdurar ni dejar recuerdo (If you don't talk about love, it vanishes like masturbatory pleasure, unreflected in another, it doesn't stay or leave a memory; p. 72)."

The wife evaluates the total interchange as a victory for the husband, because he has compelled her to speak as he would have her speak. The reader, though, sees a more disturbing "victory" in Raúl's influence over his wife's unuttered statements. She has internalized his negative portrait of her, as evidenced by her unquestioning assent to his various accusations. Indeed, she states that Raúl has never spoken to her irrationally. Such a judgment is incompatible with the evidence of their transcribed dialogues, in which both spouses become unreasonable. Nonetheless, Blanca concludes from her husband's scolding that "soy una basura (I'm no good; p. 72)," a thoroughgoing submission to the man's authority. Again, she has betrayed her profound implication in the mechanisms of reciprocal denigration, despite her ostentatiously mocking detachment.

The progression in the two previously noted exchanges is the woman's gradual loss of control over the discourse situation and over her own behavior with it. This deterioration reaches an extreme in the third episode in this series: the couple's evening together. Their encounter is basically a testing situation in which the wife must prove that she can meet the husband's announced standard. He has announced beforehand what he expects from her: that she forego complaining and demonstrate "buena voluntad (good will; p. 72)." Blanca comes to the meeting grimly determined to sustain a pleasant-sounding conversation, but fails to do so.

Again the wife doubles as unhappy participant and distanced, or pseudo-distanced, commentator. She wittily describes the first impediment to agreeable discourse. When complaints and quarreling are excluded, the couple has no topic around which to structure their conversation. Blanca's analysis of this impasse, though clever-sounding, is nonetheless quite favorable to herself and notably reliant on sex-role stereotypes. Her husband likes to speak of the more grossly material aspects of his medical practice. She cares more for the "finer things in life," artistic and leisure activities which her husband is incapable of discussing.

The conversation goes seriously amiss when Blanca, catching sight of herself in a restaurant mirror, suffers a fresh attack of anxiety over the marks of aging. Although the signs of her disturbance are patent, Blanca refuses to tell her husband what is troubling her. At this point, the wife realizes that her evasive speech is damaging to the couple's relations. Yet, she denigrates her husband's capacity to be her confidant. In her judgment, he is too well socialized into patterns of gallantry to converse honestly about aging: "si digo lo que siento objetará que nunca me ha visto más hermosa y tendré que tragar esa mentira . . . (if I tell him how I feel he'll just say he's never seen me more beautiful and then I'll have to swallow that lie . . . ; p. 77)."

The blockage of communication pushes both spouses into yet more rigidly ritualized speech. All of Blanca's remarks take the form of complaints about the weather, the restaurant, the food and so forth. Raúl's responses, comically unsuited to Blanca's querulous remarks, are vigorous displays of conversational agreeability.

The absurd exchange of disparate comments is interrupted by Blanca's unvoiced formulations of her experience. Here the reader sees the true sources of her unease—an unease that remains opaque to the husband. For example, Blanca is inwardly lucid concerning her resentment of her husband's profession. She expertly contrasts his satisfyingly productive existence with her own household stagnation. Unfortunately, when she begins to externalize this insight, it emerges as yet another formulaic complaint: "Trabajas demasiado (You work too hard; p. 78)." The husband further deflects the conversation from the real issue by treating the accusation as if it were an inoffensive item of "small talk." His incongruous reply is "Posiblemente atienda desde mañana al doctor Lafuente (Maybe I'll have Dr. Lafuente as a patient starting tomorrow; p. 78)."

During the final portion of this scene, Blanca moves from querulous speech to silence. She finally provokes Raúl into abandoning his forbearing attitude and demanding an explanation for her conduct. The wife's outward response is hostile silence, but inwardly she formulates an adequate response. Her unspoken explanation is that the situation was too forced and strained to allow truly pleasurable discourse, no matter how earnestly that conversational goal was sought. Here is the type of impasse that leads Silvina Bullrich to describe the Lynch heroine as a "ratón que quisiera salir de una trampa y no ve la salida (mouse trying to get out of a trap and not finding a way out)."[16]

The wife's control of the narration leaves several issues uncertain. In particular, the reader finds it difficult to assess Raúl's competence as recipient of Blanca's confidences. His wife claims that she cannot speak to him freely because he is too insensitive, too limited and too "bourgeois." Since she suppresses all the material he supposedly cannot grasp, one cannot know how well he would have reacted. Indeed, Raúl gives signs of being a willing confidant. He repeatedly invites his wife to disclose the source of her anguish and even moves the conversation into her terrain by attempting to discuss Alberto Moravia's fiction. Each of these overtures elicits a rebuff or silence.

Raúl's receptive capacity continues to be a puzzling matter throughout the work. One discovers that his original role in his wife's life was that of skilled confidant. Raúl helped Blanca recover from an hysterical paralysis by providing a "sympathetic ear." In his professional life, he is known for his tactful and reassuring manner with patients. From this mass of information, only a tautological conclusion emerges. The man cannot do a good job of listening to his wife so long as she refuses to speak to him in any meaningful fashion.

Another troubling point is the degree to which other persons, especially Raúl, are able to control Blanca's speech and actions. In Blanca's view, Raúl can compel her to say things she does not mean. Conversely, he can manipulate the situation, making it "imposible contestar (impossible to answer; p. 80)." Especially telling is her metaphor for him: a verbal predator gifted with "sutiles artimañas (subtle ruses)," determined "de no soltar la presa que te da tanto poder (not to let go of the prey that gives you such power; p. 72)." Raúl, on the other hand, objects that his wife's speech and actions cannot be controlled, either by him or by socialized constraints she should have internalized.

What the reader sees is a consistent pattern of Blanca's following the lead of some other person. The way in which this influence is subsequently discussed creates massive confusion around the issue of domination. This confusion comes to the fore in another quarreling episode, again narrated by Blanca.

On this occasion, Raúl is upset over his wife's imminent opening of a one-woman art show. It is difficult to know whether the man is seeking to change his wife's plans in this respect. When the reader comes in upon the dispute, Blanca claims that Raúl has been "asegurando que no estaba decidido a emprender otra de mis locas aventuras (making it clear he wasn't prepared to go along with another of my mad ventures; p. 15)." Raúl's transcribed remarks, though, are considerably less bullying. Rather than make his wife alter her course of action, his goal is to express general dissatisfaction with her conduct and attitudes. Blanca proceeds as if Raúl were, in fact, ordering her about and shouts "Voy a intentarlo aunque vos te opongás (I'm going to try it even if you stand in my way; p. 147)." No sooner has she spoken these melodramatic words than she must inwardly admit their utter incongruity. Raúl is too sophisticated and "modern" to exercise such overt domination.

Raúl now shifts around the terms of the discussion. So far, Blanca has been positing her artistic enterprise as a sign of autonomous self-expression; Raúl's discomfiture is an index to his need to control her. Raúl insinuates that Berta's "liberated" undertaking is symptomatic of another subjugation, from which he would save her: "¿Es Berta la que te ha calentado la cabeza, esta vez? (Is Berta the one who's been putting you up to things, this time? p. 147)."

Raúl's remark is not only successful in displacing the topic of dispute but also is fairly descriptive of Blanca's characteristic behavior. His suggestion that she must continually be "put up to things" sends her into a state of inner turmoil. Her unspoken remarks are no longer mocking and pseudo-insightful, but wild. Against all evidence, she insists that "no necesitaba el impulso de otros para las magras cosas de mi vida. El impulso siempre había estado en mí (I didn't need other people to get me to do what little I did in life. I had always been self-motivating; p. 147)." Her proof of this assertion is unimpressive: she persuaded her husband to marry her after he had impregnated her and she procured a rich patient for his practice.

Raúl, too, abandons his habitual care to sound reasonable. He states, alternately, that he likes his wife's artistic efforts, that her recent activities have been an aggression toward him and that he trusts her. The couple's utterances lack a clear interrelation with one another, producing a disjointed, disorienting discourse. The only unifying element is that everything said refers back to the question of Blanca's "controllability," an issue so key to the couple's conflict as to cause near-panic. The closure of the dispute further clouds this issue. Raúl unexpectedly agrees to attend Blanca's showing in the role of supportive husband. For Blanca, this apparent accommodation of her wishes is actually a paradoxical form of domination: "accediendo y a la vez sacando su ventaja (giving in and at the same time coming out ahead; p. 148)."

This chaotic exchange brings home a point made by Robin Lakoff. Lakoff sees women as lacking in the types of verbal strategies that would allow them to exercise control over situations. In consequence, women are frequently conflicted over their malleability and inability to produce change. Women's attempts to speak assertively may elicit a poor response, either because women are inept in their presentation, or because they violate their listener's expectations. While Blanca illustrates the problem of incompetence, Berta is representative of the assertive, and therefore unacceptable woman. Raúl views her with suspicion and sees in his wife's friendship with her a threat to the order of the household. Later Blanca finds that the forceful Berta is under suspicion of homosexuality and receives warnings to beware of her excessive influence. As Lakoff observes, a woman must often choose between dissatisfied compliance and socially unacceptable self-assertion.[17] Blanca's disputes with Raúl show her in an unpredictable and wholly unsatisfactory fluctuation between these two alternatives.

V

Conventional expectations are evident when Blanca speaks with her family and her bourgeois friends. Because of her insistence that these constraints are alien to her, the reader becomes curious to see how Blanca performs in an unconventional discourse situation. Such an opportunity arises when Blanca enters a liaison with Rocky, whose very name signals his "foreignized" pseudo-sophistication. Many factors place this relation outside predetermined patterns. There are the couple's disparate ages, her respectability versus his marginality, the man's bisexuality and the extreme difficulty of placing him in any social context. Rocky not only lacks family and career identification but avoids association with any neighborhood of Buenos Aires by inhabiting an unused railway station. Blanca's art-world acquaintances cannot accept Rocky as an artistic Bohemian; they distrust his aberrance, unpredictability, and disaffiliation. Blanca's involvement with him strikes all concerned as highly irregular and incongruous.

Yet, when one begins to look at this anomalous bond, what emerges are strong uniformities of experience with bourgeois society. Rocky, like Raúl, works to reform Blanca's habits of discourse. Each man would accommodate the woman to a preexisting model. Raúl wants his wife to be charmingly loquacious and demonstrative, "sociable." Rocky would teach her the counter-cultural virtue of "cool." Blanca, apparently unaware of this parallelism, describes Rocky's reformism with more delight than irritation:

> . . . se empeñó en enseñarme a hablar.
> —No hagas teatro.
> O más secamente:
> —No dramatices.
> Le exasperaba mi apego a tantas palabras como yo usaba.
> —Son cursis—decía burlándose de mi grandilocuencia.
> Como tantas otras cosas, ese aprendizaje quedó en la cuenta de mi gratitud. Conforme: no había que hablar de amor, no había que usar tantas palabras, no declamar, no gemir, no exagerar.

> . . . he was determined to teach me how to talk.
> "Don't make everything into a big deal."
> Or more curtly:
> "Don't dramatize everything."
> It exasperated him that I need to use so many words to get things said.
> "That's so hokey-sounding," he said, making fun of my grandiloquence.
> Along with so many other things, that training became part of my debt of gratitude. So, all right: no talking about love, no using so many words, no declamations, no moaning, no exaggeration (p. 202).

Lying has a special affective importance for Blanca. The excitation produced by false statements is present in many of her relations with others, but the liaison with Rocky brings it to the fore. Rocky lies to her in two major areas. On the one hand, he creates a glamorous and travel-filled past for himself; he gives himself a social position far above any status he may possess. In another vein, he denies his obvious sexual involvement with partners ranging from young women to aging male protectors. These falsifications are easy to discover by simply checking Rocky's assertions against more reliable sources.

When Blanca discovers Rocky's untruthfulness, she feels a powerful attraction. The less expertise the liar displays, the more potent his appeal. The woman imagines her lover as a child who cannot separate private imaginings from "objective" reality. She insists that his thorough falseness is, paradoxically the sign of an underlying innocence: "Ese era mi Rocky, mi tierno y vergonzante Rocky, ingenuamente corrumpido, cándidamente infame . . . (That was my Rocky, my sweet and shameful Rocky, naively corrupt, innocently vile . . .; p. 208)." For her, Rocky is less the perpetrator of deception than its helpless victim: "sin reparar que era trampeado casi siempre (unaware that he almost always ended up getting fooled; p. 206)."

From Blanca's commentary, one might gather that Rocky's lying is merely some private ceremony from which both lovers can derive stimulation. She can incorporate the untruths into her expectations about their relations and thus achieve a measure of detachment. However, she also voices some concern lest her involvement in Rocky's lying become so intense as to jeopardize her inner stability (p. 203). This apprehension, largely suppressed in Blanca, becomes overt in the remarks of the third-person narrator. The duplicitous lover receives much less favorable treatment from this narrator, who has the obvious advantage of not being in love with the young man. In the third-person relation, Rocky appears as a "cautivante mistificador (captivating razzle-dazzle artist)" whose lying is part of a coherent strategy to take emotional possession of Blanca. The reader is alerted to the fact that Blanca's discussion of lying may itself be extremely untrustworthy discourse, that the woman is lying to herself about her ability to deal with mendacity.

Despite her illusions of detachment, Blanca makes one point that the reader recognizes as accurate. She sees her excited response to Rocky's fabrications as an extension of a pattern found in her more conventional interactions. The woman is able to trace her attitude back to her family of origin, where lying had value as a "resorte milagroso que hace menos miserable el paso por la vida (miracle device that makes getting through life less wretched; p. 203)."

This observation shows more insight than Blanca's earlier claim to be an honest person surrounded by false ones. Blanca does not go far enough, however, in her comments. She really values lying not only as a cosmetic procedure, but as a thrilling stimulus to liar and listener. In her mind, this pleasure is an important dimension of the sexual relation of the couple. Her compulsive misrepresentations to her husband provide her with, by her own admission, "una catarsis de mentiras (a catharsis of lying; p. 148)." Her earlier marriage reveals a like procedure. As the third-person narrator remarks of the first husband, "Como la amaba creía en ella (Because he loved her he believed in her; p. 191)" despite her vague self-accounts. Blanca applies these notions in assessing her friends. In Alicia, she finds only one fascinating trait. Alicia's contented-wife persona is clearly a work of artifice. Berta's unvarnished truth-telling, on the other hand, inhibits her allure. In addition, Blanca feels the powerful excitement of the highly mannered homosexual. In short, feigning is what makes a man or woman interesting.

When one views the total design of Blanca's affair with Rocky, what emerges is a laying-bare of her vulnerability and inability to "hold her own." As in her interactions with Raúl, there is a progressive loss of control on the woman's part. This loss becomes more devastating because Blanca expects a liberation from the inequities of socialized discourse, only to find them reiterated within a context of social marginality. Her experience with Rocky is the final discrediting of her notions and habits of discourse, all of which work to her disadvantage in her relationships with men.

The first stages of the attachment are narrated by both Blanca and the third-person narrator. The former expresses confidence in her ability to govern the new situation and claims to have "la cabeza fría (my wits about me; p. 185)." The other narrator tells quite a different story. Here, Blanca figures as the object of Rocky's art of verbal seduction. Despite his studied nonconformism, the young man's wooing style is the conventional one of "sweet nothings," pseudo-intimate flattery in an agreeably nonsensical vein. Tellingly, his claim to have "discovered" Blanca's eyes (p. 173) is virtually identical to Blanca's father's amorous phrase-making: "Pasé una tarde como tantas, y allí estaban sus ojos (I was going about my usual business one afternoon, and there were her eyes; p. 21)." Though it should be familiar, this rhetoric has a devastating effect on its object. Blanca is so overwhelmed she can scarcely speak.

The third-person narrator includes material unfavorable to Rocky. As the young man regales Blanca with his "sweet talk," he brings along a witness to the courtship. This eavesdropper is an older man whom Rocky knows to be enamored of him. The narrator, generally omniscient only for Blanca, reveals the jealous man's inner travail. His profound unhappiness stands as documentation of Rocky's penchant for manipulating the emotions of others unethically.

The divergence between Blanca's view and that of the other narrator grows wider. The woman continues to receive information tending to discredit Rocky. On each occasion, she rewords and restates the evidence, transmuting it into a confirmation of her lover's appeal and worth. She insists that this transformation is an operation of the logical mind: "Cuando conseguía pensarlo fríamente, más lo veía como a un pobre niño desvalido ingeniándose para aprovechar lo que se le ofrecía (When I managed to think things through calmly, I could see him as a poor little waif doing what he could to get hold of what the world offered; p. 207)." The woman's earlier ironic manners are notably diminished in these passages. Her inadvertent self-betrayals, formerly occasional lapses, now are in the foreground. The reader no longer finds wit and caustic merriment in her words, but rather the symptoms of her disordered state.

The cause of Blanca's deterioration grows clearer in the commentary of the third-person narrator. One sees Rocky gaining control over his lover through his incessant talking. The narrator details Rocky's procedures for manufacturing an illusion of childlike artlessness. The young man's discourse is "plagado de errores, de giros que se contradecían (full of mistakes, of places where he contradicted himself)" but, at the same time, "preciso (precise)." The pseudo-blunders impart to the entire discourse a rough, naturalistic quality that, para-doxically, makes the speaker more to be trusted. The result is the construction of "una fábula con la que pretendía confesarse a la mujer, reclamando su auxilio y asistencia (a fable good for seeming to open himself up to the woman, demanding her help and support; p. 219)."

Her lover's feigned lack of sophistication has a devastating effect on Blanca, who is described as a woman in a trance. The enrapturing is not shared by the narrator, who speaks of Rocky's "aire permanente de titiritero (perpetual puppet-master quality; p. 219)" and "encantamiento (bewitchment; p. 220)" of the heroine. The very detail with which this narrator describes Rocky's pseudo-infantile tactics constitutes an implicit denunciation of the man's cunning.

Subsequent segments chronicle Blanca's degradation in the unequal relation. Utilizing the powers the narrator has described, Rocky obtains money from Blanca, torments her by eliciting her jealousy, strikes her and perversely disrupts her bonds with other persons. Eventually, even the bewitched Blanca must confront the issue of domination. Seeing her daughter's relations with a brutal social climber, Blanca recognizes the analogy with her own case.

VI

The liaison with Rocky raises many complex questions. For this study, the most interesting one is Blanca's failure to speak out against her subjugation. Some illumination comes from the segments intercalated between episodes in the affair. These segments cohere in a design of structural parataxis by interweaving various threads in the heroine's life. The recurring features in these threads show that Blanca's passive surrender is no unique occurrence. She cannot rightly attribute it to Rocky's charisma, her own distress at turning forty, uncontrollable love or any other current circumstance.

Indicative of the problem is Blanca's history of pseudo-political involvements. In her original home, "political" discussion is, essentially, the pronouncements of the father. The rise of Perón angers him. However, his objections are hardly more than expressions of revulsion toward persons of lower social class. The visibility of such persons under the new régime exacerbates his preexisting hatred. Socio-political issues are avoided in favor of crude characterizations of lower-class dress and hygiene. The role of the females in the household is to avoid further angering the male; assent or silence are their only options.

Blanca's first political involvement outside her family comes as part of her first sexual attachment. An ardent Peronist, her first husband is a member of a specialized subgroup (La Alianza) requiring participation in clandestine and potentially violent endeavors. In addition, he occupies a visible place in the régime. Thus, Blanca experiences a wide spectrum of Peronist-related undertakings, ranging from underground militance to a gala performance at the celebrated Buenos Aires opera house, presided over by Eva Perón.

Given her extensive contact with political phenomena, one must be surprised by Blanca's own statements. What stands out is an avoidance of voicing political opinions of her own. The woman must resort to a variety of maneuvers to evade the overt expression of affiliation or belief. One of her favored strategies is to claim, if pressed, to be a "nationalist." While her listener can generally be counted on to take this as the equivalent of "Peronist," Blanca's own meaning for the term is considerably vaguer. The success of this ploy depends on Blanca's general presentation of self. In a noisy meeting, she makes this substitution "encendiéndome de bríos (sparkling with enthusiasm; p. 13)." In an audience with Eva Perón, Blanca switches around the terms, "fingiendo muy bien mi confusión (doing a very good job of pretending to get mixed up; p. 216)." Her assumption is that, since she is pretty, unassertive, and accompanied by her husband, no one will inquire too closely into the character of her political beliefs.

Blanca has no interest in an accurate expression of her beliefs. Her goal is a display that will satisfy the expectations of others, and thus of her husband. For this reason, she can shout slogans in unison even when she could not enunciate the same notions as an individual (p. 134).

Her evasive stance becomes more patent when she enters a relationship with a youthful anti-Peronist. In a familiar pattern, the man seeks to influence Blanca by "liberating" her from the influence of others: "Te han arrastrado a todo eso (They've dragged you into all this; p. 134)." The woman manages to sustain her relations with both politically involved men. She is able to do so because she makes political matters into a convenient topic for an implicitly amorous exchange. As in her original home, the goal of a woman's political remarks is to control her relations with her man.

Blanca's evasive pseudo-Peronism reaches an absurd crisis only many years after these events. After her husband's death in action, Blanca becomes politically inert. The fall of the Peronist régime leaves her remarkably indifferent. When it becomes possible for her old colleagues to reassemble, Blanca receives an invitation to a party congress. Her conversation with her former associates shows her typical attitude: that she need only announce herself as the widow of a fallen party member. On this occasion Blanca's well-practiced equivocations prove inadequate. She is asked to define her own position vis-à-vis the party and its current reorganization. This demand is entirely outside the range of Blanca's skills. She must leave the conference without ever voicing an individual commitment to any point of view. The highlight of this episode is a conversation between Blanca and a male party official assigned to clarify her situation. Their interchange has a ridiculous quality at first because of Blanca's reluctance to believe that the man is talking to her about politics *qua* politics.

Excessive docility also mars Blanca's efforts in other areas. In her sporadic artistic career, she seeks the approval of her art-world connections. The production of work becomes ancillary to "sounding serious" about her projects. The goal is no longer expression, but being taken seriously, winning admission to artistic discussion. Blanca's distraction follows a characteristic feminine pattern described by Adrienne Rich. Rich sees women as vulnerable to a loss of control over their own creative labors. Self-governance is impossible when women displace their focus from productivity to the meeting of other persons' expectations. In Rich's judgment, men are less subject to this malaise because they are more often able to set or enforce standards of speech and behavior.[18] The same analysis is equally applicable to Blanca's production of children and various attempts to effect intellectual or social good. The question of how her activities are perceived and judged becomes much more important than the activities and their results. To cite an extreme case, all one learns of Blanca's classical studies is the irritation they produced in her husband. Blanca shows insight into this entire mechanism when she speaks of her "ansiosa necesidad de halago y de confirmación (anxious need for flattery and confirmation of my worth; p. 250)."

VII

After observing the ways in which Blanca continues to meet with frustration, one still has an important question to ask. Where does the novel place the blame for this blockage? It is indicative of the work's complexity that no one answer to this question emerges. Rather, there are two principal areas of denunciation.

In many ways, Blanca has condemned herself to a life full of trivial and inefficacious discourse. The self-frustration appears, for example, when the

92

woman rebuffs well-meant invitations to dialogue. Raúl and Berta both try to discuss important issues with Blanca, but find her unamenable to their overtures. To avoid thinking about certain topics, Blanca makes an exhibition of "feminine" behavior. Thus, when Berta issues pragmatic warnings about Rocky, Blanca's response is an inappropriately "high-minded" disquisition concerning love. Also in this category are Blanca's fits of complaining, declarations of helpless weakness, self-pitying ruminations and silent sulkings.

In other instances, specific male characters work to banalize the heroine's attempts at self-expression. A spectacular example is provided by Blanca's encounters with a licentious priest. Breaking with her usual patterns, the newly-wed Blanca tries to reform the priest's political beliefs. She finally overcomes her intimidation to produce a more or less coherent statement, but the response is hardly encouraging:

> Priesso se rió a carcajadas.
> —Divina Blanquita, exclamó sin mucha reticencia. Es un placer tan grande verte mover los labios que no interesa demasiado lo que dices.

> Priesso burst into peals of laughter.
> "Blanca, you beautiful doll," he exclaimed with undisguised feeling. "It's such a pleasure to watch you move your lips it hardly matters what you're saying" (p. 158).

On a more sophisticated level, Blanca is relegated to a trivial status by an art expert. In a café conversation on art, this man appears to be addressing Blanca about her artistic production. In fact, he is giving signals to the other discussants concerning how they should consider Blanca:

> —Después de todo esto, tu deber consistirá en reintegrarte a la creación de tus objetos.
> Que fuera claro su discurso: la señora Ordóñez no descubriría nada nuevo en materia de arte, pero era una mujer encantadora por la que se sentía inclinado.

> "After all this, what you'll really need to do is get back into creating your objects."
> Let there be no doubt what he was saying: Mrs. Ordóñez wouldn't discover anything new as far as art went, but she was an enchanting woman and he was quite taken with her (p. 173).[19]

The above-described behavior points to the individual as the source of the sex-role problem: the woman who avoids adult responsibility and the man who refuses to consider her as fully human in status. The major burden of guilt, though, falls neither upon men nor upon women but upon the structuring of the entire social arrangement. The novel illustrates Robin Lakoff's premise that "women prejudice the case against themselves by their use of language," that "women's speech is designed to prevent the expression of strong statements."[20] Blanca's ineffective efforts at self-expression reveal, to use Lakoff's description, many a "device you'd use if you felt it unseemly to show you had strong emotions, or to make strong assertions, but felt you had to say something along those lines anyway."[21] When the woman does manage to speak energetically, her force is deflected into uselessly melodramatic statements, further undermining her right to be listened to seriously.

As Lakoff makes clear, it is idle to blame women for being poor speakers or men for being poor listeners. Women's devious stratagems really do "give the impression that the speaker lacks authority or doesn't know what he's talking about," and the listener quite rationally draws just such a conclusion. But the blame cannot lie with the speaker, either, because "the use of these hedges arises out of a fear of seeming too masculine by being assertive and saying things directly."[22] These features are common to men and women in Western culture and not at all dependent upon Blanca's indolence, Raúl's stodginess or other idiosyncratic characteristics.

Blanca Ordóñez is, beyond any doubt, a woman deeply in conflict with herself. Her paradoxical behavior is symptomatic of the "double-bind" in which social conventions place women speakers. To quote Lakoff again:

> If she doesn't learn to speak women's language, in traditional society she's dead: she is ostracized as unfeminine by both men and women. So that is not a possible option, unless a young girl is exceedingly brave—in fact, reckless. But what if she opts to do as she ought—learn to talk like a lady? She has some rewards: she is accepted as a suitable female. But she also finds that she is treated—purely because of the way she speaks and, therefore, supposedly thinks—as someone not to be taken seriously, of dim intelligence, frivolous, and incapable of understanding anything important. It is true that some women adapt to this role quite nicely, and indeed it has apparent advantages: if you're not taken seriously, if you can't understand anything, you then have no responsibility for important ideas, you don't have to trouble your pretty little head about deep problems. Maybe this is nice for a while, but surely it's hard to be a child forever. If a woman learns and uses women's language, she is necessarily considered less than a real, full person—she's a bit of fluff.
>
> Now that means . . . that a woman is damned if she does and damned if she doesn't.[23]

Notes

1. Marta Lynch, "Testimonio: con mi obra," *Hispamérica*, 3, 7 (1974), 61-64. See also her interview, *Hispamérica*, 4, 10 (1975), 34-36: Martha Paley de Francescato, interviewer.
2. Eduardo Gudiño Kieffer, interviewed by Juan Armando Epple, *Hispamérica*, 6, 18 (1977), 51.
3. David Viñas, *Literatura argentina y realidad política: de Sarmiento a Cortázar*, rev. ed. (Buenos Aires: Siglo Veinte, 1971), p.201.
4. On the question of foreign cultural models, it is interesting to see Lynch's set of observations about her travels, *Apuntes para un libro de viajes* (Buenos Aires: Editorial Cástor y Pollux, 1977).
5. Ernesto Goldar, *El peronismo en la literatura argentina* (Buenos Aires: Editorial Freeland, 1971), pp. 103-104. David W. Foster notes the political theme in Lynch's work "never becomes very clear," but finds this lack of explicitness literarily justifiable; see his "Marta Lynch: The Individual and the Argentine Political Process," *Latin American Digest*, 13, 3 (1978), 8-9.
6. See, for example, Amy Kaminsky, "The Real Circle of Iron: Mothers and Children, Children and Mothers in Four Argentine Novels," *Latin American Literary Review*, 4, 9 (1976), 77-86.
7. These stories have received feminist analysis. See Naomi Lindstrom, "Woman's Voice in the Short Stories of Marta Lynch," in Rose S. Minc, ed., *The Contemporary Latin American Short Story* (Montclair, NJ: Senda Nueva de Ediciones, 1978), 101-111, and "The Literary Feminism of Marta Lynch," *Critique: Studies in Modern Fiction*, 20, 2 (1978), 49-58; Gwendolyn Díaz, "Presentación," in *Páginas de Marta Lynch seleccionadas por la autora* (Buenos Aires: Celtia 1983), pp. i-xxii. H. Ernest Lewald points out the prominence of the sex-role question in Lynch's short-story production and examines the title story from her 1970 *Cuentos de colores*. See his "Aspects of the Modern Argentine Woman," *Chasqui*, 5, 3 (1976), 24-25. Lewald had a longstanding interest in the special role of the Argentine woman writer as a social critic. See, for example, his anthologies *Escritores platenses: ficciones del siglo XX* (New York: Houghton Mifflin, 1971), especially pp. 20-21; *Diez cuentistas argentinas* (Buenos Aires: Ediciones Riomar, 1968), pp. 5-6, 8, 88.
8. Kaminsky, in her above-cited article, 78-79, 84-85, looks at the portrayal of women in *El cruce del río*. Guidiño Kieffer's commentary, also cited above, situates *La señora Ordóñez* and *Un árbol lleno de manzanas* as the two impressive Lynch portraits of middle-class Argentine women.

9   Lewald, 19-20, 23-24. The critic also mentions the scandalized reaction of readers unaccustomed to the verisimilitude of the bedroom scenes in the novel, another factor in its impact.

10 Lynch, interview with Paley de Francescato, 38.

11 See Lewald, 23. It is significant that the 1967 edition of the novel was published by Editorial Jorge Alvarez, a publishing house known for its willingness to print innovative works whose sexual thematics might occasion legal difficulties. The novel was subsequently (1968) brought out by Sudamericana, a more mainstream publisher.

12 The concept of the "unreliable narrator" is developed by Wayne C. Booth in his 1961 *The Rhetoric of Fiction* (Chicago: University of Chicago Press).

13 Marta Lynch, *La señora Ordóñez* (Buenos Aires: Jorge Alvarez, 1967), p. 14. Subsequent page numbers in the text refer to this edition.

14 Mary Louise Pratt, *Toward a Speech Act Theory of Literary Discourse* (Bloomington: Indiana University Press, 1977).

15 Roland Barthes, *Système de la mode* (Paris: Seuil, 1966).

16 Silvina Bullrich, *La mujer argentina en la literatura* (Buenos Aires: Centro Nacional de Documentación e Información Educativa, 1972), p. 17. Bullrich is here generalizing about the composite figure of Argentine women that emerges from Lynch's writings.

17 Robin Lakoff, *Language and Woman's Place* (New York: Harper and Row, 1975).

18 Adrienne Rich, *Of Woman Born* (New York: Norton, 1976). Rich's specific area of examination is the production of children. At the same time, she makes it clear that her analysis of women's alienation from their creative enterprises is a generalized phenomenon under the prevailing social order. A poet, Rich includes interesting commentary on the relations between artistic production and women's role.

19 These passages suggest that part of the heroine's difficulty in receiving serious treatment is attributable to her attractive physical appearance—a notion common in feminist thought. Lakoff, p. 40, expreses the belief that pretty women are more often trivialized in a male-dominated society. The same premise is key to Alix Kates Shulman's novel, *Memoirs of an Ex-Prom Queen* (New York: Knopf, 1972).

20 Lakoff, p. 19.

21 Lakoff, p. 55.

22 Lakoff, p. 54.

23 Lakoff, p. 61.

Silvina Bullrich

Silvina Bullrich:
Making Feminism Accessible

I

Two constants stand out in the literary career of Silvina Bullrich. One is her success in reaching a very wide and variegated audience. H. Ernest Lewald, Bullrich's enthusiastic supporter in the U. S., considers her the "most successful" of Argentina's contemporary novelists for her extensive readership and ability to claim public attention.[1] Several of her novels have enjoyed exceptional sales, notably the 1968 *Mañana digo basta* (*Tomorrow I'll Tell Them I've Had It*), the novel to be discussed here. [2] Bullrich's effort to affect numbers of people goes beyond her literary output to include journalistic and essay writings as well as personal appearances. Her outlets vary widely in prestige, ranging from women's magazines like *Para Ti* to quite respectable publishing houses; she has also collaborated with Jorge Luis Borges.[3] Because of her amorous-feminist thematics, women's magazines take a keen interest in the writer's work and person. Because her social criticism has an elitist basis, she does not alienate "establishment" readers; witness her favorable notices in the "oligarchic" *La Nación* and *La Prensa* literary supplements.[4] There has also been a fair amount of academic criticism on her work, principally by Lewald but also by other commentators.[5] This last fact makes her inclusion here especially apropos.

Given Bullrich's broad-spectrum, wide-appeal approach, it is not surprising that her relation to the literary enterprise as such has been in question at times. The issues raised by disputants include the ready visibility of Bullrich's thematic statements and a concomitant lessening of novelistic complexity and ambiguity. For example, one disgruntled critic writes of "black-and-white judgments on morality," "stereotypes" and "pasteboard ethics."[6] The scandalous anecdotes with which Bullrich illustrates her critique of Argentine society have led other commentators to call her work gossipy and frivolous.[7] One may easily surmise that the characteristics mentioned above have much to do with Bullrich's widespread audience. In sum, there is agreement concerning the "accessibility" of her writings. What is occasionally at issue is whether this feature constitutes a praiseworthy forthrightness or a banalization.

The second most notable aspect of Bullrich's work is its constituent of denunciation. The principal target of her novelistic aggression is the Argentine upper class, particularly as it loses its specifically aristocratic qualities and becomes essentially bourgeois. Much of her critique is individualistic and elitist in character. Bobs M. Tusa identifies this component of her work with the philosophical stance of personalism. For Tusa, Bullrich belongs with such essayists as Ezequiel Martínez Estrada because of her willingness to see social problems as manifestations of an underlying spiritual malaise.[8] At the same time, there is an unmistakable vein of purely social commentary in Bullrich's writing, though it is more prominent in some works than others. Francisco Herrera finds this the most valuable portion of her novelistic effort.[9] The desire for concrete structural change becomes apparent in Bullrich's treatment of poverty in *La redoma del primer ángel* (*The First Angel Goes Under*, 1943). Class divisions are the topic of protest in the 1973 *Mal don* (*The Loser*), a work Lewald sees as too influenced by a fashion for "radical chic" writing.[10] The social patterning of sex role is often a topic, most impressively in *Mañana digo basta*.

What is most characteristic of Bullrich's perspective is a simultaneous preoccupation with spiritual style and socio-economic equity. This fusion finds a clear illustration in her observation on the advent of social welfare legislation in Argentina: "En cuanto al pueblo, su vida entonces [1943] era difícil e injusta; no era protegido por leyes sociales, pero había en sus componentes tal confianza en el porvenir, que soportaban con más entereza la casi miseria de entonces que lo que soportan en la actualidad las comodidades bastante evidentes traídas por las nuevas conquistas sociales (As for the lower classes, their life then [1943] was hard and unjust, they were unprotected by social legislation, but among them there was so much confidence in the future, that they bore up with greater integrity under almost wretched conditions than they now bear up under the obvious comforts brought by the new social advances)."[11]

Of all the areas in which Bullrich applies her eclectic analysis, the one of interest to this study is the issue of women. Lewald identifies as "her favorite topic and characters: the relationship of male and female among the Argentine upper classes."[12] The author herself has been overt about this component of her work. In 1967, her 1943 *La redoma del primer ángel* was reissued. The author's preface to the new edition is an unmistakably feminist analysis of the novel. Of the novel's dissatisfied, wealthy heroine, the author writes: "Cuando Mercedes se subleva ante la idea de ser madre supongo que es porque en cierta medida los hijos eran la prueba flagrante de la inferioridad de ser mujer, del yugo aceptado. No aceptarlo era una manera de rechazar a la vez la inferioridad y el yugo, es decir de parecerse al hombre (When Mercedes rebels against the idea of becoming a mother I suppose the reason is that to some extent children were the obvious proof of the inferiority of being a woman, of accepting the yoke. Not to accept it was a way of rejecting both the inferiority and the yoke, that is, of being like a man)."[13] She affirms that the heroine's unhappiness over sex roles is justifiable because it corresponds to the author's first-hand experience. Bullrich claims that in her own family "nada, ni el Premio Nobel, podría borrar la mancha original de ser mujer (nothing, not even the Nobel Prize, could wipe away the original stigma of being a woman)."[14] The same feminist analysis appears in Bullrich's commentary on the works of other authors. Because of Bullrich's well-known preoccupation with the conjunction of feminism and literature, a government agency commissioned from her a study on the image of women in Argentine literature.[15]

My study is concerned with how Bullrich transmits her trenchantly feminist views through the medium of the novel. The question of the novelist's quality, though it has been discussed, is not very germane to this inquiry. What is relevant is that Bullrich adopts a fundamentally different strategy than the three authors discussed so far. Her goal is to make her sex-role analysis plainly visible to readers: as critics agree, her work is markedly instructive in nature. Of course, one could argue that there are other ways to reach and teach a large audience other than the one chosen by Bullrich; however, Bullrich's procedure has had undeniable success. Taking as a given the pragmatic justification for her method, one can look at how she proceeds to present her case for women with a maximum of unmistakability.

II

Mañana digo basta takes the form of a diary written by a female art critic and occasional painter, a woman who very much wants to look critically at her own life situation. The diary chronicles an experiment she makes in order to gain a perspective on herself and on others around her. Breaking with her conventional habits, she elects to spend a protracted summer vacation at a Uruguayan beach resort which is neither modish nor very accessible. This course of action is especially anomalous in that the woman belongs to a well-off Buenos Aires set whose vacationing practices follow rigidly predetermined patterns: nearly all go to Punta del Este, some miles to the south. Moreover, while summer vacation is widely regarded as a time of enforced socializing and gaiety, the heroine aspires to a hermit-like existence. Thus, the very fact of being in her current circumstance requires an explanatory effort of introspection, which the heroine approaches through a paradox: "me he propuesto una sola cosa: aislarme para no ser una mujer sola (I have just one thing in mind: to isolate myself in order not to be a woman alone)."[16]

As the woman reviews the factors that have led to her current deviance, the reader begins to form an opinion of her character and capabilities. Hers is an ironic voice, given to witty formulations and characterized by a markedly cynical outlook. She has a good grasp of the potential for self-delusion inherent in the diary form: in consequence, she is continually monitoring and correcting her own performance: "Yo que tuve . . . bueno, me he jurado evitar toda mentira y toda exageración. No fueron tan importantes los hombres de mi vida (And here I've had . . . well, I swore I'd avoid any lying and any exaggeration. The men in my life were not that important; p. 20)." The result is a self-representation that wins the reader's confidence. The narrator's detachment, apparent objectivity and self-vigilance seem to bespeak great competence. Indeed, one may initially fear that her undistorted, fully-explicated account will leave the reader with little to do. After all, convention holds that one of the pleasures of reading epistolary or pseudo-dairy fiction is that of discovering the "unreliabilities" of the speakers.[17] This narrator seems to lack any element of distortion or reticence.

In the heroine's introspective commentary, it becomes evident that sex role is a key issue in her current turmoil. In a very programmatic fashion, she lays out the factors that constrain her existence. Argentine society, in her analysis, allows few variant roles to upper-class, middle-aged women. Essentially, a woman in this category can choose between a glamorous, frivolous self or a benevolent grandmotherliness. Neither of these roles is adequate to the heroine's need to exercise her intellectual and creative capacities; moreover, both strike her as posed and unnatural, unsuited to the potential varieties of human beings.

In seeking to represent this dilemma to herself, the heroine structures her subject-matter in a variety of ways. Most impressively, she sets up a discourse between herself and an imaginary discussant. Her phantom interlocutor is a collective entity, comprised of all those who shape and enforce sex-role expectations: "un interlocutor invisible que tiene trescientos millones de bocas (an invisible conversation partner who has three hundred million mouths; p. 19)." The dialogue created through this construction synthesizes the heroine's key concerns:

> Yo pertenezco a esa clase de la cual salen los cónsules, los embajadores, los agregados culturales, los directores de los directorios. Pero son hombres. Pero yo he trabajado como un hombre. Pero no es hombre. ¿Y qué debo hacer? No sé, es lamentable que no le divierta llevar a su nieto a la calesita. No hablo de divertirme, hablo de cumplir una misión, de ocupar un lugar que me corresponde, no, no, no me gusta la calesita ni los caballitos ni ningún otro diminutivo. Les daré a mis nietos un nombre de qué enorgullecerse . . . Eso déjelo para los hombres. ¿Y qué hay para las mujeres? Hay calesitas.

> I belong to that class that produces consuls, ambassadors, cultural attachés, board chairmen. But they're men. But I worked like a man. But you're not a man. And what am I supposed to do? I don't know, too bad you don't enjoy taking your grandchild to the merry-go-round. I don't mean for fun, I mean to carry out a mission, to occupy a place that's really mine, no, no, I don't like merry-go-rounds or horsey-go-rounds or anything else with a cutesy name . . . I'll give my grandchildren a name to be proud of . . . That's only for men. And what is there for women? There's the merry-go-round (pp. 18-19).

This complicated discourse with an abstract being appears as a spontaneous musing on the heroine's part. The fact that she can structure such a debate without forethought underscores her very great control over her private formulations of experience. The same mastery is evident in her well-informed and methodical approach to her subject-matter. She compares the status of Latin women with that of non-Latin women, looks at the new generation of assertive young women and deplores the lack of true change for older women. Rather than a private and sentimental document, her expression often resembles the semiconfessional essay that has become a favored form among feminist writers.[18]

The heroine's almost superhuman detachment and mastery, though, only appear in her diary entries. As soon as she begins to converse with other persons, she reveals her helplessness to exercise control over the discourse situation. This incompetence first becomes patent in her encounter with a local painter at his beachside studio. The woman has no strategy by which she may deflect the man's ritualized sexual-courtship discourse. All she can do is elaborate ironic commentaries, which remain unspoken: "Este parece hacerme la corte pero sólo cuando paso y el resto del día es largo (So now it seems he's courting me but only if I happen to drop by and there's not much else to do; p. 22)." Trained in art criticism, the woman would make the encounter an occasion for inspecting and appraising the man's production. He, though, insists on making the esthetic discussion a mere displacement of courtship. The man's conception of their interaction imposes itself completely. Though feeling absurd and theatrical, the woman must go through a series of clichés in which she rebuffs the man, he reproaches her with frigidity, and so on. Again one finds a sharp disjuncture between her manifest speech and behavior, immersed in the male-defined situation, and her ironic inner voice with its detached reflection: "Finjo defenderme de un sátiro en celo (I pretend I'm defending myself from a satyr in heat; p. 26)."

Alone, the diarist regains her mastery and makes a number of telling critical points. Reflecting on the lives of her daughters, she points out that the "career girl" and the "hippie" are, essentially, as constrained in their roles as the daughter who has chosen a conventional marriage. In each woman's life, societal factors and individual males prevent true self-determination and self-realization from occuring. The mode of discourse is again essay-like, full of measured observations, calculated mockery and conceits.

A rupture with the diarist's polished presentation comes with the arrival of the conventional daughter, her husband and son. In a repetition of the earlier pattern, the reader sees the heroine plunged into a discourse situation not of her own choosing. Chaos and strife supplant the distanced tone of the social critic; the heroine's attempts to speak in her own voice exacerbate the tensions of the encounter.

The daughter's goal is to push the mother back into expected habits of discourse and interaction. Failing that, she would like to expose the woman's reprehensible deviance. Arriving on Christmas Eve, grimly determined to celebrate, she denies the legitimacy of her mother's desire for silence and solitude. In the daughter's scheme of things, the maintenance of family ritual is a woman's duty. As such, it must override the personal urge to experiment with new patterns of communication and withdrawal. The older woman accedes to the force of convention; resentfully, she surrenders her right to remain *incomunicada*.

Having decreed a family reunion, the daughter exploits it to question the mother's "unmotherly" communication with a younger daughter. She suggests that the mother should be pressuring the younger daughter to come home for Christmas and to follow prescribed patterns of courtship and marriage. The model of family discourse that emerges from these remarks is one in which female family members labor to constrain one another's potential aberrance. The mother, revolted by this scenario of mutual repression, can only manage evasive replies. Inwardly, though, she is afire with repressed eloquence: "Tengo ganas de gritarles que no sólo los jóvenes tienen derecho a ser rebeldes, también hay viejos rebeldes. ¿Si me da la gana ser una madre rebelde, una abuela rebelde y no festejar las fechas que a ellos se les antoja decretar Fiestas de Familia? Pero es un desgaste inútil de energías (I feel like yelling at them that it's not just young people who are entitled to be rebellious, there are rebellious old people too. What if I just feel like being a rebellious mother, a rebellious grandmother and not celebrating the days they've decided to make official Family Holidays? But that's a useless waste of energy; p. 39)."

Through successive provocations, the daughter finally succeeds in forcing the mother into a "womanly" mode of expression. This triumph occurs while the younger woman attempts to badger the older one into attending mass. The daughter's arguments are both trivial and sly. One the one hand, she claims to be upholding family tradition; on the other, she suggests that her mother has cause to avoid taking communion. The mother seeks to address the substantive issue underlying her refusal to attend: "No me gustan las exteriorizaciones colectivas . . . soy inmune al sacrificio de la misa, no lo siento, al menos hoy (I don't care for group worship, the sacrificial meaning of mass doesn't get through to me, I don't feel it, at least not today; p. 40)."

Ultimately, the mother recognizes the impossibility of engaging the daughter in rational discourse. She changes tactics, claiming she cannot attend because she is wearing pants. This frivolous and clearly illogical remark strikes a responsive chord. The daughter is more than willing to start a quarrelsome discussion concerning dress. Her implication is that clothing is a proper topic for family discussion. A woman's private notions of worship are anomalous and, therefore, unspeakable. The diarist emerges from this skirmish surer than ever of the grievous error of society's notions of verbal interaction. The reader notes something more: the ease with which the woman capitulates to the tenets she claims to reject. Clearly, convention has a more powerful grip on her than she initially cares to admit.

A pattern of rhythmic repetition begins to characterize the novel's structure. Retreating into her diary-writing, the heroine is lucid and controlled in her exposition. Contact with other persons shatters this self-possession. In effect, the high degree of repetition is key to the novel's "accessibility." This redundancy is, without doubt, one of the features that dismay negative critics of Bullrich's writing. However, it has a rationale if one remembers the character of Bullrich's widespread readership. The novel is in conformity with the conventions of the "best-seller," constructed to accommodate even idle or inattentive readers, those who may read at a purely anecdotal level. Redundancy helps make the writing insistent and therefore unmistakable in its statements.

For instance, the heroine's encounter with Freddy is almost a repetition of her earlier interaction with the painter. Again, the man has read the woman's art criticism and initially strikes up a dialogue on this topic. Shortly, it becomes clear that critical discussion is a substitute topic. The man seeks to turn the conversation into a hackneyed form of verbal courtship. The diarist is again stricken with a feeling of absurdity and falsity.

The Freddy episode presents a minor variation: the heroine attempts to present Freddy with a critique of his "seductive" discourse. In the midst of his declarations, she reprimands him: "No digas cosas comunes (Don't talk in clichés; p. 62)." She hopes to expose his ridiculous hyperbole through persistent and abrasive irony. The intended confrontation meets with failure. Freddy evidently likes the way he speaks to women and cannot recognize criticism of his "line."

The key to the early encounters between the heroine and her suitors is monotony. The woman has no choice but to play the resisting maiden to the man's Don Juan role. The diarist's attempts to introduce authentic or individualistic notes into this pre-programmed scenario consistently fail. The men are too heavily socialized into their role to stand outside their behavior and examine it critically. As these encounters repeat themselves, the novel's redundancy becomes a denunciation of the redundancy produced by sex-role stereotyping.

III

However, the novel is not without a marked progression. The change that first occurs is within the heroine's inner musings. At the outset, she expresses confidence in her new experiment. Her self-doubts are relatively minor. In her self-critiques, she notes a reluctance to forswear socialized chit-chat. Her attitude is that she can attack the problem by identifying it and analyzing her weaknesses. Thus she scolds herself: "Las preguntas tontas las había hecho yo (I was the one who was asking silly questions; p. 17)."

Repeated failures in interpersonal contacts cast doubt upon the efficacy of the heroine's procedure. Though she continues to assess situations, she is no closer to being able to control them. The reader must necessarily see this dilemma in the woman's failure to assert herself on Christmas Eve. The woman's own recognition, though, seems somewhat delayed. Only during the Freddy episode does she really look at the failure of her experiment.

As the woman's outer voice rebuffs Freddy's advances, her inner voice speaks of a massive personal defeat. Addressing her unuttered speech to the insensitive man, she fumes: "lo que no sabes, Freddy, es que yo vine decidida a decir, ¡basta! (what you don't know, Freddy, is that I came out here determined to call a halt to this nonsense; p. 64)." In short order, she moves from fulminating at Freddy to reproaching herself: "Cuando uno dice basta debe cumplirlo, ésas no son cosas que se dejan para mañana (When you announce you're calling a halt you should just up and do it; it's not something you can keep putting off; p. 64)." She looks at her situation plainly, but does not act to change the course of events. In effect, she and Freddy spend the evening engaged in the routines of sociable interaction she would avoid.

Subsequent passages diminish the heroine's illusion of competence and control. A visible sign of her weakening resolve is her excitement over Freddy's continuing courtship. There is a violent contrast between this acritical enthusiasm and her earlier negative assessment of the man. Previously, she mocked her suitor's "mod" clothing and his trite speech. She dismissed his display of ardor as "machismo por encargo (the old macho routine; p. 63)." Now she suddenly assigns him the feature of sincerity and views his persistence as one human being's attempt to know another.

The reader, of course, cannot revise his opinion of Freddy this drastically. Instead, it is evident that the young man has triumphed over the older woman's good sense. Her trivialization is evident as she anxiously primps before answering his knock on her door. One sees that Freddy's attentions have allayed the woman's fears about advancing age. The diarist moves from being a highly reliable narrator to being an untrustworthy one, ridiculously self-deluded in her effusions: "Cuando abrí la puerta su cara de felicidad me llenó de ternura. Me sentí indispensable, otra vez mi presencia iluminaba una vida (When I opened the door his happy face filled me with tenderness. I felt indispensable, once again my being there lit up someone's life; p. 71)."

The heroine's intoxication, however, fluctuates. Soon after Freddy's "enthralling" arrival, one of his remarks brings her back to reality. Her ironic tone returns as she speculates on the banality of the young man's predictable life. In this mood, she sees how idly he pursues her and how little she likes him. She even succeeds in naming the factors that underlie her interest in him: fear of "una vejez solitaria y . . . esta madurez desorientada (a lonely old age and . . . this disoriented middle age; p. 72)." The recuperation of her endangered lucidity and detachment is a partial triumph, for no remedial action proceeds from it.

IV

This episode, with its patent loss of control, marks a change in the heroine's life and the novel's structure. The passages of solitary reflection dwindle to a minimum. Their disappearance is a consequence of the heroine's surrender to the demands of sociability. What now appears is an uninterrupted sequence of chaotic events involving numerous characters.

The diarist herself has predicted this change in her writing: "Si de veras continuara mi estadía en La Paloma, el diario que intento llevar se convertiría en un folletín (If I were to stay on in La Paloma, the diary I mean to keep would turn into a trashy romance; p. 44)." In effect, the new section of the novel has an unmistakable—and, one may argue, purposeful—resemblance to extremely popular writings aimed at a female audience. The intertextuality is signaled by the exasperated heroine's complaints to the effect that she is living in a soap-opera environment. However, it is also patent in many features of the writing itself. The beleaguered diarist is torn between the several "men in her life." Side plots abound as two of the daughters turn out to have equally complicated amorous lives. Characters storm in and out of the heroine's house, making passionate declarations or terrible accusations. As a final Gothic-melodramatic touch, there is a stunning coincidence. One daughter's name is the same as the mother's, Alejandra; her married lover has the same name as the mother's long-lost married lover. It is almost needless to say that this situation permits a mix-up of the two couple's love letters with appropriately traumatic consequences.

From a negative point of view, one could attribute the soap-opera quality to Bullrich's novel itself. Beyond any doubt, the work seeks to retain reader interest through a time-honored best-seller convention: the tricky, scandal-filled plot. But along with the evident need to capture mass-reader attention, there is a strong irony in the adoption of trashy-romance devices. The heroine's unwilling participation in the hackneyed scenario generates a mocking commentary on the trivialization of women by means of socialized expectations. Though at first glance chaotic and turbulent, the melodramatic events all point to serious deficiencies in the social delineation of male and female.

The first unifying issue to emerge is that of the couple, that is, of the ideal sexual and affective bond between man and woman. In her earlier periods of reflection, the heroine gives two models for her concept of the couple. One is the early years of her marriage, although this relation deteriorated well before her widowhood. The other is an affair with a married man. This second liaison terminated through renunciation, leaving the heroine with the intensity of her feeling intact. As a sign of the value of this attachment, she still occasionally addresses herself to the absent lover in moments of stress or self-revelation. The distinguishing characteristic of these bonds is the partners' ability to realize themselves with a minimum of interference from social stereotyping and socialized constraints.[19]

Upon entering the most melodramatic section of the novel, the reader sees repeated instances of attachments that fail to meet this high standard. Examplary of a faulty couple is the pair formed by the heroine and an "old flame," Rolando. Rolando appears unexpectedly, impelled to the heroine's house by an inchoate need to resume contact. The interaction that results, however, is terribly uncomfortable for both parties concerned.

The encounter suffers from the effects of Rolando's peculiar manifestations of physical vanity. By refusing to admit that he is subject to attacks of hives, the man creates a ridiculous disruption of the couple's seaside idyll. The woman may not speak of the man's undignified ailment, but must make many accommodations to it, including supplying medicine. When the pair visit the beach, the man is completely covered with clothing, an anomaly that arouses no little curiosity. He is horrified that his partner would attempt a truthful explanation of his behavior. Instead, it is her womanly duty to support his improbable explanations. Implicit in this farcical episode is the man's belief that his woman should help him in his efforts to deceive himself and others. Rolando's notions of the couple fall notably short of the heroine's ideal of total communication and honesty.

If Rolando worries that Alejandra will damage his "image," she also sees a threat in what he may say. In particular, she realizes how little support he can give to her efforts at self-realization and self-expression. For this reason, the most important aspects of her stay in the isolated town must remain concealed. Neither solitude, nor introspection, nor art is a safe topic.

Rolando's brief stay brings home to the heroine several negative aspects of male and female roles: men's vanity, women's anxiety over men's opinions, and men's ability to determine and define a situation and its appropriate discourse. These factors reappear in her encounters with the other men who continually come to court her.

A further reiterated element runs through these encounters. The diarist, immersed in the interaction, regains her sarcastic detachment. The result is inevitably insight into the feigning and fixed patterning that characterize male-female relations. "Yo, la verdadera yo, liberada de mi estructura terrestre, miraba irónicamente a esa pareja cincuentona que fingía tener ganas de hacer el amor (I, the true I, free of my earthly enclosure, watched ironically as that fifty-ish couple pretended to feel like making love; p. 106)."

V

Men, however, create only half the unwelcome drama in the diarist's existence. The other half arises from her woman-to-woman relations with her grown daughters. Each daughter brings with her an ongoing personal drama. Two of them have the "dime-novel romance" quality that disgusts the heroine. With their convoluted past chronicles and present dilemmas, the daughters impede the mother's search for a retreat. Between them, they feature two affairs with married men, a pregnancy begun out of wedlock, parents-in-law who oppose a marriage, a couple in transition from the counterculture to the bourgeoisie as well as sudden engagements to be married and a deplorable case of childrearing.

Like the topic of the heroine's "love life," the daughters' dramas constitute part of the novel's feature of readability. Once the complicated interrelations between characters have presented themselves, the reader must persist in his reading to discover the resolution and thus to enjoy some sense of novelistic closure. But, at the same time, the individual chronicle loses its value. In her moments of detachment, the heroine defines her daughters' dilemmas as depressing and monotonous farce, denying them any unique importance: "me contó su drama que cree muy original: está enamorada de un hombre casado que no se resuelve a dejar a su mujer. Por supuesto me cuido muy bien de decirle que a lo largo de toda la costa uruguaya y argentina miles de mujeres están llorando por el mismo motivo (she told me her drama, which she thinks is really original: she's in love with a married man who can't bring himself to leave his wife. Of course I refrain from telling her that all along the coast of Uruguay and Argentina thousands of women are crying over the same thing; p. 86)." In effect, the daughter's presentation of her affair is overwhelmingly stereotypical, complete with reiterated cries of "Es un canalla (he's a rat; p. 87)." On those occasions when the diarist does become involved in the daughters' emotional turmoil, she ends up feeling humiliated for descending to the level of a soap opera. The total result is that the entire topic of the troubled daughters becomes nothing more than a constant element of chaos and disruption, lacking in lasting effects or significance.

What is important about the daughters' intervention is their uniform ability to control their mother in discourse situations. In this respect, each daughter is a reiteration of the others, and all three essentially repeat the work of the men in the diarist's life. Conventional expectations about the heroine's role in life permit them to converse with her purely on their terms. Whether she is the object of amorous pursuit or the ever-available mother, the heroine finds no grounds on which she may begin to state her own case.

Her relegation to a less than fully human status is partially apparent in the Christmas Eve quarrel described above. The arrival of the daughter with the unhappy love affair, though, brings the problem to the fore. To begin with, the daughters all expect that, by virtue of a societal "contract," they may contact the mother at any time and consult her on any matter. Thus, while the daughters understand they must be invited to visit one another, the mother is expected to have an "open door."

The idea of permanent availability for mother-daughter interaction is in conflict with the diarist's own life plan. The daughters, however, are unlikely to discover this contradiction. They never inquire about the mother's attempts at self-realization and artistic and intellectual expression. Their belief is that the mother should display concern for others in her speech and action; talk of self is unseemly and out of role.

It is easy to see why the daughters behave as they do. They engage their mother in dialogue chiefly in order to seek some advantage. Variously, they demand lodging, consolation, maid service, motherly praise and more conventional comportment on the older woman's part. Each daughter is also determined to alter the mother's financial arrangements for selfish reasons. What remains to be explained, however, is the mother's inability to resist the predation of her offspring.

The first deficiency in the mother's self-presentation is an obvious one: a lack of assertive strategies. Part of a tradition of genteel and ladylike women, she cannot externalize her resentment, even when she knows it is justified. For example, here is her unuttered indignation over her daughters' unceasing demands on her time and energy: " 'Merde, merde, trois fois merde,' masculle en francés por ser una palabra que estoy más habituada a usar en ese idioma que en castellano pero no lo dije en voz alta, claro está ('Merde, merde, trois fois merde,' I muttered in French, because I'm more used to using the word in that language than in Spanish—but of course I didn't say it out loud: pp. 109-110)." The daughters, even the conventional matronly one, are much less constrained in their speech. They set forth their opinions and demands without much consideration for gentility, decorum or even bare civility. The mother is here disadvantaged by generational changes in discourse habits as well as by her sex.

Less obvious than the factor of gentility is that of feminine "chattiness." The trait is generationally determined, for the heroine finds that only women of her own age are locked into a pattern of loquacity, a pattern that serves them badly. The diarist discovers that her daughters can appear more efficacious and significant than she simply by the ability to remain silent: "Ese dominio de sí misma, esa capacidad de silencio es la gran conquista de las mujeres de la nueva generación. Nosotras hablábamos siempre, hasta por los codos (That self-control, that capacity for silence is the great achievement of women of the new generation. We were always talking, chattering away like a bunch of parrots; p. 119)."

Chattiness, though, is only one aspect of a larger system that trivializes the heroine's speech. During her enforced period of melodramatic situations, she begins to uncover the workings of this system. The socialized discourse required by festive occasions is key to her frustration. Continually plunged into party-like situations, she broods bitterly over the sterility of such events, the impossibility of saying anything substantive: "llegué a preguntarme si un enorme ventrílocuo no nos obligaba a hablar contra nuestra voluntad (I started wondering if some enormous ventriloquist wasn't forcing us to speak against our will; p. 138)." She becomes increasingly able to see the constraints against which her attempts at self-assertion fail.

Complicating the picture is the diarist's lack of control once she does succeed in breaking loose from social restraints. This problem becomes apparent in a terrible quarrel involving two daughters and the mother. The mother, in the excitement, forgets herself and makes an "unmotherly" demand, not to be visited without a preliminary warning. She is struck by her own inadvertant deviance: "¡Otra frase al parecer prohibida! (Another apparently forbidden phrase! p. 140)." In her ensuing remarks, she abandons all her ladylike habits, but finds no effective new patterns by which to present her case. Consequently, all she can produce is a chaotic mass of grievances and demands, aggressive but notably inefficacious. Here one sees the implication that women cannot manage to "speak up" effectively merely by resolving to do so. The ability to set forth one's needs to others requires a mastery of forceful rhetorical techniques, but because of the diarist's role, she has no practice in these techniques.

Most significantly, the woman begins to see signs of her own complicity in her much-lamented inefficacy. As she abandons her search for hermitage and gives in to the press of social obligations, this thought comes to her: "¡Pero es tan difícil que una mujer sola tome decisiones heroicas! Los rieles establecidos dan una cierta paz, quitan responsabilidad (But it's so hard for a woman alone to make heroic decisions! The established patterns give you a certain peace, they take away responsibility; p. 134)."

Her growing awareness leads the heroine to another insight: that her own discourse can inadvertantly repeat the stereotypical patterns she deplores in others' remarks. An unpleasant shock of recognition results from the critical examination of much of her own speech. This discovery takes the diarist far from her original position, in which she imagined herself to stand apart from societal patternings. Her achievement is to see her own profound implication in these structures, particularly as they perpetuate sex-role and generational inequities. The triumph remains, however, untranslated into remedial action.

VI

The "soap opera" section of the work ends, not with a confrontation, but with a form of escape. The diarist temporarily abandons her demanding daughters and suitors for the company of two eccentric strangers. These two are considered marginal figures in the resort community and, in fact, that is their self-definition. Their great appeal for the diarist is their apparent ability to speak without fear of offending social custom. The question is whether she can learn anything from these women's untrammeled expressive practices.

One of these two, Diana, conscientiously exposes the most disagreeable and potentially unfavorable aspects of her family history and her personal experiences. The former effort is represented by a family history Diana has written, highlighting whatever one would conventionally disguise or suppress. The chronicler lends out her account as a form of implicit instruction in truth-telling. Its impact upon Alejandra is so great that she transcribes it into her diary as a document in her own search for authenticity. The continuation of the family's story and Diana's personal memories appear in the form of long confessional monologues, also recorded in the diary.

These passages show clearly how Bullrich works to accommodate her feminist-individualistic subject matter to the conventions of the best-seller format. Diana's ancestral story is a repository of slavetrading, piracy, manias, incest, miscegenation, sadism and a family curse. Her personal experience includes a torrid amorous triangle with a black jazz musician and his violent, jealous girlfriend. Here, indeed, is the potential for drawing in a mass audience eager for stimulating anecdotes.

Apart from their anecdotal value, though, these chronicles serve to change the diarist's conceptions. At first Alejandra views the confessions as a sort of game with "una gran parte de novela (a lot of fictionalizing; p. 160)." It is a shock to realize that they are part of an earnest effort at honest self-representation. This revelation causes Alejandra to rethink the value of the undistorted personal chronicle. One of her frequent complaints has been the uniformity of the persons around her. Now, through a dialogue with Diana, she decides that this apparent monotony is the result of a falsification and masking of self.

Diana's cousin presents another instance of female forthrightness. However, the cousin's specialty is the unabashed enunciation of banal, quotidian truths. When Alejandra first meets the cousin, the latter startles her by expressing a certain relief over the death of a more brilliant and successful friend.

The episode of the truth-telling women turns out to be highly relevant to the issue of socially-defined femininity. As soon as Alejandra resumes contact with her old acquaintances, she discovers that the two women are generally viewed as lesbians. One townsperson goes so far as to say of Diana: "Para mi no es mujer (To me, she's not a woman; p. 172)." No concrete evidence of homosexuality can be offered, and the entire issue becomes one of women's proper discourse. The question of sex role becoms extremely overt at this juncture. The diarist engages two of her suitors in heated debates over the concept of femininity and a woman's right to speak openly. While these passages cannot be singled out for novelistic subtlety, they definitely serve to place a feminist lesson between "reader-gripping" events.

VII

The final portion of the novel structures the heroine's conflicts over social role and selfhood into a neat and synthetic dilemma. Alejandra succeeds in developing a circle of friends—all somewhat marginal persons—with whom she can speak openly. In stark opposition to this frankness is the trivialized, routinized discourse the diarist must sustain with her daughters and her fashionable friends.

The dichotomy produces a crisis when, visiting Buenos Aires, Alejandra is entrapped in a "catty" female squabble over the disposition of the family jewels. Returning to her Uruguayan retreat, she contemplates a radical change: year-round residence in the little town. This move would offer her true isolation from the cosmopolitan crowd, few of whom would seek out a northern Uruguayan beach town in the winter. The move would involve a true commitment to her resolve to forswear the amenities of socialized chatter, gossip and self-promotion.

In a further accession to the melodramatic plot construction, Alejandra's decision remains uncertain throughout a series of swiftly changing circumstances. The turbulent period of decision features the diarist thinking with alternative lucidity and confusion about her role in society. Her moments of clarity provide the occasion for undisguised statements favoring self-determination for older women. As foreshadowed by the novel's title, the resolution of the conflict is a poor one. Alejandra succumbs to her imagined need for the conventional interaction of upper-class persons in their accustomed milieux.

Several features differentiate this novel from the works by Lispector, Castellanos and Lynch. Prominent are the high degree of redundancy, the "cliffhanger" plot construction, rather sensationalistic subplots (involving a UFO, hippies, exotic sexual liaisons, etc.), easily placed characters and overt instruction on social issues. From a critical stance that demands complexity of elaboration and purposeful ambiguity, these novelistic features are defects.

However, if one considers the novel as an entertaining device for the diffusion of a feminist-personalist social critique, the same characteristics are not so grievous. Certainly, the issues presented in the novel correspond to problems found in real-world society; moreover, they are issues that need to be publicly questioned. The novel's definition of social role is essentially congruent with that of current-day sociological thought. Indeed, many excerpts from the fictional work could serve to illustrate basic concepts (role, status, generational change) in an introductory sociology textbook.

In a sense, then, it is pointless to fault the novel for being too obvious, for lacking novelistic texture and richness. It is designed to display its subject matter openly. Bullrich's novel has succeeded in attracting a good deal of public notice and winning many readers. If even a portion of this mass audience has gained in awareness of the sex-role issue, then one must say that the work has performed a valuable service.

Notes

1. H. Ernest Lewald, *Eduardo Mallea* (New York: Twayne, 1977), p. 41. Lewald comments on Silvina Bullrich on pages 41-42.

2. Lewald comments upon Bullrich's wide impact and sales in "Aspects of the Modern Argentine Woman," *Chasqui*, 5, 3 (1976), 20; this article covers pages 19-25.

3. Jorge Luis Borges and Bullrich compiled the anthology *El compadrito: su destino, sus barrios, su música* (Buenos Aires: Fabril, 1968).

4. H. A. R. praises Bullrich as a novelistic innovator in *La Nación* [Buenos Aires], 31 May 1964, sec. 4, p. 4. His "*Los burgueses*: nueva novela de Silvina Bullrich" extends the same treatment to Bullrich as one would give a less "accessible" novelist. The same is true of Oscar Hermes Villordo in his "El friso de *Los burgueses*," *La Nación*, 9 August 1964, sec. 4, p. 4.

5. See Mauricio de la Selva, "Silvina Bullrich: *Los burgueses*," *Cuadernos americanos*, 23 (1964), 287-89; Lewald's above-cited article (his longtime research continued his interest in Bullrich as a novelistic social commentator-essayist); Bobs M. Tusa, "A structural analysis of *Los burgueses* by Silvina Bullrich," *Hispanófila*, 54 (1975), 51-60; Amy Kaminsky, "The Real Circle of Iron: Mothers and Children, Children and Mothers, in Four Argentine Novels," *Latin American Literary Review*, 4, 9 (1976), 77-86; Corina Mathieu, "Argentine Women in the Novels of Silvina Bullrich," *Letras Femeninas*, 6, 1 (1980), 3-13; and Erica Frouman-Smith, "The Paradoxes of Silvina Bullrich," in Doris Meyer and Margarite Fernández-Olmos, eds., *Contemporary Women Authors of Latin America: Introductory Essays* (Brooklyn: Brooklyn College, 1983), pp. 58-71.

6. David William Foster, review of Bullrich's 1965 *La creciente*, in *Books Abroad*, 42, 2 (1968), 243. Foster also reproaches Bullrich with lack of genuine novelistic innovation in his *Currents in the Contemporary Argentine Novel* (Columbia, Missouri: University of Missouri, 1975), p. 139.

7. Francisco Herrera, "Silvina Bullrich," in Pedro Orgambide and Roberto Yahni, *Enciclopedia de la literatura argentina* (Buenos Aires: Sudamericana, 1970), pp. 105-106, views the greater part of the novelist's work as less than serious literature. For example, he finds that in two of her most overtly social novels, the chief virtues are the gossipy anecdotal interest and frivolous mocking tone. However, Herrera has a higher opinion of *La creciente*. Similar comments on Bullrich's apparent triviality appear in Katherine K. Phillips, "Silvina Bullrich," in David William Foster, ed., *A Dictionary of Contemporary Latin American Authors* (Tempe, Arizona: Center for Latin American Studies, 1975), p. 21. Lewald, despite his generally high opinion of Bullrich, makes the same complaint as the above critics in his review of the novelist's *Será justicia* (1976) in *Chasqui*, 6, 2 (1977), 94.

113

8   Tusa, 52.

9   Herrera, p. 106. The component of the social essay is also emphasized by Lewald, especially in his general introduction to the novelist in *Escritores platenses: ficciones del siglo XX* (New York: Houghton-Mifflin, 1971), pp. 20-21.

10 Lewald, "The Social and Literary Scene in the River Plate," *Books Abroad*, 49, 1 (1975), 64.

11 Bullrich, preface to *La redoma del primer ángel* (Buenos Aires: Santiago Rueda Editor, 1967), p. 9.

12 Lewald, review of Bullrich, *Entre mis veinte y mis treinta años*, *Books Abroad*, 46, 1 (1972), 82.

13 Bullrich, p. 15.

14 *Ibid.*

15 Bullrich, *La mujer argentina en la literatura* (Buenos Aires: Centro Nacional de Documentación e Información Educativa, 1972).

16 Bullrich, *Mañana digo basta* (Buenos Aires: Sudamericana, 1968), p. 21. Further page numbers in the text refer to this edition.

17 As the terms "reliable narrator" and "unreliable narrator" are developed by Wayne C. Booth in *The Rhetoric of Fiction* (Chicago: University of Chicago Press, 1961).

18 The personal confession has often been utilized to make points concerning women's status. Rosario Castellanos' personal journalism, collected in *El uso de la palabra* (Mexico: Excélsior, 1974) contains many efforts in this vein. Castellanos, in *Mujer que sabe latín...* (Mexico: SepSetentas, 1973) points out the strong autobiographical and self-descriptive component of Betty Friedan's *The Feminine Mystique* (1965) and Simone de Beauvoir's *Le Deuxième Sexe* (1949; English translation *The Second Sex*, 1952).

19 Tusa's above-cited article traces Bullrich's concept of the ideal couple.

Summary

The four narrative works this study examines all serve to make the reader aware of how unjust social circumscription of sex role may disrupt communication. This type of analysis becomes the instrument of a critical questioning of sex role. Each work focuses attention upon a somewhat different aspect of the general problem.

Clarice Lispector's *Laços de família* makes women exemplary of those who avoid—or are kept from—confrontation with the drama of existence. In their narrowly-circumscribed role, women fail to develop the awareness needed to become fully existent beings. This diminution of consciousness is associated with a severely inhibited ability to articulate existential concerns. So great is women's insufficiency that inchoate thoughts and perceptions cannot even be represented as unuttered speech through direct or indirect interior monologue. Acute crises force these characters to question their own life patterns and to examine the fundamental problems of human existence. In so doing, they begin to develop new powers of articulation. The reader now encounters the heroines' *ipsissima verba*: the third-person narrator cites, directly and indirectly, their silent verbal formulations of experience. The women may try to communicate their vital concerns through overt speech acts. However, the acquisition of a "voice" proves a painful process; it is typically abandoned in favor of a return to muted femininity.

Rosario Castellanos' *Oficio de tinieblas* is especially concerned with the ethical dimensions of women's silencing. It presents a traditional rural society in which the constraints on female expression are both pervasive and relatively undisguised. In describing and displaying this repressive system, the novel explores issues of moral responsibility. These questions arise: who benefits from the inhibition of communication? What satisfaction does this arrangement offer? What will be necessary to break out of this pattern of suppression?

The characters prove unwilling or unable to articulate issues that underlie their communicational habits. Their silence on this subject is, paradoxically, eloquent testimony to the nature of the problem. The third-person narrator underlines the character's muteness by actively intervening to help the reader comprehend the fictional discourse situation. In the resultant analysis, both men and women receive blame for willfully preserving a blockage of communication. Open discourse entails a responsible involvement in the governance of one's personal affairs and those of the larger community. This responsibility, however, can be evaded by impeding the transmission of human messages.

In *La señora Ordóñez*, Marta Lynch portrays one woman who exemplifies a number of communicational problems related to the female role. Blanca Ordóñez makes successive attempts at self-expression, but each ends in frustration. She fails because she has not acquired the basic skills needed to participate efficaciously in activities of discourse. For her ideas to win serious consideration from others, Blanca would need to give them an impressive and purposeful verbal formulation. Yet she cannot eliminate from her discourse the frivolous digressions and flirtatiously feminine element that trivialize her remarks. In Robin Lakoff's term, Blanca is a speaker of "woman's language" and, as a result, cannot hope to earn a respectful audience of listeners.

The novel alternates scenes of Blanca's adult distress with flashbacks that help show the roots of her inefficacy. Blanca has grown up amid discourse situations that discourage women from developing strong skills of argumentation. Moreover, much of her language is "prefabricated," composed of verbal formulae and habits current in her cultural ambience. In Blanca's lower middle-class childhood home, this ready-made language comes from mass-media entertainments and the school system. As the woman becomes upwardly mobile, she assimilates her language to that of the affluent clientele of resort hotels and cosmetic establishments. Whether her linguistic models are vulgar or sophisticated, their domination of her speech inhibits inventive and meaningful personal expression.

The labor of narration falls to, alternatively, a third-person omniscient narrator and Blanca herself. This alternation permits the reader to check the heroine's assertions against the more reliable testimony of the narrator. At first, one sees few discrepancies between the two versions. Despite her difficulties in face-to-face interaction, Blanca appears to be a capable narrator with a strong ironic awareness of her own situation. Only gradually does the reader discover in Blanca's apparently insightful remarks a subtle system of falsifications.

Mañana digo basta is Silvina Bullrich's embodiment of principles of sex-role analysis in a best-selling fictional format. The heroine of this work finds herself in an unfavorable social circumstance not only by virtue of her sex but also because of her advancing age. The novel takes the form of an intimate diary chronicling this woman's attempts to analyze and to overcome the constraints imposed by her position. Such a format lends itself both to didacticism and to entertainment. In her reflective moments, the diarist provides abundant instruction in concepts of social role. In behavior intended to break out of her limited role, she encounters a number of lurid and melodramatic situations.

As in the Lynch novel, the heroine-narrator initially appears more competent and accurate than she is. The diarist of *Mañana digo basta* presents herself as one who has understood her own voicelessness and is now determined to speak out on important issues. Yet, as her diary reveals, she repeatedly fails to assert herself. Any situation of conflict sends her back to the "ladylike" speech she deplores as ineffectual.

All four works, through a use of narrative voice and discourse analysis, examine sex role while providing, to varying degrees, complex artistic representation.

Feminist Criticism of Latin American Literature: Bibliographic Notes

I

In recent years the question of socially-defined sex role has attracted great numbers of investigators, both critics and popular essayists. There have been widespread expressions of dissatisfaction with society's determination of what is properly male and what is properly female. Women's role has been criticized for the excessive number of constraints it imposes on female members of society. To remedy this situation, students of sex role have proposed a number of reforms. The consideration of this entire set of related issues might most accurately be described as a critical questioning of sex roles, but it is generally referred to as feminism.

This chapter looks at the impact of feminism on several aspects of Latin American literature, examining the diffusion and promotion of this literature, analyzing the critical response it has stimulated, and, above all, seeking to provide a guide to the feminist criticism now emerging in this field. By feminist criticism, I mean literary commentary in which principles of sex-role analysis derivable from modern-day feminism play a significant part.

Because of the diversity of elements this chapter examines, a preliminary outline of its contents is in order. The first section looks at the elements of sex-role analysis that have traditionally been present in the criticism of Latin American literature. The following segment surveys the impact of 1970s feminism on the field of Latin American letters: the tendency, early established, to promote female writers rather than to attack male ones; the attempt to reorganize literary promotion and publishing in order to give women better representation; and the creation of new literary enterprises dedicated exclusively to women's literature and feminist discussion. The third portion of the chapter lists and comments upon feminist criticism existing outside specialized feminist publishing outlets. This section deals with book-length studies as well as journal articles, and includes reference to parallel developments in the criticism of Spanish literature. After this review of the standing criticism, there is an assessment of the areas that feminist critics have neglected and some indication of how this neglect may be remedied.

II

Some sex-role commentary has long been implicit in much non-feminist discussion of Latin American writings. One need only look at characterizations of, for example, Jorge Isaacs' *María* (Columbia, 1867 or José Mármol's *Amalia* (Argentina, 1851-55). Representative examples include Enrique Anderson Imbert, "Isaacs y su romántica *María*," in his *Estudios sobre escritores de América* (Buenos Aires: Editorial Raigal, 1954), pp. 81-107, and David William Foster's discussion of *Amalia* in *Currents in the Contemporary Argentine Novel* (Columbia, Missouri: University of Missouri Press, 1975), pp. 5-6. As commentators note, these literary works rely on cultural notions of femininity. In addition, there are imaginative works and essays so focused on the sex-role issue that commentators must necessarily recognize the question. The paradigmatic instance is the 1691 "Respuesta de la poetisa a la muy ilustre Sor Filotea de la Cruz" by Sor Juana Inés de la Cruz (Mexico). An unmistakable anger over women's status stands out in many poems of the Argentine Alfonsina Storni (1892-1938).

Rather adjacent to the discussion of the sex-role theme in literature is the consideration of the "femininity" of women writers. This partially extraliterary interest finds a famous expression in Germán Arciniegas' portraits of women authors in *Las mujeres y las horas*, Volume II of his essay *América mágica* (Buenos Aires: Sudamericana, 1961).

Still outside the realm of deliberately feminist criticism, sociological criticism may examine women's status through the testimony of literature. The Argentine social critic Julio Mafud has long been interested in the literary under-representation of women in Argentina. See his "El desarraigo en la literatura: lo femenino," in *El desarraigo argentino* (Buenos Aires: Américalee. 1959). pp. 100-103, and *Contenido social del Martín Fierro* (Buenos Aires: América-lee, 1961), pp. 27-29, 38-41 and 75-77. Sexuality and sex role have also attracted commentary from another literarily-oriented Argentine social essayist, Arturo Jauretche, in his *El medio pelo en la sociedad argentina* (Buenos Aires: A. Peña Lillo, 1966), which discusses fiction, pp. 193-211. A lesser-known sociologist, Alfredo Moffatt, analyzes both literary and popular-culture material in his *Estrategias para sobrevivir en Buenos Aires* (Buenos Aires: Jorge Alvarez, (1967). An inquiry into women's status through an examination of very popular writings is found in Juan José Sebreli, the Argentine social polemicist; one may consult especially his *Eva Perón:¿aventurera o militante?*, 4a ed. rev. (Buenos Aires: La Pléyade, 1971).

The examples listed above represent the variety of sex-role commentary found outside of overtly feminist discussion. A tradition of more direct commentary has long existed in the writings and statements of literary women. The special position of the outspoken woman writer far antedates the emergence of women's studies, although the most recent practitioners of this form of discussion are influenced by the so-called "women's liberation movement." Victoria Ocampo, the celebrated matriarchal figure of the Argentine literary establishment, has long practiced an essayistic feminist criticism. Of particular relevance are her "Literatura" and "La mujer" in her *Testimonios: Segunda Serie* (Buenos

Aires: Sur, 1941), pp. 122-34 and 237-86, respectively. A special number of her magazine *Sur* |Buenos Aires], 326-28 (1970-71), presents the views of many prominent women on the subject of sex role. Doris Meyers' biographical *Victoria Ocampo: Against the Wind and Tide* (New York: Braziller, 1979) emphasizes the feminist aspect of Ocampo's writings. Less "genteel" is the criticism of Rosario Castellanos (Mexico). Her 1973 *Mujer que sabe latín . . .* (Mexico: SepSetentas) is the best-known manifestation of her literary feminism, but the same concepts recur throughout her work. Especially impressive is her feminist analysis of Choderlos de Laclos' *Les liaisons dangereuses* in her 1966 *Juicios sumarios* (Xalapa, Veracruz: Universidad Veracruzana), pp. 221-30. In connection with Castellanos' method, one may see Naomi Lindstrom, "Rosario Castellanos: Pioneer of Feminist Criticism," in the anthology *Homenaje a Rosario Castellanos*, Maureen Ahern and Mary Vásquez, eds. (Valencia: Estudios de Hispanófila, 1980), pp. 65-73. Silvina Bullrich has also published feminist essays on literature. Examples are *George Sand: una mujer como yo* (Buenos Aires: Emecé, 1972) and *La mujer argentina en la literatura* (Buenos Aires: Centro Nacional de Documentación e Información Educativa, 1972). Interviews and journalistic writings often provide women writers with an opportunity to diffuse feminist thought. Two forthright women who have made wide use of mass-media outlets are Marta Lynch (Argentina) and the Mexican novelist-journalist, Elena Poniatowska.

III

With the advent of the decade of the 1970s, there arises a deliberate attempt to extend feminist principles to the discussion of literary texts. From its inception, feminist criticism faces certain fundamental questions of orientation. What corpus of literary work is most suitable for consideration by feminists? Is an essentially value-free sex-role analysis a proper critical ideal, or should the committed feminist promote and/or attack works of literature? In English-speaking countries, feminists have often guided themselves by the model of Kate Millett's 1970 *Sexual Politics* (Garden City: Doubleday). The greater part of this work is dedicated to taking male writers to task for allegedly disseminating prejudicial, yet powerful, images of women.

This denunciatory labor has not become widespread in Latin American studies. The validity of the Millett model and its applicability to Hispanic studies is the topic of a polemic in *Journal of Spanish Studies: Twentieth Century*. Patricia O'Connor's Millett-patterned "Francisco García Pavón's Sexual Politics," 1, 1 (1973), 65-81, draws a rebuttal from Birgitta Vance in the latter's "The Great Clash: Feminist Literary Criticism Meets up with Spanish Reality," 2, 2 (1974), 109-14; an ensuing exchange of letters appears in 2, 3 (1974), 193-96.

Instead of an attack on male authors, there has been a renewed interest in and a vigorous promotion of female writers. Various activities have sought to bring women's writings the critical reader attention they have often lacked. The first Congreso Internacional de Escritoras Latinoamericanas was held at Carnegie-Mellon University in 1975 (Yvette Miller, organizer); the proceedings were issued as a special publication of the Latin American Literary Review Press under the title *Latin American Women Writers: Yesterday and Today* (1978). The Congreso has since met at irregular intervals and given rise to other similar events. For a recent example of selected material from one of these meetings, see Patricia González and Eliana Ortega, eds.. *La sartén por el mango: actas del Congreso de Escritoras Latinoamericanas*, 1982 (San Juan, Puerto Rico: Huracán, 1983). The principal drawback to these as to other volumes of selected conference papers is that they tend to be diverse in aims and methods.

An alternative is to bring together critics who agree upon a common approach and produce papers on a given topic. Such an enterprise is Vicente Cicchitti et al., *La mujer: símbolo del mundo nuevo* (Buenos Aires: Fernando García Cambeiro, 1976), which evaluates womanly images without concern for the sex of the author. The essays are all aligned with an attempt to create a hermeneutical, Peronist criticism following a pattern set by Leopoldo Marechal. Whatever one may make of this extremely interpretive system with its heavy load of religious and political doctrine, it does make the volume original and unique among such collections.

Journals, more accessible than proceedings, have also sprung up around the women's literature issue. The Asociación de Literatura Femenina publishes the journal *Letras Femeninas*. This organization, which was headed by Victoria Urbano until her death in 1984, has sponsored a variety of activities: meetings on women's literature, readings of poetry, publications of critical studies and creative works, and special sessions at various regularly held conferences and study tours. *fem*, the Mexico City feminist journal, has been successful in bringing together literary work, cultural criticism, and social analysis from writers living and working in many countries; it also carries news of interest to feminists and some examples of visual art by women.

A related enterprise is the organization of bulletins, circulars and bibliographies to disseminate news about women writers and their work. Kathleen O'Quinn originated the San Francisco-based Clearinghouse on Latin American Women Authors, active in the early and middle seventies. Diane Marting first organized a bibliographic enterprise at Rutgers University. Xeroxed listings were circulated until a bibliography in book form appeared. Marting's goal has been to centralize information about English translation of Latin American women's writing: which works have been translated, which of these translations are available, and which works deserve translation or re-translation.

Feministas Unidas is a group organized during the meetings of the Modern Language Association, although not directly under the aegis of that learned society. It sponsors a newsletter and brings together feminists attending the Modern Language Association conference for the sessions on Spanish and Latin American Literature. Indiana University's Chicano-Riqueño Studies program offices coordinate information on U.S. Latin women authors and produce a journal, *Third Woman* (ed. Norma Alarcón).

IV

In recent years, it has been common to devote an entire issue of a journal to women's writing or discussions of women writers and women's issues in literature. An early Latin American example is *Revista/Review Interamericana*, 4, 2 (1974). An unusually coherent effort of this type is the collection of alternative and Third World criticism of Chilean women's culture, with suitable creative writings. in *Literatura Chilena, Creación y Crítica*, Autumn, 1982 (Marjorie Agosín; guest editor, David Valjalo, regular editor).

The production of anthologies of female-authored works has been greatly stimulated by the new interest in women's literature. Amalia Martin Gamero, ed., *Antología del feminismo* (Madrid: Alianza Editorial, 1975) is outstanding because of its consistency in choosing selections that contain commentary on women's role. English-translation anthologies include Doris Meyer and Margarite Fernández Olmos, eds., *Contemporary Women Authors of Latin America: New Translations* (Brooklyn: Brooklyn College, 1983); and Nora Jacquez Wieser, ed., *Open to the Sun: A Bilingual Anthology of Latin American Women Poets* (Van Nuys, California: Perivale Press, 1981).

There has also been considerable feminist criticism that stands somewhat outside the strictly "women's studies" category. An example is the recent criticism on the Chilean novelist María Luisa Bombal. These new studies are more part of the critical examination of Bombal than part of feminist discussion, yet they contain many insights clearly provoked by the feminists' rereading of literature. The major examples are: Hernán Vidal, *María Luisa Bombal: la femineidad enajenada* (Barcelona: Aubí, 1976); Lucia Guerra-Cunningham, *La narrativa de María Luisa Bombal: una visión de la existencia femenina* (Madrid: Playor, 1981), and Marjorie Agosín *Las desterradas del paraíso, protagonistas en la narrative de María Luisa Bombal* (New York: Senda Nueva, 1982), and Marjorie Agosín et al., eds., *María Luisa Bombal* (Tempe: Bilingual Press/Editorial Bilingüe, 1987) Examples of this type of criticism on a Peruvian and an Argentine writer, respectively, are Wolfgang Luchting, *La mujer o la revolución* (Lima: Ecoma, 1974) on Enrique Congrains Martin, and Rachel Phillips, *Alfonsina Storni: From Poetess to Poet* (London: The Lost Rib: Female Characters in the Spanish American Novel* (Lewisburg, Pennsylvania: Bucknell University Press/Toronto: Associated University Presses, 1985), and Samuel G. Saldívar, *La evolución del personaje feminino en la novela mexicana* (Lanham, Maryland: University Press of America, 1985).

The limited representation of women authors and women's issues in literary histories and anthologies of criticism has prompted the production of such volumes with a special or exclusive concentration of women. Two reference works are Lucia Fox-Lockert, *Women Novelists of Spain and Spanish America* (Metuchen, New Jersey: Scarecrow, 1979) and Julie Greer Johnson, *Women in Colonial Spanish American Literature: Literary Images* (Westport, Connecticut: Greenwood Press, 1983). Doris Meyer, *Victoria Ocampo: Against the Wind and Tide* (New York: Braziller, 1979) is a biography, but also an effort to emphasize a woman's importance in modern Argentine literary life. Anthologies of feminist criticism on Spanish and Latin American writers include: Meyer and Margarite Fernández Olmos, eds. *Contemporary Women Authors of Latin America: Critical Essays* (Brooklyn: Brooklyn College, 1983); Beth Miller, *Mujeres en la literatura* (Mexico: Fleischer, 1978) and her edition, *Women in Hispanic Literature: Icons and Fallen Idols* (Berkeley: University of California Press, 1983); and Gabriela Mora and Karen S. Van Hooft, eds., *Theory and Practice of Feminist Literary Criticism* (Ypsilanti, Michigan: Bilingual Press/Editorial Bilingüe, 1982).

H. Ernest Lewald was notable for his early enthusiasm for Latin American and especially Argentine women writers. He was especially careful to represent women amply in his many anthologies, two of which are entirely of women's writing: *Diez cuentistas argentinas* (Buenos Aires: Riomar, 1968), and *The Web: Stories by Argentine Women* (Washington, DC: Three Continents Press, 1983).

A complex form of literary-historical research has as its goal the identification of criticism of women's status in works written before the advent of current-day literary feminism. In some cases, researchers categorize their subjects as feminists in literature; in others the authors studied can only be described as concerned with women's situation. Among these studies are: Teresa A. Cook, *El feminismo en la novela de la Condesa de Pardo Bazán* (La Coruña: Diputación Provincial, 1976), on a declared feminist; Ruth El-Saffar, *The Recovery of the Feminine in the Novels of Cervantes* (Berkeley: University of California Press, 1984); Sandra M. Fox, *Feminismo y forma literaria: estudio del tema y las técnicas de María de Zayas y Sotomayor* (Valencia: Hispanofila, 1979); Malveena McKendrick, *Woman and Society in the Spanish Drama of the Golden Age* (London: Cambridge, 1974); and Patricia O'Connor, *Gregorio and María Martínez Sierra* (Boston: Twayne, 1975).

The largest number of items is in the area of articles published in mainstream journals which treat a literary work or works with special attention to the reflection of women's place in society. Under "mainstream," one may classify journals aimed at Hispanic and Latin American literary critics. A typical concern is the identification of those qualities most frequently assigned to women in literature. The female character is identified as having the attributes of weakness, strength, mysterious power, treachery, innocence, and so forth. A productive relation with the central sex-role issue is not always in evidence. For example, George O. Schanzer's below-cited study on Rubén Darío has the term *Ms.* in the title and begins with a citation from a feminist group statement. However, the ensuing discussion is akin to other analyses of Darío's feminine theme with its fusion of religious and erotic elements. The connection with the current-day question of role is disproven in the course of the analysis. Schanzer concludes: "If Darío were alive today, rather than supporting Betty Friedan or Sister Margaret Traxler, I could imagine him benefiting from occasional contributions to *Playboy* or *Cosmopolitan*" (p. 151). One wishes all critics would be as honest as Schanzer in stating the lack of relation between Darío's critical analysis and feminist thought.

The following listing includes no articles from *Letras Femeninas* or *fem*, because the reader needs no bibliographic aid to locate feminist criticism in a feminist journal. Its basic purpose is to show the appearance of feminist criticism in journals read by a broad cross-section of Hispanists. Articles have been judged to be feminist if they reveal a marked conceptual relation and/or explicit reference to the debate over women's role as that debate has been formulated in the 1960s, 1970s and 1980s.

Before listing articles in the Latin America area, one should note the emergence of feminist journal criticism on peninsular authors. Here is a listing of journal criticism:

Bluestine, Carolyn. "The role of women in the *Poema de Mio Cid.*" *Romance Notes*, 18, 3 (1978), 404-409.

Boring, Phyllis Zatlin. "Carmen Martín Gaite, feminist author." *Revista de estudios hispánicos*, 11, 3 (1977), 323-38.

_____. "Delibes' two views of the Spanish mother." *Hispanófila*, No. 63 (1978), 79-87.

Cambria, Rosario. "Women's rights in Spain: it all began with Concepción Arenal." *The American Hispanist*, 2, 17 (1977), 7-10.

Cook, Teresa A. "Emilia Pardo Bazán y la educación como elemento primordial en la liberación de la mujer." *Hispania*, 60, 2 (1977), 259-65.

El-Saffar, Ruth. "Tres imágenes claves de lo femenino en el *Persiles.*" *Revista canadiense de estudios hispánicos*, 3, 3 (1979), 219-36.

Fontanella, Lee. "Mystical diction and imagery in Gómez de Avellaneda and Carolina Coronado." *Latin American Literary Review*, 9, 19 (1982), 47-55.

Galerstein, Carolyn L. "Carmen Laforet and the Spanish spinster." *Revista de estudios hispánicos*, 11, 2 (1977), 303-315.

Gastón, Nélida Vientós. "Concepción Arenal." *Sin nombre [San Juan, Puerto Rico]*, 7, 3 (1976), 46-61.

Giles, Mary E. "Feminism and the feminine in Emilia Pardo Bazán's novels." *Hispania*, 63, 2 (1980), 356-67.

Griswold, Susan C. "Topoi and rhetorical distances: the 'feminism' of María de Zayas." *Revista de estudios hispánicos*, 14, 2 (1980), 97-116.

Halsey, Martha T. "Olmo's '*La pechuga de la sardina*' and the oppression of women in contemporary Spain." *Revista de estudios hispánicos*, 8, 1 (1979), 3-20.

Ibarra, Fernando. "Clarín y la liberación de la mujer." *Hispanófila*, No. 51 (1974), 27-33.

Kirkpatrick, Susan. "On the threshold of the realistic novel: gender and genre in *La gaviota.*" *PMLA*, 93 (1983), 323-40.

Marcus, Roxanne B. "An application of Jungian theory to the interpretation of Doña Inés in Valera's *Juanita la larga*," *Revista canadiense de estudios hispánicos*, 3, 1 (1979), 259-74.

O'Connor, Patricia. "A Spanish precursor to women's lib: the heroine in Gregorio Martínez Sierra's theater." *Hispania*, 55 (1972), 865-72.

_____. "José Ruibal: feminist unaware in *La secretaria*?" *Revista de estudios hispánicos*, 8, 3 (1974), 413-17.

_____. Eros and Thanatos in Francisco García Pavón's *El último sábado.*" *Journal of Spanish Studies: Twentieth Century*, 4, 1 (1976), 175-85.

_____. "Gregorio Martínez Sierra's maternal nuns in dramas of renunciation and revolution." *The American Hispanist*, 2, 12 (1976), 8-12.

_____. "Spain's first successful woman dramatist: María Martínez Sierra." *Hispanófila*, 60 (1979), 87-108.

Ordóñez, Elizabeth. "The decoding and encoding of sex roles in Carmen Martín Gaite's *Retahílas.*" *Kentucky Romance Quarterly*, 27, 2 (1980), 237-44.

_____. "The female quest pattern in Concha Alos' *Os habla Electra.*" *Revista de estudios hispánicos*, 19, 1 (1985), 21-34.

124

Ortega, José. "La frustración femenina en *Los mercaderes* de Ana María Matute." *Hispanófila*, No. 54 (1975), 31-38.

Richards, Catherine G. "Social criticism in Lorca's tragedies." *Revista de estudios hispánicos*, 17, 2 (1983), 35-53.

Rodríguez, Alfred, and John Timm. "El significado de lo femenino en *La familia de Pascual Duarte*." *Revista de estudios hispánicos*, 11, 2 (1977), 251-64.

Rovira, Rosalina R. "La función de la mujer en la literatura contemporánea española." *Explicación de textos literarios*, 3, 3 (1974-75), 21-24.

Schmidt, Ruth A. "Woman's place in the sun: feminism in *Insolación*." *Revista de estudios hispánicos*, 8, 1 1974), 68-81.

Seator, Lynne Hubbard. " 'Ana Kleiber' and the traditional nature of Sastre's unconventional women." *Revista de estudios hispánicos*, 12, 2 (1978), 287-302.

_____. "Women and men in the novels of Unamuno." *Kentucky Romance Quarterly*, 27, 1 (1980), 469-77.

Sims, Edna N. "Resumen de la imagen negativa de la mujer en la literatura española hasta mediados del siglo XVI," *Revista de estudios hispánicos*, 11, 3 (1977), 443-49.

Spieker, Joseph B. "El feminismo como clave estructural en las *novelle* de doña María de Zayas." *Explicación de textos literarios*, 6, 2 (1978), 158-60.

Sullivan, Constance A. "Re-reading the Hispanic literary canon: the question of gender." *Ideologies and Literature*, 16 (1983), 93-101.

Van Beysterveldt, Anthony. "Revisión de los debates feministas del siglo XV y las novelas de Juan de Flores." *Hispania*, 64, 1 (1981), 231-33.

Ziomek, Hendryk. "La dramatización veleceña de la mujer guerrera en *El amor en vizcaíno*." *Revista de estudios hispánicos*, 17, 3 (1983), 363-70.

Journal articles about Latin American literature:

Araújo, Helena. "Narrativa femenina latinoamericana," *Hispamérica*, No. 23 (1982), 23-24.

Arias de la Canal, Fredo. "Feminismo y homosexualidad." *Norte* [Mexico], No. 265 (1975), 25-31.

Arrom, José Juan. "Cambiantes imágenes de la mujer en el teatro de la América virreinal." *Latin American Theatre Review*, 12, 1 (1978), 5-15.

Barradas, Efraín. "El machismo existencialista de René Marqués," *Sin nombre*, 8, 3 (1977), 69-81.

Barros, Alcides João de. "A situação da mulher no teatro de Consuelo de Castro e Leilah Assunção." *Latin American Theater Review*, 9, 2 (1976), 13-20.

Beer, Gabriella de. "Feminismo en la obra poética de Rosario Castellanos." *Revista de crítica literaria latinoamericana*, No. 13 (1981), 105-112.

Bischoff, Efraín U. "La mujer en el *Martín Fierro*," *Letras de Buenos Aires*, 2, 6 (1982), 35-53.

Boschetto, Sandra María. "El canto de las sirenas: aproximación al mundo femenino en algunos relatos de Juan Carlos Onetti." *Explicación de textos literarios*, 7, 2 (1983-84), 3-18.

_____. "La inversión de la figura femenina en 'El güero' de José Donoso." *Crítica Hispánica*, 6, 1 (1984), 1-10.

Corteau, Joanna. "The image of woman in the novels of Graciliano Ramos," *Revista/ Review Interamericana*, No. 4 (1974), 161-71.

Fisherova Beck, Vera. "Las heroínas en la novelística argentina." *Revista hispánica moderna*, Nos. 3-4 (1944), 111-24.

Fitz, Earl E. "Freedom and self-realization: feminist characterization in the fiction of Clarice Lispector," *Modern Language Studies*, 10, 3 (1980), 51-61.

Foster, David William. Discussion of women's writing in his "The demythification of Buenos Aires in selected Argentine novels of the seventies." *Chasqui*, 10, 1 (1980), 11-14.

Ginsberg, Judith. "From anger to action: the avenging female in two *Lucías.*" *Revista de estudios hispánicos*, 14, 1 (1980), 51-64.

González, José Emilio. "Julia de Burgos: la mujer y la poesía," *Sin nombre*, 7, 3 (1976), 86-100.

Guerra-Cunningham, Lucía. "Algunas reflexiones teóricas sobre la novela femenina." *Hispamérica*, No. 28 (1981), 29-39.

Gyurko, Lanin A. "The pseudo-liberated woman in Fuentes' *Zona Sagrada.*" *Journal of Spanish Studies: Twentieth Century*, 3, 1 (1975), 17-43.

_____."The vindication of La Malinche in Fuentes' 'Todos los gatos son pardos'," *Ibero Amerikanisches archiv* 3, 3 (1977).

_____."Women in Mexican society: Fuentes' portrayal of oppression." *Revista hispánica moderna* 38, 4 (1974-75), 206-29.

Hancock, Joel. "Elena Poniatowska's *Hasta no verte, Jesús mío*: the remaking of the image of woman." *Hispania*, 66, 3 (1983), 353-39.

Hoberman, Luisa. "Hispanic American women as portrayed in the historical literature: type or archetype?" *Revista/review interamericana*, No. 4 (1974), 131-35.

Johnson, Julie Greer. "A caricature of Spanish women in the new world by the Inca Garcilaso de la Vega." *Latin American Literary Review*, 9, 18 (1981), 47-51.

Kaminsky, Amy. "The real circle of iron: mothers and children, children and mothers, in four Argentine novels." *Latin American Literary Review*, 4, 9 (1976), 77-86.

Kirsner, Robert. "De doña Bárbara a Luisiana: feminismo refinado." *Caribe*, 1, 2 (1976), 57-64.

Leal, Luis. "Mujer que sabe latín." *Letras de Buenos Aires*, 2, 7 (1982), 35-53.

Lemaître, Monique J. "Jesusa Palancares y la dialéctica de la emancipación femenina." *Hispamérica*, No. 30 (1981), 131-35.

Levine, Linda Gould. "María Luisa Bombal from a feminist perspective." *Revista/review interamericana*, No. 4 (1974), 148-61.

Lewald, H. Ernest. "Aspects of the modern Argentine woman." *Chasqui*, 5, 3 (1976), 19-25.

_____. "Two generations of River Plate women authors." *Latin American Research Review*, 15, 1 (1980), 231-36.

Lima, Robert. "Cumbres poéticas de erotismo femenino en Hispanoamérica." *Revista de estudios hispánicos* [Alabama], 18, 1 (1984), 41-59.

Lindstrom, Naomi. "A discourse analysis of 'Preciosidade' by Clarice Lispector," *Luso-Brazilian Review*, 19, 2 (1982), 187-94.

_____. "Feminist criticism of Latin American literature: bibliographic notes," *Latin American Research Review*, 15, 1 (1980), 151-59.

_____. "A feminist discourse analysis of Clarice Lispector's 'Daydreams of a Drunken Woman'," *Latin American Literary Review*, 9, 19 (1982), 7-16.

Llamas, María del Refugio. "Sor Juana Inés de la Cruz," *Norte*, No. 265 (1975), 25-31.

López, Yvette. " 'La muñeca menor': ceremonias y transformaciones en un cuento de Rosario Ferré." *Explicación de textos literarios*, 11, 1 (1982-83), 49-58.

Magnarelli, Sharon. "Gatos, lenguaje y mujeres en *El gato eficaz* de Luisa Valenzuela," *Revista iberoamericana*, Nos. 108-109 (1979), 603-611.

_____. "*La ciudad y los perros:* women and language," *Hispania*, 64, 2 (1981), 215-225.

Martin, Eleanor J. "Carlota O'Neill's *Cuarta dimensión [Fourth Dimension]*: The role of the female and the imagination in everyday existence," *Latin American Literary Review*, 8, 15 (1979), 1-11.

Martínez, Z. Nelly. "*El gato eficaz* de Luisa Valenzuela: la productividad del texto," *Revista canadiense de estudios hispánicos*, 4, 1 (1979), 73-80.

McCracken, Ellen. "Manuel Puig's *Heartbreak Tango*: women and class culture," *Latin American Literary Review*, 9, 18 (1981), 27-35.

Meyer, Doris. "Woman's space, woman's text: a new departure in Inés Malinow's *Entrada libre.*" *Latin American Literary Review*, 12, 23 (1983), 41-50.

Miller, Beth. "Avellaneda, nineteenth-century feminist." *Revista/review interamericana*, No. 4 (1974), 131-35.

_____, "Historia y ficción en *Oficio de tinieblas* de Rosario Castellanos," *Texto crítico*, No. 28 (1984), 131-42.

_____. "Rosario Castellanos' *Guests in August*: critical realism and the provincial middle class." *Latin American Literary Review*, 7, 14 (1979), 5-19.

Minc, Rose S. "Guadalupe Dueñas: texto y contexto de la nueva alquimia del poder." *Discurso literario*, 1, 2 (1984), 231-41.

Mora, Gabriela. "La otra cara de Ifigenia: una reevaluación del personaje de Teresa de la Parra." *Sin nombre*, 7, 3 (1976), 130-44.

_____. "*Los perros* y *La mudanza* de Elena Garro: designio social y virtualidad feminista," *Latin American Theatre Review*, 8, 2 (1975), 5-14.

Nigro, Kirsten F. "Rosario Castellanos' debunking of *The Eternal Feminine.*" *Journal of Spanish Studies: Twentieth Century*, 8, 1-2 (1980), 89-102.

Novães Coelho, Nelly. "A presença da 'Nova mulher' na ficção brasileira atual." *Revista iberoamericana*, No. 126 (1984), 141-54.

Nunes, Maria Luisa. "Clarice Lispector: artista andrógina ou escritora?" *Revista ibero-americana*, No. 126 (1984), 281-89.

Pescatello, Ann. "The special issue in perspective: the Hispanic Caribbean woman and the literary media." *Revista/review interamericana*, No. 4 (1974), 131-35.

Pontiero, Giovanni. "Testament of experience: some reflections on Clarice Lispector's last narrative *A hora da estrela.*" *Ibero Amerikanisches archiv*, 10, 1 (1984), 13-22.

Rodríguez-Peralta, Phyllis. "Images of women in Rosario Castellanos' prose." *Latin American Literary Review*, 6, 11 (1977), 68-80.

_____. "María Luisa Bombal's poetic novels of female estrangement." *Revista de estudios hispánicos*, 15, 1 (1980), 139-55.

_____. "Narrative access to a feminine childhood world: a new Peruvian novel." *Latin American Literary Review*, 9 (1980), 1-8.

Schanzer, George O. "Rubén Darío and Ms. Christa." *Journal of Spanish Studies: Twentieth Century*, 3, 2 (1975), 145-52.

Schlau, Stacy. "Conformity and resistance to enclosure: female voices in Rosario Castellanos' *Oficio de tinieblas (The Dark Service).*" *Latin American Literary Review*, 7, 24 (1984), 45-57.

Steele, Cynthia. "Toward a socialist feminist criticism of Latin American literature." *Ideologies and Literature*, No. 16 (1983), 323-329.

Urbistondo, Vicente. "El machismo en la narrativa hispanoamericana." *Texto crítico*, 4, 9 (1978), 165-83.

Valdivieso, Mercedes. "Social denunciation in the language of *El árbol [The Tree]* by María Luisa Bombal." Trans. Ellen Wilkerson. *Latin American Literary Review*, 4, 9 (1976), 70-76.

Vásquez Arce, Carmen. "Sexo y mulatería: dos sones de una misma guaracha." *Sin nombre*, 12, 4 (1982), 51-63.

Williams, Lorna V. "*The Shrouded Woman*: Marriage and its constraints in the fictions of María Luisa Bombal." *Latin American Literary Review*, 10, 20 (1982), 21-30.

Wilson, S. R. "Art by gender: the Latin American woman writer." *Revista canadiense de estudios hispánicos*, 6, 1 (1981), 135-37.

Zapata, Celia de. "One hundred years of women writers in Latin America." *Latin American Literary Review*, 3, 6 (1975), 7-16.

Zavala, Iris M. "Dos mujeres contra el mundo: Flora Tristán y Louise Michel," *Sin nombre*, 7, 3 (1976), 37-45.

Selected Bibliography

Before presenting bibliographic listings on criticism of the four women authors studied, I should explain the criteria of selection.

First, there has been a general exclusion of book reviews and of journalistic criticism appearing in literary supplements and newspaper columns. The reason for this procedure is that journalistic criticism tends to be rather sketchy and non-analytical; in addition, many libraries either do not order or do not retain newspaper materials. The exception to this rule is review criticism that (a) includes a substantial amount of analytic discussion; (b) is significant because of its place of appearance, for example, attention to Clarice Lispector in *Saturday Review*; and/or (c) is noteworthy because of the critic writing, for example, a journalistic commentary on Lispector by the celebrated critic Affonso Romano de Sant'Anna. Although many reviews cannot be listed, one should note the persistent efforts of journalists and academic reviewers to draw notice to the work of women authors. In this country, H. Ernest Lewald has been active in promoting River Plate women writers. In Brazil, the literary supplement of *Minas Gerais* (a newspaper) has been a source of well-written reviews of female-authored writings.

A second area of exclusion is passing mention of any of these authors in books or articles. Briefer comments have only been listed when there is a particular attempt to focus upon the writer in question and her specific literary achievements, along with some analysis of these achievements. Simple, in passing remarks have not merited listing.

There is always some question whether to list dissertation materials. In the cases of Bullrich and Lynch, critical attention is recent enough that book-length studies are few or none as yet. In view of this circumstance, it seems fitting to include dissertations as indicative of more extended consideration to come. Lispector, however, is a longstanding topic of Brazilian literary discussion. Her work has received book-length commentary from such established figures as Assis Brasil and Benedito Nunes. Castellanos' writings are more recently rising to such major status. Consequently, one could expect dissertation material of sufficiently widespread interest to appear in the journal articles and discussion in books.

The women authors in this study are all frequent subjects of interviews. Many of these conversations are about personal, political or general cultural matters rather than the literary production of the subject. In this listing, interviews have only been included if they appear in a major publication and have direct bearing on the analysis of the author's work.

To sum up, my goal has been to provide listings of materials that are relatively accessible to interested readers and that make a significant comment upon the work of the four women authors.

Guide to Abbreviations Used in Bibliography

Bs. As.	Buenos Aires
M	Mexico City
ALetM	*Anuario de letras*
BBib	*Boletín bibliográfico*
BA	*Books Abroad*
CA	*Cuadernos americanos*
CBA	*Cuadernos de Bellas Artes*
CHA	*Cuadernos hispanoamericanos*
DAI	*Dissertation Abstracts International*
ICACH	Instituto de Ciencias y Artes de Chiapas
LAD	*Latin American Digest*
LALR	*Latin American Literary Review*
LARR	*Latin American Research Review*
LFem	*Letras femeninas*
MGSL	*Minas Gerais suplemento literário*
N	*Norte* (Amsterdam)
PH	*La palabra y el hombre*
PPNWCFL	*Proceedings of the Pacific Northwest Conference on Foreign Languages*
RBMex	*Recent Books in Mexico*
RBA	*Revista mexicana de literatura*
RCLL	*Revista de crítica literaria latinoamericana*
REH	*Revista de estudios hispánicos* (Alabama)
RI	*Revista iberoamericana*
RML	*Revista mexicana de literatura*
RUM	*Revista de la Universidad de México*
UNAM	Universidad Nacional Autónoma de México
VidaL	*Vida y letras*

Lispector, Clarice (1924-1977)

BIBLIOGRAPHY

Fitz, Earl E. "Bibliografía de y sobre Clarice Lispector." *RI*, No. 126 (1984), 293-304.

CRITICAL MONOGRAPHS

Borelli. Olga. *Clarice Lispector, esboco para um possivel retrato.* Rio: Nova Fronteira, 1981.
Brasil, Assis. *Clarice Lispector.* Rio: Simões, 1969.
Nunes. Benedito. *O mundo de Clarice Lispector.* Manaus· Edicões do Governo de Estado, 1966.
. *Leitura de Clarice Lispector.* São Paulo: Quirón, 1974.
Pereira. Teresinha *Estudo sôbre Clarice Lispector.* Coimbra: Nova Era. 1975.
Sá, Olga de. *A escritura de Clarice Lispector.* Petrópolis: Vozes, 1979.

ARTICLES AND DISCUSSION IN BOOKS

|Aguiar|, Adonias Filho. "O conto e o monólogo." In his *Modernos ficcionistas brasileiros.* 2nd ser. Rio: Tempo Brasileiro, 1965, pp. 81-82.
Baden, Nancy T. "Clarice Lispector." In *A Dictionary of Contemporary Brazilian Authors.* Ed. David William Foster and Roberto Reis. Tempe: Center for Latin American Studies. 1982. pp. 73-74.
Bruno, Haroldo. "Solilóquio de Clarice Lispector sobre o ser." In his *Novos estudos de literatura brasileira.* Rio: Josè Olympio/Instituto Nacional do Livro, 1980, pp. 12-20.
Castellanos, Rosario. "Clarice Lispector: la memoria ancestral." In her *Mujer que sabe latin...*M: SepSetentas. 1973. pp. 127-30.
Castro. Silvio. *A revolução da palavra.* Petrópolis: Vozes, 1976. pp. 263-67.
Cook. Bruce. "Women in the Web." *Review 73,* (Spring 1973). 65-66.
Costa Lima, Luis. "Clarice Lispector." In *A literatura no Brasil.* Ed. Afrânio Coutinho. 2nd ed. Rio: Sul Americana, 1970, V, pp. 468-72.
."A mística ao revés de Clarice Lispector." In his *Por quê literatura.* Petrópolis: Vozes, 1966, p. 100.
. "O modernismo na ficção." In *A literatura no Brasil.* Ed. Afrânio Coutinho. 2nd ed. Rio: Sul Americana, 1970. V, pp. 468-72.
Coutinho, Edilberto. "Uma mulher chamada Clarice Lispector." In his *Criaturas de papel.* Rio de Janeiro: Civilização Brasileira, 1980, pp. 165-70.
Fitz, Earl E. "Clarice Lispector and the Lyrical Novel: A Re-examination of *A maçã no escuro.*" *Luso-Brazilian Review,* 14, 2 (1977), 153-60.
. "Freedom and Self-realization: Feminist Characterization in the Fiction of Clarice Lispector." *Modern Language Studies,* 10, 3 (1980), 51-61.
. "The Leitmotiv of Darkness in Seven Novels by Clarice Lispector." *Chasqui,* 8, 2 (1977), 18-27.
Gilio, María Ester. "Mis libros son mis cachorros." *Crisis* |Bs. As.|, No. 59 (1976), 41-44.
Goldman, Richard Franko. Review of Lispector's *The Apple in the Dark.* *Saturday Review,* 19 August 1967, 47-48.
Guimarães Hill, Amariles, prologue and annotations, and Renato Cordeiro

Gomes, selection and arrangement of materials. *Seleta de Clarice Lispector* (passages from her works with commentary). Brasilia: Instituto Nacional do Livro/Ministério da Educação e Cultura, 1975.

Hecker Filho, Paulo. "Clarice Lispector/alguns contos." In his *A alguma verdade*. Porto Alegre, 1952. Vol I, pp. 94-95.

Helena, Lúcia. "*Aprendizagem* de Clarice Lispector." *Littera*, 5, 13 (1975), 99-104.

Herman, Rita. "Existence in *Laços de família*." *Luso-Brazilian Review*, 4, 1 (1967), 67-74.

Jozef. Bella. "Chronology." *Review*. No. 24 (1979). 24-26.

_____. "Clarice Lispector: la recuperación de la palabra poética." *RI*, No. 126 (1984), 239-57.

_____. "Clarice Lispector: la transgresión como acto de libertad." *RI*, Nos. 98-99 (1977), 20-27.

Lindstrom, Naomi. "Clarice Lispector: Articulating Women's Experience." *Chasqui*, 8, 1 (1978), 43-52.

_____. "A Discourse Analysis of 'Preciosidade' by Clarice Lispector." *Luso-Brazilian Review*, 19, 2 (1982), 187-94.

_____. "Feminist Discourse Analysis of 'Amor' by Clarice Lispector." *LALR*, 9, 19 (1982), 7-16.

Linhares, Temístocles. "Clarice Lispector e sua experiência." In his *22 diálogos sobre o conto brasileiro atual*. Rio: José Olympio, 1973, pp. 117-20.

Lins, Alvaro. "Clarice Lispector." In his *Os mortos de Sobrecasaca*. Rio: Civilização Brasileira, 1963, pp. 186-93.

Lorenz, Günter W. *Die zeitgenössische Literatur in Lateinamerika*. Tübingen: Horst Erdmann, 1971. p. 250.

Lowe, Elizabeth. "The Passion According to C. L." *Review*, No. 24 (1979), pp. 24-37.

Lucas. Fábio. "Guimarães Rosa e Clarice Lispector: mito e ideologia." MGSL, 26 August, 1972, No. 313, 4-5.

_____. Lispector discussion in *Contemporary Latin American Literature*. Ed. Harvey L. Johnson and Phillip B. Taylor. Houston: University of Houston, Office of International Affairs, 1973, pp. 64-66.

Martins, Wilson. "O romance brasileiro contemporâneo." *Inti*, No. 3 (1976), 27-36.

Millet, Sérgio. "Clarice Lispector." In his *Diário Crítico*. São Paulo: Brasilense, 1955, Vol. 8, pp. 235-37.

Moisés, Massaud. "Clarice Lispector: ficção e cosmovisão." *Humboldt*, 11, 23 (1971), 49-53.

_____. "Clarice Lispector: Fiction and Cosmic Vision." Trans. Sara McCabe. *Studies in Short Fiction*, 7, 1 (1971), 268-81.

_____. Lispector commentary in his *Temas brasileiros*. São Paulo: Conselho Estadual de Cultura, 1964, pp. 119-24.

Nunes, Benedito. "O mundo imaginário de Clarice Lispector." In his *O dorso do tigre*. São Paulo: Perspectiva, 1969, pp. 93-139.

Nunes. Maria Luisa. "Narrative Modes in Clarice Lispector's *Lacos de família*: The Rendering of Consciousness." *Luso-Brazilian Review*, 14, 2 (1977), 174-84.

132

_____ . "Clarice Lispector: artista andrógina ou escritora?" *RI*, No. 126 (1984), 239-57.

Patai, Daphne. "Clarice Lispector and the Clamor of the Ineffable." *Kentucky Romance Quarterly*, 27, 2 (1980), 133-57.

Pereira, Teresinha. "Coincidencia de la técnica narrativa de Julio Cortázar y Clarice Lispector." *Nueva narrativa hispanoamericana*, 3, 1 (1973), 102-111.

Perez, Reynard. In his *Escritores brasileiros*, 2nd ser. Rio: Civilização Brasileira, 1964, pp. 69-76.

Pontiero, Giovanni. "The drama of existence in *Laços de família*." *Studies in Short Fiction*, 7, 1 (1971), 256-67.

_____ . "Introduction." *Review*, No. 24 (1979), 37-38.

_____ . "Testament of Experience: Some Reflections on Clarice Lispector's Last Narrative *A hora da estrela*." *Ibero Amerikanisches Archiv*, 10, 1 (1984), 13-22.

_____ . Preface to *Family Ties*, his translation of *Laços de família*. Austin: University of Texas Press, 1972, pp. 13-23.

Rodriguez Monegal, Emir. "The Contemporary Brazilian Novel." In *Fiction in Several Languages*. Ed. Henri Peyre. Boston: Beacon, 1969, p. 15.

_____ . Lispector discussion in *Borzoi Anthology of Latin American Literature*. Ed. Monegal and Thomas Colchie. New York: Knopf, 1978, p. 77.

_____ . "Clarice Lispector en sus libros y en mi recuerdo." *RI*, No. 126 (1984), 231-28.

Sá, Olga de. "Clarice Lispector: processos criativos." *RI*, No. 126 (1984), 259-80.

Sant' Anna, Affonso Romano de "O relatório do mistério." *MGSL*. 6-XXII-74, No. 408, 11.

Seniff, Dennis. "Self Doubt in Clarice Lispector's *Laços de família*." *Luso-Brazilian Review*, 14, 2 (1977), 161-73.

Silveira, Alcântara. "Renovação de Francisco Alves." In his *Excitantes e relaxantes*. São Paulo: Conselho Estadual de Cultura, 1970, pp. 129-31.

Silverman, Malcolm. "A ficção brasileira. Rio: Civilização Brasileira, 1979, pp. 70-84.

Youssef Campedelli, Samira, and Benjamim Abdala, Jr., eds. *Clarice Lispector, antologia comentada*. São Paulo: Abril, 1981.

Zaguri, Eliane. "Clarice Lispector e o conto psicológico brasileiro." In her *A palavra e os ecos*. Petrópolis: Vozes, 1971, pp. 20-27.

Castellanos, Rosario (1925-1974)

CRITICAL MONOGRAPHS

Ahern, Maureen, and Mary Vásquez, eds. *Homenaje a Rosario Castellanos*. Valencia: Estudios de Hispanófila, 1980. Individual essays are listed below.

Baptiste, Víctor N. *La obra poética de Rosario Castellanos.* Santiago de Chile: Exégesis, 1972.

Calderón, Germaine. *El universo poético* de Rosario Castellanos. Mexico City: UNAM, 1979.

Reyes Venares, Beatriz. *Rosario Castellanos.* M: Secretaría de la Presidencia, Departamento Editorial, 1976.

ARTICLES AND DISCUSSION IN BOOKS

Ahern, Maureen. "A Critical Bibliography Of and About the Works of Rosario Castellanos." In *Homenaje a Rosario Castellanos.* Ed. Ahern and Mary Vásquez. pp. 121-74.

Anderson, Helene M. "Rosario Castellanos and the Structures of Power." In *Contemporary Women Authors of Latin America: Introductory Essays.* Ed. Doris Meyer and Margarite Fernández-Olmos. Brooklyn: Brooklyn College, 1983, pp. 22-32.

Arellano, Jesús. "Las ventas de don Quixote: revisión de algunos nombres de la literatura mexicana. La obra de Rosario Castellanos." *Nivel,* No. 42 (1962), 2-4.

Beer, Gabriella de. "Feminismo en la obra poética de Rosario Castellanos." *RCLL,* No. 13 (1981), 105-111.

Benedetti, Mario. "Rosario Castellanos y la incomunicación racial." In his *Letras del continente mestizo.* 2nd ed. Montevideo: Arca, 1969 (orig. 1967), pp. 165-70.

Brushwood, John S. *The Spanish American Novel: A Twentieth Century Survey.* Austin: University of Texas Press, 1975, pp. 237-38.

_____. *Mexico In Its Novel: A Nation's Search for Identity.* Austin: University of Texas Press, 1966, p. 36.

Campo de Gómez, Aurora R., and Ernesto Prado Velásquez. "Rosario Castellanos." In their *Diccionario de escritores mexicanos.* Mexico City: UNAM, 1967, pp. 68-70.

Campos, Jorge. "Novelas e ideas de Rosario Castellanos." *Insula,* No. 211 (1964), 11.

Carballo, Emmanuel. "Rosario Castellanos." In his *Diecinueve protagonistas de la literatura mexicana del siglo XX.* Mexico City: Empresas Editoriales, 1965, 409-24.

Carreno, Mada. *Album de familia, Justine* y el ángel." *VidaL.* No. 30 (1972), 12-13.

Castro, Dolores. *"Balún-Canán."* *PH,* No. 7 (1958), 33-36.

_____. "Rosario Castellanos." *Nivel,* No. 12 (1959), 3.

Castro Leal, Antonio. "Dos poemas dramáticos [en] *Poesía no eres tú* ['Judith' y 'Salomé']." *VidaL,* No. 30 (1972), 5-6.

El centavo, No. 56 (1964), entire issue.

Cresta de Leguizamón, María Luisa. "En recuerdo de Rosario Castellanos." *PH,* No. 19 (1976), 3-18.

134

Domínguez, Luis Adolfo. "Entrevista con Rosario Castellanos." *RBA*, No. 25 (1969), 16-23.

Durán, Manuel. "In memoriam: Jaimes Torres Bodet, Salvador Novo, Rosario Castellanos." *RI*, No. 90 (1975), 79-83.

Fox-Lockert, Lucía. "Rosario Castellanos: *Balún-Canán* (1957)." In her *Women Novelists in Spain and Spanish America*. Metuchen, N. J.: Scarecrow Press, 1979, pp. 202-15.

Franco, Jean. *The Modern Culture of Latin America*. Rev. ed. Middlesex, England: Penguin, 1970, pp. 124-25.

Fuentes, Aquiles. "Escritores contemporáneos." *LvP*, 17, 19 (1955), 53-58.

García-Barragán, Guadalupe. "Rosario Castellanos en la novela y el cuento indigenistas." *PPNWCFL*, 20 (1969), 113-20.

Godoy, Emma. "Rosario Castellanos." *Abside*, 39 (1975), 350-54.

González, Alfonso. "La soledad y los patrones del dominio en la cuentística de Rosario Castellanos." In *Homenaje a Rosario Castellanos*. Ed. Ahern and Vásquez. pp. 107-113.

_____. "Lenguaje y protesta en *Oficio de tinieblas*." *REH*, 9 (1975), 441-450.

González Guerrero, Francisco. "Rosario Castellanos: *De la vigilia estéril*." In his *En torno a la literatura mexicana*. M: SepSetentas, 1976, pp. 179-84.

Guillén, Pedro. "Rosario la de Chiapas." *VidaL*, 30 (1972), 14-15.

Jozef, Bella. "Rosario Castellanos: o resgate dos mitos eternos." *MGSL*, 7-XXI-1974, p. 2.

Langford, Walter M. "Rosario Castellanos (1925)." In his *The Mexican Novel Comes of Age*. Notre Dame, Indiana: University of Notre Dame Press, 1971, pp. 182-85.

Leiva, Raúl. "*Oficio de tinieblas*." *Nivel*, No. 48 (1962), 3.

_____. "Rosario Castellanos (1925)." In his *Imagen de la poesía mexicana contemporánea*. Mexico City: UNAM. Centro de Estudios Literarios. 1959, pp.333-41.

_____. "Tres grandes novelas mexicanas en 1962." *CBA*, 4, 1 (1963), 25, 28-31.

Lindstrom, Naomi. "Narrative Technique and Women's Expression in a Novel by Rosario Castellanos." *Modern Language Studies*, 8, 3 (1983), 71-80.

_____. "Rosario Castellanos: Pioneer of Feminist Criticism." In *Homenaje a Rosario Castellanos*. Ed. Ahern and Vásquez. pp. 65-73.

Lorenz, Günter. "Rosario Castellanos." In his *Diálogo con América Latina*. Santiago de Chile: Editorial Pomaire, 1972, pp. 185-211. Originally published in his *Dialog mit Latein-amerika*. Tübingen und Basel: Horst Erdmann, 1970, pp. 275-315.

Macdonald, Regina Harrison. "Rosario Castellanos: On Language." In *Homenaje a Rosario Castellanos*. Ed. Ahern and Vásquez. pp. 41-64.

Millán, María del Carmen. "En torno a *Oficio de tinieblas*." *ALetM*, 3 (1963), 287-99.

_____. "Tres escritoras mexicanas del siglo XX." *CA*, No. 202 (1975),

163-81. (María Enriqueta Camarillo de Pereyra, Concha Uriquiza Rosario Castellanos).

Miller, Beth. "El feminismo mexicano de Rosario Castellanos." In her *Mujeres en la literatura*. M: Fleischer, 1978, pp. 9-19.

_____."Historia y ficción en *Oficio de tinieblas.*" *Texto Crítico*, No. 28 (1984), 131-42.

_____."Personajes y personas: Castellanos, Fuentes, Poniatowska y Sainz." In her *Mujeres en la literatura*. M: Fleischer, 1978, pp. 65-75.

_____."La poesía de Rosario Castellanos: tono y tenor." *Diálogos* [M], No. 74 (1977), 28-31.

_____. "The Poetry of Rosario Castellanos: Tone and Tenor." In *Homenaje a Rosario Castellanos*. Ed. Ahern and Vásquez. pp. 75-83.

_____. "The Poetry of Rosario Castellanos: Tone and Tenor." *Proceedings of the Pacific Coast Council of Latin American Studies*, 6 (1977-79), 49-57.

_____. "Rosario Castellanos' *Guests in August*: Critical Realism and the Provincial Middle Class." *LALR*, No. 14 (1979), 5-19.

_____. "Voz e imagen en la obra de Rosario Castellanos." *RUM*, 30, 4-5 (1975-76), 33-38.

_____, and Alfonso González. "Rosario Castellanos." In their *Veintiséis autoras del México actual*. M: Costa-Amic, 1978, pp. 115-38.

Moirón, Sara. "Rosario Castellanos." *PH*, No. 11 (1974), 17-18.

Murúa, Rita. "Oficio de tinieblas." *RML*, Nos. 3-4 (1963), 62-63.

Nigro, Kirsten F. "Rosario Castellanos' Debunking of the *Eternal Feminine*." *Journal of Spanish Studies: Twentieth Century*, 8, 1-2 (1980), pp. 89-102.

Nivel, No. 30 (1961), entire issue.

O'Quinn, Kathleen. " 'Tablero de damas' and 'Album de familia': Farces on Women Writers." In *Homenaje a Rosario Castellanos*. Ed. Ahern and Vásquez, pp. 99-105.

Pacheco, José Emilio. "Rosario Castellanos o la rotunda austeridad de la poesía." *VidaL*, No. 30 (1972), 8-11.

Paley Francescato, Martha. "Transgresión y apertura en los cuentos de Rosario Castellanos." In *Homenaje a Rosario Castellanos*. Ed. Ahern and Vásquez, pp. 115-120.

Passafari, Clara. "Rosario Castellanos y 'El ciclo de Chiapas'." In her *Los cambios en la concepción y estructura de la narrativa mexicana desde 1947*. Rosario, Argentina: Universidad Nacional del Litoral, Facultad de Filosofía, 1968, pp. 171-87.

Plaza, Dolores. "El culto a 'los otros' en la obra de Rosario Castellanos." *PH*, No. 11 (1974), 13-15.

Poniatowska, Elena. "Rosario Castellanos: las líneas de la vigilia." *La gaceta* [Mexico], No. 165 (1984), 98-103. Also as foreword to Julián Palley, ed. *Meditación en el umbral*. M: Fondo de Cultura Económica, 1975, xi-xx.

Portal, Marta. "Narrativa indigenista mexicana de mediados de siglo." *CHA*, No. 298 (1975), 196-207.

136

Rivero, Eliana. "Visión social y feminista en la obra poética de Rosario Castellanos." In *Homenaje a Rosario Castellanos*. Ed. Ahern and Vásquez, pp. 85-97.

Robles Sasso, Daniel. "Rosario Castellanos." *ICACH*, No. 13 (1964), 5-8.

Rodríguez Chicharro, César. "Rosario Castellanos: *Balún-Canán.*" *PH*, No. 9 (1959), 61-67.

Rodríguez-Peralta, Phyllis. "Images of Women in Rosario Castellanos' Prose." *LALR*, No. 11 (1977), 68-80.

_____. "Rosario Castellanos." In *Los narradores ante el público*. M: Joaquín Mortiz, 1966-67, I, pp. 87-98.

Rosser, Harry L. "The Structure and Psyche of Provincial Society in Transition: Magdaleno, Fuentes, Galindo, Castellanos." In his *Conflict and Transition in Rural Mexico*. Boston: Crossroads Press, 1980, pp. 119-60.

Schlau, Stacy. "Conformity and Resistance to Enclosure: Female Voices in Rosario Castellanos' *Oficio de tinieblas.*" *LALR*, 7, 24 (1984), 45-57.

Selva, Mauricio de la. "*[Balún-Canán]*." *CA*, No. 97 (1958), 272-73.

Shedd, Margaret. "On Rosario Castellanos." *RBMex*, 7, 5 (1960), 3; 8, 5 (1961), pp. 6-11.

Sierra, Carlos J. "Silueta de Rosario Castellanos. *BBib*, No. 500 (1974), 10-13.

Silva Villalobos, Antonio. "La poesía de Rosario Castellanos." *Metáfora*, No. 19 (1958), 3-9. Also *Nivel*, No. 30 (1961), 2, 5.

Sommers, Joseph. "Changing View of the Indian in Mexican Literature." *Hispania*, 47 (1964), 47-55.

_____. "El ciclo de Chiapas: nueva corriente literaria." *CA*, 133 (1964), 246-61.

_____. "Forma e ideología en *Oficio de tinieblas* de Rosario Castellanos." *RCLL*, Nos. 7-8 (1978), 73-91.

_____. "The Indian-Oriented Novel in Latin America: New Spirit, New Forms, New Scope." *Journal of Inter-American Studies*, 6 (1964), 249-65.

_____. "Rosario Castellanos." In his *After the Storm: Landmarks of the Modern Mexican Novel*. Albuquerque: University of New Mexico, 1968, pp. 83-88.

_____. "Rosario Castellanos: nuevo enfoque del indio mexicano." *PH*, No. 29 (1964), 83-88.

Speratti Piñero, Emma Susana. "*Balún-Canán.*" *RUM*, 12, 5 (1958), 30.

Urbano, Victoria E. "La justicia femenina de Rosario Castellanos." *LFem*, 1, 2 (1975), 9-20.

Vásquez, Mary. "Rosario Castellanos, Image and Idea (An Introduction to *Homenaje a Rosario Castellanos*)." In *Homenaje a Rosario Castellanos*. Ed. Ahern and Vásquez, pp. 15-40.

Xirau, Ramón. "The New Poetry of Mexico—Rosario Castellanos." *RBMex*, 10, 3 (1963), 1-2.

Lynch, Marta (1930-1985)

CRITICAL MONOGRAPHS AND DISSERTATIONS

Billman, Lynne Lois. *The Political Novels of Lucila Palacios and Marta Lynch.* Diss: Catholic University, Washington D.C., 1976.

Kaminsky, Amy Katz. *Marta Lynch: The Expanding Political Consciousness of an Argentine Woman Writer.* Diss: Pennsylvania State, 1976.

Shaw, Lee Roberts. *The Feminine Principle in a Masculine World: A Study of Contemporary Argentine Fiction by Women Writers.* Diss: University of Tennessee, 1978.

ARTICLES AND DISCUSSION IN BOOKS

Cornejo Polar, Antonio. *"Los dedos de la mano." RCLL*, No. 3 (1976), 114-15.

Díaz, Gwendolyn. "Estudio preliminar." In *Páginas de Marta Lynch seleccionadas por la autora.* Buenos Aires: Celtia, 1983, pp. 11-40.

Foster, David William. "Marta Lynch: The Individual and the Argentine Political Process." *LAD*, 13, 3 (1979), 8-9.

Goldar, Ernesto. *El peronismo en la literatura argentina.* Buenos Aires: Freeland, 1971, pp. 46, 55, 59-60, 103-104, 145 on Lynch.

Herrera, Francisco. "Marta Lynch." In *Enciclopedia de la literatura argentina.* Ed. Pedro Orgambide and Roberto Yahni. Buenos Aires: Sudamericana, 1970, pp. 406-407.

Kaminsky, Amy Katz. "The Real Circle of Iron: Mothers and Children, Children and Mothers, in Four Argentine Novels." *LALR*, 4, 9 (1976), 19-26.

Lewald, H. Ernest. "Aspects of the Modern Argentine Woman." *Chasqui*, 5, 3, 1 (1976), 19-26.

_____. "Marta Lynch." In his anthology *The Web: Stories by Argentine Women.* Washington, DC: Three Continents Press, 1983, pp. 83-84.

_____. "Two Generations of River Plate Women Writers." *LARR*, 15, 1 (1980), 231-36.

Lindstrom, Naomi. "The Literary Feminism of Marta Lynch." *Critique*, 20, 2 (1978), 49-58.

_____. "Woman's Voice in the Short Stories of Marta Lynch." In *The Contemporary Latin American Short Story.* Ed. Rose S. Minc. Montclair, NJ: Senda Nueva de Ediciones, 1978, pp. 148-53.

Lynch, Marta. "Con mi obra." *Hispamérica*, 3, 7 (1974), 61-64.

Paley de Francescato, Martha. "Marta Lynch." *Hispamérica*, No. 10 (1975), 33-44.

Phillips, Katherine Kayper. "Marta Lynch." In *A Dictionary of Contemporary Latin American Authors.* Ed. David William Foster. Tempe: Center for Latin American Studies, 1975, p. 61.

Viñas, David. "Un viaje contradictorio: de *Los premios* a *Rayuela*. Y también: Marta Lynch, Daniel Devoto y Vanni Blengino." In his *Literatura argentina y realidad política: de Sarmiento a Cortázar*. rev. ed. Buenos Aires: Siglo Veinte, 1971, pp. 199-202.

Bullrich, Silvina (b. 1915)

DISSERTATIONS AND THESES

Birkmore, Diane Solomon. *Contemporary Women Novelists of Argentina (1945-67)*. Diss: University of Illinois, 1968. Bullrich inter alios.

Shaw, Les Roberts. *The Feminine Principle in a Masculine World: A Study of Contemporary Argentine Fiction by Women Writers*. Diss: University of Tennessee, 1978.

Tusa, Bobs McElroy. *The Work of Silvina Bullrich*. Thesis: Tulane University, 1972.

ARTICLES AND DISCUSSION IN BOOKS

Cócaro, Nicolás. "Estudio preliminar." In *Páginas de Silvina Bullrich, seleccionadas por la autora*. Buenos Aires: Celtia, 1983, pp. 11-22.

_____. "La pequeña comedia humana en la obra de Silvina Bullrich." In his anthology *Silvina Bullrich*. Buenos Aires: Ediciones Culturales Argentinas, 1979, pp. 11-23.

Frouman-Smith, Erica. "Entrevista con Silvina Bullrich." *Chasqui*, 8, 2 (1979), 37-46.

_____. "The Paradoxes of Silvina Bullrich." In *Contemporary Women Authors of Latin America: Introductory Essays*. Ed. Doris Meyer and Margarite Fernández Olmos. Brooklyn: Brooklyn College, 1983, pp. 58-71.

Goldar, Ernesto. *El peronismo en la literatura argentina*. Buenos Aires: Freeland, 1970, pp. 105-106.

Herrera, Francisco. "Silvina Bullrich." In *Enciclopedia de la literatura argentina*. Ed. Pedro Orgambide and Roberto Yahni. Buenos Aires: Sudamericana, 1970, pp. 105-106.

Kaminsky, Amy Katz. "The Real Circle of Iron: Mothers and Children, Children and Mothers in Four Argentine Novels." *LALR*, 4, 9 (1976), 77-86.

Lewald, H. Ernest. "Aspects of the Modern Argentine Woman." *Chasqui*, 5, 3 (1976), 19-25.

_____. "Silvina Bullrich." In his *Escritores platenses: ficciones del siglo XX*. New York: Houghton-Mifflin, 1971, pp. 20-21.

_____. "Silvina Bullrich." In his *Diez cuentistas argentinas*. Buenos Aires: Riomar, 1968, p. 8.

_____. "Silvina Bullrich." In his anthology *The Web: Stories by Argentine Women*. Washington, DC: Three Continents Press, 1983, pp. 35-36.

_____. "Two Generations of River Plate Women Writers." *LARR*, 15, 1 (1980), 231-32.

Lindstrom, Naomi. "Sex Role Analysis and Best Seller Conventions in a Novel by Silvina Bullrich." *REH*, 17, 2 (1983), 227-38.

Mathieu, Corina. "Argentine Women in the Novels of Silvina Bullrich." *Letras Femeninas*, 6, 1 (1980), 3-13.

Phillips, Katherine Kayper. "Silvina Bullrich." In *A Dictionary of Contemporary Latin American Authors*. Ed. David William Foster. Tempe: Center for Latin American Studies, 1975, p. 21.

Reyes García, Ismael. Note on Bullrich, *Será justicia*, *REH* [Río Piedras, PR], No. 4 (1977), 105-107.

Selva, Mauricio de la. "Silvina Bullrich: *Los burgueses*." *Cuadernos americanos*, No. 23 (1964), 287-89.

Tusa, Bobs M. "A Structural Analysis of *Los burgueses* by Silvina Bullrich." *Hispanófila*, 54 (1975), 51-60.

Selected Bibliography of Primary Sources:
Writings of the Four Women Authors

Criteria of Selection

These four bibliographies have been assembled to aid the reader seeking access to copies of the author's creative writings and important essays. To suit this purpose, two related criteria of selection have been applied: significance and accessibility.

As have many writers, these authors have been participants in writing and publishing projects of an ephemeral character. Journalistic activity, including rather routine and pedestrian newspaper and magazine writing, has been a constant in all four women's careers. In addition, they have published detailed answers to survey questions, statements on literary and social questions, rejoinders and rebuttals to criticism, press releases and open letters.

To list the original periodical sources for these writings would not be useful in the present context. Beyond the difficulty of obtaining these materials in the U.S., one must consider that much of the writing is only of interest for a particular time and place. Moreover, the best of this journalistic production is very likely to find its way into books, such as Castellanos' distinguished *El uso de la palabra* (*Speaking Up*). Lispector and Bullrich have also published collections of their most worthwhile journalistic essays. Lynch published only one such work—her traveler's sketches in *Apuntes para un libro de viajes* (*Notes for a Travel Book.*) Lynch's typical practice was to elaborate her social concerns in newspaper and magazine writings, then to give the same subject-matter a polished literary elaboration in her fiction.

As well as excluding uncollected journalism, I have omitted most literary writing of an occasional nature. These writers have been invited to write matter for particular literary events. For instance, Castellanos prefaced a new edition of Saint Theresa's autobiography, and Lynch was part of a collective project in which several writers experimented with the same crime story. Such endeavors are indicative principally of the authors' ongoing involvement in literary activity, but tend to result in "made-to-order" texts not characteristic of their finest work.

Also excluded are: translations into languages other than English; the author's own work as translation; and children's books, other than three excellent and well-known examples by Lispector. Short fiction in periodical sources has not been listed because of the degree to which this work has been included in book format, often in a refined definitive version.

Bullrich's literary production presents a special case. While early editions of her first works are difficult to obtain, she has made a massive effort to republish these writings with major presses and to obtain a better distribution and promotion for them. A note prefacing the Bullrich bibliography explains the handling of this particular situation.

Because the bibliographies are selective rather than exhaustive, I have supplemented each with a reference to the source of the most complete bibliographic listing available on that author.

Silvina Bullrich [Palenque]: A Bibliography of Her Works

Note: Although Silvina Bullrich is now Argentina's best-selling author, she initially experienced difficulty in obtaining adequate publication and distribution of her work. During the late thirties and early forties, many times her writing went unpublished or was poorly distributed by private or obscure publishers. After her rocognition came, the author carefully oversaw the republication, or first printing, of these neglected works in accessible editions. The 1970 volume *Entre mis veinte y treina años (When I Was In My Twenties)* is explicitly dedicated to establishing available versions of early writings.

Because of this circumstance, the unavailable editions and manuscripts will not be listed separately, but under the entry for more readily obtainable editions. Brief annotations provide information about the circumstances involved. Only the two early works that the author has not brought back into circulation are given independent listings.

La aventura interior [The adventure within]. Buenos Aires, Merlín, 1970. Essay.

La aventura interior. Buenos Aires: Emecé, 1977.

Bodas de cristal [Crystal anniversary]. Buenos Aires: Sudamericana, 1959. Novel, composed 1951.

Los burgueses [The bourgeois]. Buenos Aires: Sudamericana, 1965. Novel.

El calor humano [Human warmth]. Buenos Aires: Merlín, 1970. Novel.

Calles de Buenos Aires [Streets of Buenos Aires]. Buenos Aires: Emecé, 1979. Reissue of Bullrich's first novel, originally published privately 1939, then made generally available in her *Entre mis veinte y treinta años*, listed here.

Carta a un joven cuentista [Letter to a young short story writer]. Buenos Aires: Santiago Rueda, 1968. Essay.

El compadrito, su destino, sus barrios, su música [The gangster: his fate, his home turf, his music]. Buenos Aires: Emecé, 1945. Anthology compiled in collaboration with Jorge Luis Borges.

El compadrito, su destino, sus barrios, su música. Buenos Aires: Fabril, 1968.

La creciente [The flood]. Buenos Aires: Sudamericana, 1967. Novel.

Los despiadados [The merciless]. Buenos Aires: Emecé, 1978. Novel.

Después del escándalo [After the scandal]. Buenos Aires: Emecé, 1981. Novel.

Entre mis veinte y treinta años [When I was in my twenties]. Buenos Aires: Emecé, 1971. Collection of Bullrich's writings 1935-40.

Escándalo bancario [Banking scandal]. Buenos Aires: Emecé, 1980. Novel.

Flora Tristán, la visionaria [Flora Tristan, the visionary]. Buenos Aires: Riesa Ediciones, 1982. Biography.

George Sand: una mujer como yo [George Sand: a woman like myself]. Buenos Aires: Emecé, 1946. Fictionalized biography.

El hechicero [The spellbinder]. Buenos Aires: Editorial Goyanarte, 1961. Novel.

Historia de un silencio [Story of a silence]. Caracas: Monte Avila, 1976. Novel. Accessible edition of 1949 publication by Medina del Río.

Historias inmorales [Immoral stories]. Buenos Aires: Sudamericana, 1965. Short stories.

Un hombre con historia [A man with a past]. Buenos Aires: Merlín, 1973. Long short story.

Mal don [The loser]. Buenos Aires: Emecé, 1973. Novel.

Mañana digo basta [Tomorrow I'll tell them I've had it]. Buenos Aires: Sudamericana, 1968. Novel.

Mis memorias [My memoirs]. Buenos Aires: Emecé, 1980.

Mientras los demás viven [While the others live]. Buenos Aires: Sudamericana, 1958. Novel.

Un momento muy largo [A very long moment]. Buenos Aires: Sudamericana, 1961. Novel.

Los monstruos sagrados [The sacred monsters]. Buenos Aires: Sudamericana, 1971. Novel.

La mujer argentina en la literatura [The Argentine woman in literature]. Buenos Aires: Centro Nacional de Documentación e Información Educativa, 1972. Essay.

La mujer postergada [The woman who didn't get her turn]. Buenos Aires: Sudamericana, 1982. Novel.

El mundo que yo vi [The world I saw]. Buenos Aires: Merlín, 1969. Essay.

El mundo que yo vi: documentos de época a través de los viajes (1949-1976) [The World I saw: documents of an era through travels (1949-1976)]. Buenos Aires: Emecé, 1976. Essay. Amplification of 1969 work.

Páginas de Silvina Bullrich seleccionadas por la autora [Pages from Silvina Bullrich chosen by the author]. Buenos Aires: Celtia, 1983. Reader.

Los pasajeros del jardín [Those who pass through the garden]. Buenos Aires: Emecé, 1971. Novel.

La redoma del primer ángel, crónica de los años 40 [The breaking of the first angel: chronicle of the 40s]. Buenos Aires: Santiago Rueda, 1967. Reissue of 1943 work.

Reunión de directorio [Board meeting]. Buenos Aires: Emecé, 1977.

Saloma. Buenos Aires: Sudamericana, 1979. Novel. Available edition of work written in 1940.

Los salvadores de la patria [The saviors of the fatherland]. Buenos Aires: Sudamericana, 1965. Novel.

Será justicia [Just deserts]. Buenos Aires: Sudamericana, 1976. Novel. Written 1949; first made available in *Entre mis veinte y treinta años* under original title of *Hágase justicia* [Let justice be done].

Silvina Bullrich. Ed. Nicolás Cócaro. Buenos Aires. Edicones Culturales Argentinas, 1979. Sampler of her work.

Su excelencia envió el informe [His excellency sent the report]. Buenos Aires: Emecé, 1974. Novel.

Su vida y yo [His life and I]. 1941. Novel. Not included in 1970 collection of early work. No available edition.

Te acordarás de Taorima [You will remember Taorima]. Buenos Aires: Emecé, 1975. Novel.

Teléfono ocupado [Busy signal]. Buenos Aires: Emecé, 1955. Short novel.

Teléfono ocupado. Buenos Aires: Goyanarte, 1963.

La tercera versión [The third version]. Buenos Aires: Emecé, 1953. Novel. Reissue of 1944 work.

La tercera versión. Buenos Aires: Santiago Rueda, 1969.

La tercera versión. Buenos Aires: Emecé, 1978.

Tres novelas [Three novels]: *Bodas de cristal, Mientras los demás viven, Un momento muy largo*. Buenos Aires: Sudamericana, 1968.

Vibraciones [Vibrations]. Buenos Aires: 1935. Poetry. Not included in 1970 collection of early works. Privately published.

Sources for Complete Bullrich Bibliography Including Inaccessible Editions

Cócaro, Nicolás, ed. *Silvina Bullrich*. Buenos Aires: Ediciones Culturales Argentinas, p. 146.

Tusa, Bobs McElroy. *The Works of Silvina Bullrich*. Diss. Tulane University, 1972, n.p.

Rosario Castellanos: A Bibliography of Her Works (*Works translated into English)

Al pie de la letra [Taking it literally]. Xalapa, Mexico: Universidad Veracruzana, 1979. Poetry.

Album de familia1 [Family album]. Mexico: Joaquín Mortiz, 1971. Short stories.

Balún-Canán [trans. as *The Nine Guardians*]. Mexico: Fondo de Cultura Económica, 1957. Novel.

Ciudad Real [place name]. Mexico: Novaro, 1974. Short stories.

Los convidados de agosto [Encounter in August]. Mexico: Era, 1964. Short stories.

La corrupción [Corruption]. Mexico: Nuestro Tiempo, 1969. Social criticism by Castellanos and others.

El eterno femenino [The Eternal Feminine]. Mexico: Fondo de Cultura Económica, 1975. Comedy.

The Eternal Feminine. Trans. Diane Marting and Betty Tyree Oziek.
Juicios sumarios [Summary judgments]. Xalapa: Universidad Veracruzana, 1966. Essays.
Lívida luz [Pale light]. Mexico: UNAM, 1960. Poetry.
Looking at the Mona Lisa. Trans. Maureen Ahern. Unpublished. From *Poesía no eres tú*.
El mar y sus pescaditos [The Sea and its little fishes]. Mexico: Secretaría de Educación Pública, 1975. Essays.
Materia memorable [Memorable matter]. Mexico: UNAM, 1969. Poetry.
Meditación en el umbral [Meditation on the threshold]. Ed. Julián Palley. Mexico: Fondo de Cultura Económica, 1985. Reader (poetry).
Mujer que sabe latin... [A Woman who knows Latin...] Mexico: SepSetentas, 1973. Essays.
The Nine Guardians. Trans. Irene Nicholson. New York: Vanguard, 1960. Original title: *Balún-Canán*.
Poemas (1953-55). Mexico: Colección Metáfora, 1957. Poetry.
Poesía no eres tú; obra poética 1948-1971 [Poetry isn't you: poetic work 1948-1971]. Mexico: Fondo de Cultura Económica, 1972. Poetry.
Salomé y Judith; poemas dramáticos [Salomé and Judith: dramatic poems]. Mexico: Editorial Jus, 1959. Poetry.
Tablero de damas [The Ladies' game]. Mexico: Revista América, 1952. Drama.
El uso de la palabra [Speaking Up]. Mexico: Excélsior, 1974. Articles appearing originally in the newspaper *Excélsior* and its supplement *Diorama*.

Source for Complete Listings

Ahern, Maureen, and Mary Vásquez, eds. *Homenaje a Rosario Castellanos* [Homage to Rosario Castellanos]. Valencia: Ediciones de Hispanófila, 1980, pp. 167-175.

Clarice Lispector:
A Bibliography of Her Works
(*Works translated into English)

Agua viva [Running water]. Rio de Janeiro: Artenova, 1973. Mixed-genre work combining fictional and essay-like features.
Alguns contos [Some stories]. Rio de Janeiro: Ministério da Educação e Saúde, 1952. Short stories.
The Apple in the Dark. Trans. Gregory Rabassa. New York: Knopf, 1967, c. 1957. Original title *A maçã no escuro*.
Uma aprendizagem; ou, O livro dos prazeres [An Apprenticeship: or, The Book of Pleasures]. Rio de Janeiro: Sabiá, 1969. Novel.

An Apprenticeship or The Book of Delights. Trans. Richard A. Mazzarra and Lorri A. Parris. Austin, Texas: University of Texas Press, 1986.

A bela e a fera [Beauty and the beast]. Rio de Janeiro: Nova Fronteira, 1979. Novel.

A cidade sitiada [The Beseiged city]. Rio de Janeiro: Editôra A Noite, 1948. Novel.

Clarice Lispector, antologia comentada [Anthology with commentary]. Ed. Samira Youssef Campedelli and Benjamim Abdala, Jr. São Paulo: Abril Editôra, 1981. Reader.

De corpo inteiro [Full-length portrait]. Rio de Janeiro: Artenova, 1975. Interview format.

Family Ties. Trans. Giovanni Pontiero. Austin: University of Texas, 1972.

Felicidade clandestina [Secret Happiness]. Rio de Janeiro: Sabiá, 1971. Short stories.

A hora da estrela. Rio de Janeiro: José Olympio, 1977. Novel.

The Hour of the Star. Trans. Giovanni Pontiero. New York: Carcanet, 1986. Novel. Original title: *A hora da estrela*.

A imitação da rosa [The Imitation of the Rose]. Rio de Janeiro: Artenova, 1973. Short stories.

Laços de família. São Paulo: F. Alves, 1960. Short stories.

Laços de família. Rio de Janeiro: Sabiá, 1970.

Laços de família. Rio de Janeiro: José Olympio, 1978.

A legião estrangeira [The Foreign Legion]. Rio de Janeiro: Editôra do Autor, 1964. Contains short stories and journalistic essays.

O lustre [The Chandelier]. Rio de Janeiro: AGIR, 1946. Novel.

O lustre. Rio de Janeiro: J. Alvaro, 1963.

O lustre. Rio de Janeiro: Paz e Terra, 1976.

A maçã no escuro. Rio de Janeiro: F. Alves, 1961. Novel.

A maçã no escuro. Rio de Janeiro: José Alvaro, 1970.

A maçã no escuro. Rio de Janeiro: Paz e Terra, 1974.

O mistério do coelho pensante [The Mystery of the thinking rabbit]. Rio: J. Alvaro, 1967. Children's fiction.

A mulher que matou os peixes [The Woman who killed the fishes]. Rio de Janeiro: Sabiá, 1968. Children's fiction.

A mulher que matou os peixes. Rio de Janeiro: José Olympio, 1974.

Onde estivestes de noite? [Where were you that night?] Rio de Janeiro: Editôra Artenova, 1974. Short stories.

A paixão segundo G. H. [The Passion according to G. H.] Rio de Janeiro: Editôra do Autor, 1964.

A paixão segundo G. H. Rio de Janeiro: José Olympio, 1974.

Para não esquecer [To Keep from forgetting]. São Paulo: Editôra Atica, 1978.

Perto do coração selvagem [Near the savage heart]. São Paulo: Livraria Francisco Alves, 1963. Novel. Reissue of c. 1944 work.

Perto do coração selvagem. Rio de Janeiro.: José Olympio, 1974.

Quase de verdade [Almost true]. Rio de Janeiro: Roco, 1974. Mixed-genre work.

Seleta de Clarice Lispector [A Clarice Lispector reader]. Comp. Renato Cordeiro Gomes. Essay by Amariles Guimarães Hill. Rio de Janeiro: José Olympio, 1975. Anthology.
Um sopro de vida: pulsações [A Breath of life: pulsations]. Rio de Janeiro: Nova Fronteira, 1978. Mixed-genre work.
A via crucis do corpo [The Via crucis of the body]. Rio de Janeiro: Artenova, 1974. Short stories.
A vida íntima de Laura [The Private life of Laura]. Rio de Janeiro: José Olympio, 1974. Animal story for children.
Visão do esplendor: impressões leves [Vision of splendor: slight impressions]. Rio de Janeiro: F. Alves, 1975. Essays and sketches.

Source for Complete Listings

Cordeiro Gomes, Renato, comp. *Seleta de Clarice Lispector.* Rio de Janeiro: José Olympio, 1975, pp. 148-149.
Fitz, Earl E. "Bibliografía de y sobre Clarice Lispector." *Revista iberoamericana*, No. 126 (1984), 293-304.
Sá, Olga de. *A escritura de Clarice Lispector* [The Writing of Clarice Lispector]. Petrópolis: Vozes, 1979, pp. 382-84.

Marta Lynch
A Bibliography of Her Works

Al vencedor [To the victor]. Buenos Aires: Losada, 1965. Novel.
La alfombra roja [The Red carpet]. Buenos Aires: Fabril, 1962. Novel.
Los años de fuego [The Years of fire]. Buenos Aires: Sudamericana, 1980. Short stories.
Apuntes para un libro de viajes. [Notes for a travel book]. Buenos Aires: Cástor y Pollux, 1977. Essay.
Un árbol lleno de manzanas [A Tree full of apples]. Buenos Aires: Sudamericana, 1974. Novel.
El cruce del río [The River crossing]. Buenos Aires: Sudamericana, 1972. Novel.
Los cuentos de colores [The Colored stories]. Buenos Aires: Sudamericana, 1971.
Los cuentos tristes [The Sad stories]. Buenos Aires: Centro Editor de América Latina, 1967. Short stories.
Los cuentos tristes. Buenos Aires: Merlín, 1971.
Los dedos de la mano [The Fingers of the hand]. Buenos Aires: Sudamericana, 1976. Short stories.
Los dedos de la mano. Madrid: Ediciones Alfaguara, 1977.
Informe bajo llave [Top secret report]. Buenos Aires: Sudamericana, 1983. Novel.

No te duermas, no me dejes [Don't go to sleep, don't leave me]. Buenos Aires: Sudamericana, 1985.

Páginas de Marta Lynch seleccionadas por la autora [Pages from Marta Lynch chosen by the author]. Buenos Aires: Celtia, 1983. Reader.

La penúltima versión de la Colorada Villanueva [The Penultimate version of Colorada Villanueva]. Buenos Aires: Sudamericana, 1978. Novel.

La señora Ordóñez. [Mrs. Ordóñez]. Buenos Aires: Jorge Alvarez, 1967. Novel.

La señora Ordóñez. Buenos Aires: Sudamericana, 1968.

Toda la función; *La despedida* [The Whole show; The Good-bye]. Buenos Aires: Abril, 1982. Two novellas.

Index

Kaminsky, Amy, 5, 19, 94, 113, 125
Kellerman, Owen, 24, 44
Kirkpatrick, Susan, 123
Kirsner, Robert, 125

Laclos, Choderlos de, 9, 11-12, 119
Laforgue, Jules, 2
Lakoff, Robin, 15, 29, 86, 92-93, 95, 116
Laforet, Carmen, 123
Langford, Walter M., 69
Lawrence, D.H., 9
Leal, Luis, 125
Lemaître, Monique, 125
Levine, Linda Gould, 125
Lewald, H. Ernest: on Argentine women writers, 2, 18, 19, 122; on Lynch and Bullrich, 5, 125; on Lynch 94, 95-99; on Bullrich, 6, 100, 113, 114
Lima, Robert, 125
Lindstrom, Naomi, 43, 69, 94, 119
Lins, Alvaro, 43
Lisboa, Henriqueta, 7
Lispector, Clarice: career and literary concern with women, 3-4; analysis of stories from Laços de família, 23-45; compared and contrasted with other authors in study, 17, 112; criticism on, 43-45, 125, 126.
Llamas, María del Refugio, 125
Loos, Anita, 18
López, Yvette, 125
Lorca, Federico, García, 124
Lorenz, Günter, 69
Luchting, Wolfgang, 121
Lynch, Marta: career and interest in women's issues, 5-6, 7, 16-17, 19, 119; analysis of La señora Ordóñez, 73-95; compared and contrasted with Bullrich, 7, 112, 116; criticism on 5, 94-95, (Kaminsky article) 125

Mafud, Julio, 7, 18, 118
Magnarelli, Sharon, 126
Mailer, Norman, 9
Malinche, La, 125
Malinow, Inés, 126
Mallea, Eduardo, 18
Marechal, Leopoldo, 120

Mármol, José, 118
Marqués, René, 124
Martínez, Z. Nelly, 126
Martín Gaite, Carmen, 123
Martínez Estrada, Ezequiel, 100
Martínez Gamero, Amalia, 121
Martínez Sierra, Gregorio, 122, 123
Martínez Sierra, María, 122, 123
Marting, Diane, 120
Martins, Wilson, 43
Mathieu, Corina, 113
Matute, Ana María, 124
McCarthy, Mary, 6, 15
McCracken, Ellen, 126
McCullers, Carson, 6
McKendrick, Malveena, 122
Mead, Margaret, 6, 8
Meireles, Cecília, 7
Mendoza, María Luisa, 5, 8, 18
Meyer, Doris, 119, 121, 122, 126
Michel, Louise, 127
Miller, Beth, 69, 122
Miller, Henry, 9
Miller, Yvette, 119-120
Millett, Kate, 1, 2, 9-10, 18, 55-56, 68, 70, 119
Minc, Rose S., 126
Mistral, Gabriela, 7
Mitchell, Julie, 1
Moffatt, Alfredo, 118
Moisés, Massaud, 41, 43
Montherlant, Henri de, 2
Mora, Gabriela, 122, 126
Morante, Elsa, 6
Moravia, Alberto, 84
Morin, Edgar, 3, 18
Nigro, Kirsten F., 135
Novães Coelho, Nelly, 126
Nunes, Benedito, 23, 43
Nunes, Maria Luisa, 23, 36, 43, 44-45, 126

Ocampo, Silvina, 7
Ocampo, Victoria, 7, 19, 118
O'Connor, Patricia, 10, 119, 122, 123
Olmo, Lauro, 123
O'Neill, Carlota, 126
Onetti, Juan Carlos, 124
O'Quinn, Kathleen, 120
Ordóñez, Elizabeth, 123
Ortega, José, 124